SLAVERY THROUGH
THE AGES

AN ARAB SLAVE DHOW

Slavers on a " bagaleh " photographed in the Gulf of Oman.

SLAVERY THROUGH
THE AGES

By

LIEUT.-GENERAL SIR GEORGE MACMUNN,
K.C.B., K.C.S.I., D.S.O.

EP PUBLISHING LIMITED
ROWMAN & LITTLEFIELD
1974

ISBN 0 85409 946 8 (EP Publishing)

ISBN 0-87471-463-X (Rowman and Littlefield)

Please address all enquiries to EP Publishing Limited
(address as above)

Printed in Great Britain by
Redwood Press Limited, Trowbridge, Wiltshire

FOREWORD

I am very willing to comply with Sir George MacMunn's request that I should write a few words by way of introduction to his book. It deals with a subject to the study of which I have devoted myself for many years, and to which the attention of the thoughtful public should be constantly directed.

So authoritative and detailed a survey of Slavery in the Past and in the Present should have many readers, some of whom may be surprised to discover that they are not merely gaining information about old, unhappy things of long ago, but that there is still an urgent problem which survives and calls for the best of our thought and effort before this hideous system, in one or other of its insidious forms, can be said to be banished from the earth. Kind-hearted people sometimes show themselves unwilling to be roused from their indifference by the specious plea that some of the examples of contemporary slavery do not necessarily imply that the slave is dissatisfied with his lot, and that the condition of a slave may actually provide some assurance against the hunger and destitution which might accompany freedom. Let anyone who is beguiled into complacency by such a contention study the details of the systems exposed in this book and he will see reason to change his view.

The child of a slave woman born into slavery is a creature to be bought and sold, often to be separated from its mother for ever, and to be under the uncontrolled domination of

a purchaser who claims " to do what he likes with his own."
Cruelties against which the slave has no redress are in-
separable from such a relation. The temptations of such
uncontrolled power are irresistible. No one is fit to have
undisputed domination over another human creature, to
treat man or woman or even little children as beasts of
burden, or as ministers to the owner's pleasure, without
any right in the victim to end the relationship or to claim
the protection which the law ought to give to the poorest
and weakest of human creatures.

There is something in the conception of individual
liberty as the only basis upon which the dignity of man
can be established, and the worth of human life can be
measured, which issues a flat and final challenge against
the infamy of treating as a mere chattel any human being,
whatever his race or birth or colour. If it be the fact that
some slaves to-day are content with their lot, that only
proves the more clearly the degradation to which such a
system inevitably leads. More horrible still would be the
outcome if those of us who are free should refuse to bestir
ourselves where others are in bondage.

> ". . . wherever wrong is done,
> To the humblest and the weakest, 'neath the all-
>   beholding sun,
> That wrong is also done to us; and they are slaves
>   most base,
> Whose love of right is for themselves, and not for all
>   their race."

LOWELL.

This volume will contribute to the study of a wicked
institution which in past ages spread its malign influence

over vast areas of the earth, and inflicted suffering and wrong on millions who " have no remembrance ; they are perished as though they had never been." But there is another purpose, more immediate and practical, which Sir George MacMunn's book will serve. It will, I trust, help to rouse the public conscience to the work of abolition still to be accomplished, so that we shall not rest content until present-day slavery is finally and completely abolished.

KATHLEEN SIMON.

71 ADDISON ROAD,
LONDON, W.14,
November 1937.

AUTHOR'S PREFACE

THE Western Conquest of Abyssinia, promising to abolish the last stronghold of slave-making, if not of slave-holding, seems an opportunity to review once more the whole absorbing if horrifying story of slavery from the mists of pre-history till to-day. The formation of the " Committee of Experts " within the League of Nations, will ere long add the coping-stone to the work of the British " Anti-Slavery and Aborigines Protection Society" and its children abroad, started so many years ago. Because this story of slavery from earliest days has always interested me, I have turned to such side facets, also, as the Slave Dynasties of India and Central Asia, the story of the Janissaries and the Mamelukes, and of that strange horror the emasculation of males born of slave origin. As I was writing the concluding chapters I have had put into my hands a fascinating work, *The Slave in History*, written over a generation ago by William Stevens, the well-known journalist and editor. I find that the same sequence of events and side stories interested him as much as they have me, and that we follow much the same train of thought.

GEORGE MACMUNN.

SACKVILLE COLLEGE.

TABLE OF CONTENTS

CONTENTS

xii

CONTENTS

LIST OF ILLUSTRATIONS

*The author and publishers are indebted to the following for kindly
supplying illustrations: The Anti-Slavery and Aborigines Protection
Society for the portraits of William Wilberforce and Thomas Fowell
Buxton; The British and Foreign Anti-Slavery Society for the
illustration facing p. 76; The Exclusive News Agency for the
frontispiece and the illustrations facing pp. 176, 192, 212, 228, 240.*

PART I

SLAVERY IN HISTORY

A

CHAPTER ONE

Slavery through the Ages

★

The Last Slave Country—The Slave System of the Ancient World—
Slavery in the Old Testament—The Tragedy of " The Deprived "
—Yesterday and To-day.

★

THE LAST SLAVE COUNTRY

IN the falling of Abyssinia under Italian rule there is some
hope that the last serious stronghold of slave-making—as
distinct from slave-raising—has fallen. That is to say that
the days of the raided village, and the caravans of yoked
prisoners and all the pitiful concomitants, have been driven
from the world for ever. But the end of slave-making and
slave-raiding does not unfortunately mean the end of slave-
holding and slave-raising, for that can only come when the
heart of Arabia and the Arab world changes, or Islam can
take a more humane line. This means that slave-breeding
must continue so long as the world-rule holds that a slave
mother means a slave child. It was the real trouble in the
Southern States of North America, that the slave state did
not end itself as time rolled on. It is the same in Arabia
to this day. It has been said that the Arabian form of
slavery is the most insidious form of all, in that it is bearable
and even pleasant to the lesser minds, and is not inhumane.
To those to whom the idea of any human being, existing
other than in a state of free will, is abhorrent—as indeed it
should be to us all—this easy Arabian slavery appears as
insidious and dangerous to the world, as the charming

3

paternal side of the romantic slave life under a good owner in the old Southern States of the Union.

That brings us direct to another point of view, *viz.* that slavery has apparently been a necessary condition without which, " before the moveable powers were established," the modern world of culture and civilization, industrialism and vast populations living in comfort, could not have been built. However true this may be, the fact remains that slavery in some form has existed under all the great civilizations that have existed in the past and faded away, perhaps for that very reason. Similarly there are thinkers who hold that the discipline of Islam is necessary for a few generations, before certain types can hope to absorb the Christian teaching. This might be so were the teachings and uplift of Islam freed of its slave-holding instinct.

The little grain of good in slavery is apparent when we read Rosita Forbes, who tells of an Abyssinian woman slave who told her that till she was a slave she was beaten like a camel and never fed nor clothed. In a community where women have no value, no doubt there is solace in the position of the kept woman.

" But whether or no slavery is an unthinkable evil, and whether it may have grains of good, it permeated the ancient world, and has left the modern world scarred, in some cases beyond healing, by its results.

It might intrigue those of an impish trend of thought to ask if the negro community of the United States, despite its still remaining disabilities, is not immeasurably better off in this world and even in the next, for its enforced migration from the claws of the witch-doctor. Where *Pastures Green* can be written in seriousness, all seed has not fallen by the wayside. It might even be said that had the recruitment of slaves been made under humane auspices, such forcible transfer might have had some value for populating the world's waste but fertile lands.

All that, however, is but by the way ; the fact remains that even with the matrix in Abyssinia excised, this incredible world will not yet be free of slavery for many years, and those who might attend to it are busy teaching their children how to avoid their neighbour's poison gas, which is a paradox beyond man's comprehension. Further, however little we may like the thought, this world—-with the terrible labour camps of Russia, and the concentration and instructional camps on the German method—has facets which may lead us back to slave-owning unless humanity exercises continual vigilance. That Fascism may have been necessary in certain countries whose axis of life had become dangerous, as in Italy before the apotheosis of Benito, is more than arguable, but since Fascism as yet finds it difficult to stop its authoritarian course, it can be nothing but a very temporary panacea for the evils it has apparently cured. It has, however, shown us one thing, that continual attempts to put folk into one mould can but bring us back to the *milieu* in which slavery flourished.

So though the parts of Abyssinia in which the slave trade flourished, and over which the writ of Haile Selassie did not run, or did not run sufficiently to make the people abandon their ways—which was the gravamen of the charges against him—have come under better rule, there are still world pockets to which control and civilization cannot yet spread. It should not be forgotten that it was because that ruler could not, however well intentioned, suppress slavery, that Britain was adverse to the admission of Abyssinia to the League of Nations, and that it was France and Italy who sponsored the admission. Now Italy, with none too numerous resources, is shouldering the ' White Man's Burden ' in this vast and often wild land.

Whatever may be the future of the League of Nations in this imperfect world, and however over-optimistic the aspirations of its founders, the numerous side-lines which

5

Geneva manages are alone " worth the money." The still glowing embers of the slave trade, the vigorous life of the eternal slave-producing womb, the prevention of world disease, the drug traffic, the tragedy of the White Slave traffic, all called aloud for an international body and bureau to deal with them. The League of Nations is now tackling the subject of slavery as one of the more important matters of which civilization should be aware. To all who would understand the ancient social organization of the world and how we are still affected thereby, the study of the slave system of the ancient Empires, of Carchemish, of Babylon the Whore, of Assyria, and of Egypt and China, old when the rest were young, is of supreme interest. In another epoch, that of the rise of Islam, slavery took on a different form, more ruthless and more depraved, while throwing up strange phenomena, such as the emasculated male slave, due originally, it is said, to the freakish ruthlessness of Semiramis, and the deprived odalisque, the Slave Kings, the Janissaries, and the Mamelukes. Such matters are all cognate to the subject and fascinating to study. When we come to our time, when kindly England was fast earning that epithet, we find the paradox of the systematic purchase of negro slaves developed within her gates, with none to utter protest. When that is put behind us as an old forgotten unhappy thing, we find there still remains the distressing knowledge that many million human bodies and souls, however uncouth and undeveloped, are still in bondage.

The Slave System of the Ancient World

When the increasing tribes of the prehistoric ages began to impinge on each other, and tribal war first came to the world, to enslave prisoners, in some form or other, was an obvious course so soon as there was labour to be done. When *bedu* turned *fellah*, to use the modern Arabism, and when nomad became settler, then trouble began and slaves were worth their keep. Before our eyes to-day we can see in Arab lands the age-old process of nomad becoming— reluctantly no doubt—settler, as his wants increase and his ideas develop of what makes life. The story is as old as the hills and as new as to-day, and it has been thought probable that the Bible story of Cain and Abel is a story of the trouble engendered when Cain was a settler or *fellah*, and Abel a grazier, a *bedu*. On the rivers of Mesopotamia, to this day, the same cause of quarrel occurs. The settler banks the river to save his fields from devastating floods. The grazier wants water on the desert grazing, and the *fellah* will assemble armed to protect his floodbanks. Abel the grazier would cut the banks, and Cain, after warning we are told, slew him.

Thus, we may suppose, contact and settling produced war. But it is with the rise of great conquering empires that the history of systematic enslavement begins, and from them and all that man has done unto man history turns with horror. Hittites, Khassites, Babylonians, Assyrians, Greeks, all had vast slave policies, and we see how mighty Rome founded her imperial system thereon, and fell with the decay this induced. But so much was it part of the system that we see, as consciences were pricked and economists were frightened, many statesmanlike enactments to regulate, mitigate, and in urban conditions humanize, as far as possible, the results. When we realize that much of the scientific and literary work of the Roman world was the work of an enslaved intelligentsia, and that the practice of manumitting brought brains and culture into the Roman *cosmos*, we can realize how far slavery had been woven and translated into a civilization. *Pari passu*, with a comparatively humane slave labour system within the towns, there were the horrible conditions of the estate and mine slaves, to which in another form Russia still condemns those who don't see eye-to-eye with official views.

7

We see Assyria, even more than Rome, making slavery a system, and apart from the enslavement of conquered races, also carrying out the compulsory transfer of races over many hundreds of miles, so that the conquered were sent away from their own surroundings and others transferred to their place. Such migrations have altered and complicated racial ethnology to an extent that only the laws of the Abbé Mendel can help us to elucidate.

It has been held that in struggling communities, all working hard for a livelihood, only slavery in some form, the forcing of some to do menial work, could give leisure to those with gifts to develop, or make study and art of any kind possible. So ancient, however, is civilization, a civilization that is to say so far as arts and learning go, and so constantly is it dated further down the ages by the spade of the archaeologist, that how slavery actually came about no man will ever know. The great death chamber dating from the fourth millennium before Christ, discovered a few years ago at Ur of the Chaldees, is very clear proof of an early slave system, as well as an early culture. Only slave girls and slave attendants could have been slaughtered in such numbers to make a royal funeral.

It may well be that the old Stone Age races, backward in all intelligence and development, remained alongside folk who had developed elsewhere and migrated, and the impinging of the two produced serfdom and slavery with no public conscience or human consideration to mitigate it. To domesticate by harsh methods the animal world for men's purposes must have been little different in men's minds to domesticating the ruder folk, as to this day we find rough white settlers treating aboriginals. So much is this still seen to be the case, from our knowledge of modern shortcomings, and so cruel in some of its phases is the untouchability of India or the ostracism of negro blood in the United States, that it is not unreasonable to think that

8

the world, if vigilance be relaxed and if exposed to another such shock as the World War, can go back to slavery as easily as the soil of Britain can revert to bramble and bracken.

But since slavery was a state which mankind persisted in maintaining, it does seem that it amounted almost to a law in the world's development, without which, in some form or other, men could not have progressed to civilization, given the conditions of the ages. Christianity, with its doctrine of love, first tried to inculcate mercy, and as the centuries rolled on, to create a hegemony which should keep its unruly members in the grip of a holy law. The concept, however, was too vast for mankind to live up to. In our own times we hoped that the lion and the lamb would live in peace, but as the old conception of the Church as an Empire of God failed, so an Empire of reason in the shape of the League of Nations cannot in its major rôle yet fit into our world. Science and material progress have taken us far ahead of the moral development that should march parallel. That after a " War to end War " we should be building gas shelters in our villages, and teaching our children to put on anti-gas masks, is sure evidence that there is little yet to prevent us lapsing into a condition in which slavery in some form or other could find its being.

In these days when rigorous concentration camps are used by authoritarians to force men to think alike, we may well thank our stars that we of these islands have hitherto so built our way of life and our organizations that freedom and justice provide outlets and ways of coming together not vouchsafed to the rest of the world.

It is a revelation in economics that in countries where material progress has outstripped a capacity for government, that are freer-than-they're-fit-for, slave camps and indus-tries should be re-introduced. Turning back, however, to the past, it may fairly be said that even if slavery be accepted as a concomitant of evolution in a non-Christian world, the practices and ruthlessness that went with it can never receive a coat of white-wash. A transfer of Africans under *force majeure* to labour on sugar plantations in our modern would-be Christian times, had it been wisely conceived, humanely conducted, and generously legislated for, might receive the forgiveness of posterity, despite the interference with all laws of justice and freedom involved. That it should have been in the hands of desperadoes and adventurers and have been carried out with atrocious callousness, at any rate in its earlier days, is a crime for which a comparatively humane world can never expect absolution.

When the great waves of the Teutonic and Danubic uprisings swept Roman civilization and its derivatives, good and bad, away, it was by no means the end of slavery, which only took on a worse form. In Nordic and Teuton society there were slaves galore, who perhaps in time developed into the serfs, the *adscripti glebae* in another form. Saxons, Norsemen, Danes carried off slaves from the shores they raided. The Romanized Britons became serfs and subject tribes, slavery existing in Britain till mediaeval times. It was the slave-raiding by the Dano-Irish settlements from Liffey and Waterford on the western shores of England and other piracies that first sent the Normans to conquer Ireland, leaving but one more of these modern world problems which arose out of slaving ways. In fact slave-holding and slave-making was a habit, an institution, and a vice, all through the ages, which still persists wherever the writ of humanity does not run.

Slavery in the Old Testament

Those who would in the past have defended the institution of slavery, and whose Christianity was fortified by the Old Testament, would find sanction enough therein, a sanction that specially applied to the " lesser breeds without the law." The Jewish law provided completely for the slave, and the debt-bondsman, and at any rate supported the fact that slavery was a recognized institution involving no turpitude in the eyes of the world. But in Holy Writ slave-making of Hebrews was anathema, though it may be accepted that certain races were considered as born to be enslaved—the very view of the slave traders and slave holders of the Americas.

Jews held slaves under the law of Moses, but all slaves were freed in the year of Jubilee. To enslave a freeman was to incur the death penalty. Fathers might sell their daughters under safeguard. Debtors and their families might be sold into debt-bondage. In the 21st chapter of Exodus we read that even a Hebrew might be bought for six years, and at the end of the indenture his family, if he brought them, shall go out with him. But if his master has given him a wife, presumably a slave wife, she and her children remained when he went out. The slave womb here also produced slaves. But it was also somewhat curiously enacted that if the Hebrew temporary slave refused his freedom at the end of six years, and said : " I love my master, my wife and my children, I will not go out free, then his master shall bring him unto the judges, and he shall also bring him to the door, or unto the door-post, and his master shall bore his ear through with an awl ; and he shall serve him for ever."

It was not a very humane provision that a slave wife and family should compel a man to enslave himself ; but there it was, and it was no doubt on the patriarchal lines of the Arabian family slavery of to-day.

The same chapter provides that a Hebrew might sell his daughter, as maid-servant and concubine, but that if she was not wanted she might be redeemed, and her owner must not sell her as he would an ordinary slave. If he has bought her as his own wife he must treat her as such, and if he take another the Hebrew maiden's status and treatment must not be worsened. Failure to observe this set her free. If one Hebrew was poor, and be sold to another, he was not to be treated as a bond-servant, but as an hired servant to be free in the year of Jubilee. Of the Hebrew the Lord said, " They are my servants and shall not be sold as bondmen."

The heathen had no such privileges.

" Both thy bondmen and thy bondmaids which thou shalt have shall be of the heathen that are round about you ; of them shall ye buy bondmen and bondmaids."

The children of the sojourners among them might also be bought and be their possession, and their bondmen for ever. A Hebrew who was poor, who sold himself to a wealthy sojourner, might redeem himself or be redeemed by his relatives. Equitable rates of redemption are even laid down, having due regard to the proximity or otherwise of the year of Jubilee. He must not be treated with " rigour," whatever that may mean.

The year of Jubilee that recurred after seven times seven years, _i.e._ in every fiftieth year, was the occasion on which all slaves were free men, all would be restored to their family and all bonded debt-service wiped out.

Slavery under the dispensation of Moses was thus fully legislated for—a holding of the lesser breeds—with the mitigation at the Jubilee.

THE TRAGEDY OF " THE DEPRIVED "

One of the most evil concomitants of slavery from the earliest time that has left a long smear on the world, has been that diverting of the human frame, only possible for the most part on chattels, that goes by the name of " castration."

It has been carried out on slave men and boys for many thousands of years, to fit them for certain slave purposes,

chief of which is guard and service in the harem.
In Ancient Greece there were many such, οἱ τὴν εὐνὴν
ἔχοντες. Tradition, as already referred to, has placed the
discovery of the possibility of the operation on Semiramis,
legendary Queen of ancient Babylon, *grande amoureuse*,
and powerful ruler. Semiramis is the Greek form of her
real name, Sham-mu-ra-mat, " the Dove." The tablets of
Ashurpanipal's library show an historic lady of the name
as Queen of Assyria, but there may have been a Sham-mu-
ra-mat in the early Babylon as there was a Sargon. At
any rate, much that is both good and evil have accrued
around her name, and the first making of eunuchs is one
of them. Whether or no the idea first came to her to
experiment on her slaves, it is certainly a very ancient
custom, and has been carried out on slave boys for many
a long year as enhancing their value, in what was a limited
market, limited because though in many households, where
several women resided, they were in demand, yet even then
such households could only be those of the wealthy. Where
many women, the property of a ruler, are kept for his bed
only, there are many among them whose natural rights and
needs are rarely satisfied, and to whom the presence of an
uncut male must obviously be a stimulant. To see that
his women run no such danger, the harem guards are
emasculate males who are charged under a head eunuch
with the service and protection of the large female establishment. It is part of the graveness of the charge against the
remaining slavery of Arabia, that the slave mothers must
still submit to this mutilation of their sons for the eunuch
market, many dying from bad surgery. There is little need
for the analogous operation on slave girls, as their fecundity
is desirable, save that some infecund and therefore presumably not-desirous women, have often been kept for the
service of harems, though the number is small and they are
in little general demand.

13

How ancient is the custom of male mutilation reference to both Old and New Testaments supports. It is also to be remembered that while the operation performed on the adult produces a feeble creature, that on the juvenile may direct the forces of growth into other channels, and produce giants and powerful men, especially among negroes, as among horses and cattle. In men of education it has even produced men of action, *e.g.* Nares, the Persian general. The organs and forces of generation are more productive of the good than the evil elements in mankind, and the man thus deprived may lose all sense of the milk of human kindness. Most eastern executioners are deprived men, and it is they who carried out sentences on slave girls, and then slipped the corpses in the Bosphorus, and similar oubliettes.

The eastern form of deprivement may extend to complete removal of the genitals, since the ordinary eunuch may retain sufficient attributes to be acceptable, though harmless, and eastern ruthlessness sets its face against even this easement. The classical instance of this facet of partial deprivation is the long-sustained semi-amour between Tseu-Hi, known to history as the Dowager-Empress of China, and the chief eunuch of the palace, Ngan-Te-Hai, which brought her to such power. This astounding little Manchu girl of good family was long deprived of access to the Emperor, and when admitted, found him a drunken and ineffective sot. Both before and after her becoming first favourite concubine, she had happiness and solace in the company of Ngan-Te-Hai—a strange story which illustrates the reason of ruthlessness. The Palace of the Manchus was guarded by a large corps of the deprived, who carry, preserved in spirit, the severed portions, *Les prescieuses*, to accompany them to the grave, so that they might lie complete in death. While the mutilated slave boys have no choice, the recruitment of the Manchu Palace servant was entirely voluntary. A youth anxious to secure a prosperous and certain future in the peculiar slave guard in Pekin would present himself to the chief eunuch. The latter, after carefully ascertaining that the candidate was fully aware of what he was undertaking, would suddenly deal him the knock-out blow on the jaw. The candidate would come to to find the operation over and himself enrolled in the slave guard. But this product of early slavery is used in another manner even to-day. Mediaeval choir-masters were fully alive to the value of preserving for ever a glorious boy's voice, and openly had the operation carried out.

In some eastern cities eunuchs in women's clothes appeal to certain perverted natures, and what is practically a slave male is still thus obtainable in the market, happily not a wide one. Once this deprivation became known it had, and has, uses in ruthless hands both as punishment and as an act of vengeance. The last of the Moguls to sit on the throne of Baber, the unfortunate Shah Alum, was blinded by his Pathan minister, in vengeance, be it said, for having been deprived as a youth by the Emperor's orders. Indeed the history of the ages is full of such derivatives from the discovery that men attribute to the fertile genius of the legendary Semiramis, the Dove, and the experiments she made on her slaves.

Yesterday and To-day

As we trace with horror and wonder the working of this strange world system of slavery which began in the nursery of mankind, we shall still more wonder at its persistence, and the manner in which it has remained with us. Slave-raiding and slave-selling and civilization's complaisance with it, was contemporary with John Wesley. The systems of Cuba and Brazil and the Southern States of America were contemporary with the Great Exhibition and Albert the Good. The scandals of the Belgian Congo and of Putumayo belong to our own times. The terrible drama of the Sudan that Gordon so strove against, dates almost with Queen Victoria's Jubilee. The Abyssinian horrors were with us openly till yesterday, and cannot yet have been suppressed. The world is full of vast uncontrolled tracts in which no writs of humanity can run. From outer China and inner Mongolia and the lands that fringe the Gobi, queer things still survive, the Soviets assisting.

In China, and all places east where the Chinese congregate, the system of Mui-Tsai or Pei-Nu still exists, the practice of keeping slave girls, which will be considered as we come to the evil in its modern aspects. Then also we must deal with the real slave spot still surviving, *viz.* Arabia, where slaves are bought and sold in large numbers, and the slave womb still brings forth more slaves, as it did in the United States, and where even slave-breeding studs are kept, as they were in Virginia till the days of Abraham Lincoln's tragedy.

The story of the survival of slavery to-day will not be complete, too, without some allusion to its last derivative, indentured labour, in all its forms from the early evil to the modern popular and humane evolution thereof which obtains where Governments are good.

In the history of ancient slavery there are countless instances of the brand on body and soul that the status of slavery immediately put on the slave. It is the most essential among the points that the anti-slavery enthusiast presses on us even to-day—the soul degradation of being a chattel, that all freemen recognized and to-day must strive against—the eternal taint, the destruction of caste as it were, that slavery entailed ; a priest or a prince of a cultured dominating race one day, the next captured, enslaved, branded for ever as an outcast. There is some strange psychological phenomenon here involved from earliest times which is almost unrealizable to the happily placed western mind.

CHAPTER TWO

Slavery in Ancient Greece and Rome

★

Slavery in Ancient Greece—The Slave System of Republican Rome—
Slavery under the Empire—The Servile Wars.

★

SLAVERY IN ANCIENT GREECE

THAT slavery should have been the habit of Ancient Greece is astounding when we have regard to all that name stands for in the world of culture, learning, and democratic institutions. Just as we marvel at a cultured and beautiful society made hideous by homosexuality, so are we shocked to find that slavery is the basis of its labour, and a slavery which had not the excuse of the world development and pacification which accompanied it in Rome. It had the same ruthless war origin as in the case of Assyria and Egypt, and has this same plea made for it : that slavery may be more beneficent than the immolation or slaughter that is the other alternative, or than the cannibalism that held the field in still earlier stages of the world's life. So far back as the period sung of in the Iliad we learn that prisoners of war were retained as slaves or held at ransom. From the Odyssey we learn that the men prisoners were often slain, and only the women—and presumably only the younger women—and children carried off. Also we learn in the same saga that pirates kidnapped all and sundry to sell, and we have the story of Eumaeus so treated, demonstrating that, as in Rome, slaves might be as well-born and as cultured as their masters, and indeed far more so. From the pages of Homer, however, we may equally imagine that the slavery on the homesteads was not unbearable so long as the situation was acceptable to the slave. There lies the trouble for benevolent slavery all the world over—what to do with the intractable slave. For such no remedy existed but ruthless severity.

The sources of Greek slavery, however, were not confined to prisoners of war. There was the increment of birth, since here, as elsewhere, even to Arab slavery to this day, the children of slaves are slaves. But again as in Brazil, and in all slave systems unless carefully devised and carried out with some pretensions to humanity, women are in defect, and births will not cover deaths, so that recourse must be had to more victorious war or to slave dealers. Further, the economic experience usually accepted was that it was cheaper to buy a slave than to raise one. Sale of children by free parents, by some extraordinary reasoning, was permitted, save in Attica, and even to-day encumbered parents are known to sell their children. Thus in Greece boy slaves would be bought for catamites, a practice which was not a Roman failing. Piracy and kidnapping were recognized, as with the Romans, as a source of supply. Children kidnapped were specially fed and trained. Female slaves from childhood were taught the whole gamut of courtezanry. Then since war slaves, who might be Asiatics or even from neighbouring Greek States, were not enough, the ordinary slave trade of bought and kidnapped persons handled by a highly organized dealer's ring ensured a sufficient supply. As times rolled on the same decadent conditions arose as in Rome. Landowners lived in the cities and waxed fat while slaves managed the estates. There was hardly a rôle in life in which slaves were not employed. As those familiar with Greek stories know, there were public slaves, both male and female, many of the latter being attached to the temples, charged among other things with removing all worldly desires from would-be worshippers. In Athens large numbers of Scythian slaves were employed as police. In fact, in Attica, the lot of the tractable slave was unusually benevolent. In domestic circles they were admitted to the family circle with some service of ceremony and dedication which implied that both master and slave had mutual obligations. They were not entirely excluded from public amusements and re-joicings. The position of the slave might often be a confidential one. Although the lash was in use for punishment of the refractory, serious crime had to be judged and punishment carried out as in the case of freemen, and the slave was not the pure chattel of the master as in the methods of the earlier days in Rome ; slaves could not be slaughtered to serve a mistress's whim ! A slave who was constantly ill-treated could demand to be sold in the hope of a better deal, and the law offered sanctuary while slave cases were being considered.

A Greek slave could purchase his freedom with his *peculium*, to use the Latin term for his savings, by agreement with his master. He could be liberated by will, or by notification during his owner's lifetime, or by being donated to a temple. Conditions, however, might be attached to manumission, such as service for a certain number of years to his owner or assignee. If a freedman violated such conditions, he was liable to an action at law, and might be relegated to slavery again as a penalty. Slaves were not entitled on manumission to be citizens, but could only be accepted as such by vote in a general assembly as in the case of foreigners. Again, slaves who had rendered important services, whether as soldiers or in some other capacity, were made citizens ; notable cases of such being accorded for military service being on record.

The author of *Economics*, said to be Aristotle, held slavery to be just and natural if properly carried out. He gave a practical rule for conduct towards a slave : " No outrage, no familiarity," and the latter no doubt was meant to include sex relations, normal or otherwise. He was emphatic that hope of freedom should be held out to a slave as a reward of service. Plato, on the other hand, condemned the right of a Greek to hold another Greek as a slave, while Aristotle did not. He advised the mixing of enslaved races to minimize the chance of rebellion, and considered that all slaves should be held in contempt. The later Greek writers have little to condemn in slavery, but all inculcate good treatment, while the Stoics naturally saw little difference between slavery and freedom. Euripides loudly voices praise for the general run of slaves, their faithful service, and their gratitude for kind treatment.

It will be noticed how different was the Greek attitude to that of the Roman or of the American to his slave. It is not perhaps unfair to say that Abraham Lincoln, who favoured no drastic emancipation, would have aimed at gradual extinction on the Greek lines, had there been no secession by the slave states of the Union. Certainly, except for the matter of kind treatment—and there were plenty of bad owners even then—the Greeks of old managed their business far better than the Americans ; but then the Greeks' slaves were largely white like themselves.

The Slave System of Republican Rome

However much Greek and Macedonian, Persian and Babylonian, may have fostered and developed slavery, it is to mighty Rome that we look for the great example of a ruthless and world-wide form that slowly faded into serfdom when there were no peoples left to conquer. In the Roman system we see all the evil, and all that can be said to the good, of slavery as a national principle. As conscience awoke we see more and more legislation to regulate and humanize the institution. Further, we see the modern implication—borne in at last on even the Brazilians—that under a system of slavery, or of slave-breeding, regulated by any sort of State control and responsibility, slave labour costs more than free labour—provided always that free labour could be made available —and that cheap slave labour might easily become very expensive labour indeed. The system of slavery that grew so universal when the humble Rome of the Tarquins grew to the cosmopolitan Rome of the empires, was obviously well calculated to thrive under the paternal autocracy of the Roman family organization. In the early days when Rome only warred with her small Italian neighbours, prisoners of war and conquered folk were made slaves ; but the holding was small, and slaves worked alongside their yeoman owners at the same work in reasonably good conditions, often being placed in charge of land as sub-tenants, though still slaves. The original Roman Law, however, legislated very definitely for the slave status and did give the master actual dominion over the slave, even to the power of life and death ; though to kill so valuable a piece of property as an agricultural labourer, save for persistent and aggravated recalcitrancy, would be the height of folly. A slave could not possess property, and all he acquired was legally that of his master. Actually he could collect petty savings and gifts, and his property of this kind was termed his *peculium*.

As the patricians gained possession of land, and as the number of soldiers required by the increasing military ventures of the Republic took more and more men away from agriculture or industry, the possession of slaves became of far more importance to their owner and the provisions of the law more essential for the condition of slavery. That law lacked nothing in severity. The slave, the enemy of the Republic taken in battle, had no human rights at all. He was deemed fortunate that his life had been spared and should rejoice therein for the rest of his days. Such pleasure or ease as he got out of life was due to the good-nature and long-sightedness of his master, and certainly not to the law. The law enacted, besides the provisions just recited, that no master could enter into a contract with his slave, nor could he accuse the latter of theft. Theft by a slave was but a displacement of property —a subtle lawyer's conception—and not a subtraction. The union of a male and female slave had no legal station ; cohabitation of slaves, termed *contubernium*, could be terminated at will by the master. A slave, therefore, could not commit adultery. As the years rolled on and the civilized and human sentiments of the people broadened, this attitude was tacitly relaxed. For instance, on slave tombs we do find recorded the names of husband and wife. In other relationships of life, however, the old law was still arbitrary and harsh. A slave who succeeded in enlisting in the army, or entering State service, which he could only do by false attestation, was liable to death, nor was his reputation for truthfulness sustainable. Slaves could not be examined as witnesses at law except under torture. A Roman could demand that any slave accused of a crime be thus questioned. He could also demand that his neighbours' slaves should be equally examined. A slave himself, however, was not a competent witness against his master, save in intimate matters such as adultery. In after years high treason was also a matter in which he might be called in evidence. Naturally enough the penalties to which a citizen was liable were enhanced when a slave was the offender.

As Rome developed from her original status as a small cantankerous republic and came into world power and dominion by land and sea, and as conquest extended to races of equal and often far greater culture and development than her own, the slaves were often of very different *genre* from their owners, and bore no resemblance to the fellow-peasantry of Rome's Italian neighbours who first worked under the lash in Roman fields. The cultured and educated often became domestic slaves, and the rougher folk were relegated to the fields, and later to the rigours of mining and industrial labour generally.

Slaves were servants of the State, *servi publici*, as well as of private persons, the *servi privati*. As the years rolled on slaves even became magistrates ; but for a long time were merely used as the humbler employees of Government offices and departments, for the labour of public works, and for scavenging.

SLAVERY UNDER THE EMPIRE

Under the Empire slavery increased and developed, following much the same principles as under the Republic. It has been said how suited the Roman conception of a family, and the authority of the head of it, the *patria potestas*, was to a gigantic system of slave-owning. As the great estate owners and senators became large holders of the persons of prisoners of war and their descendants, the slaves took the form referred to of estate and house slaves, which became a quite different class, viz. *familia rustica* and *familia urbana*. As in the early days of the Republic the farmer made slave sub-managers and sub-tenants, so later, superior slaves—and some came from among the noblest of the conquered—became *vilici*, managers of the estates, with wives to steady them. He was probably experienced and efficient, and the power of Rome and the servile penalties kept him faithful, as well as the comparative desirability of his employment, and the opportunities of increasing his own *peculium*. The existence of numbers of slave labourers demanded slave " lines " or barracks, and while such often became slave villages, there was room for the often benevolent conditions with which we are familiar, of the slave states in North America in the nineteenth century, and there was also room for the cruellest oppression. It is not to be anticipated, for instance, that a villein who had once been an Assyrian or Egyptian landowner would have much care for Numidians or other humbler breeds under his orders. The slave prison, *ergastulum*, on the estate, would often be in request, while slave constables and executioners would be but a normal part of such a system !

The number of slaves in Italy in the later days of the Republic and under the Empire was almost unbelievable. Among the figures that have come down to us are those for the victories of Aemilius Paullus, when it was recorded that 150,000 prisoners of war were sold, but these may easily have included the slaves of the conquered also. After Aquae, Sextae, and Vercellae, it is said that 90,000 Teutons and 60,000 Cimbri were sold ; and in Gaul Caesar sold on one occasion 63,000 captives. But the appetite for slave-holding grew, and such large numbers indicate how advantageously land could be developed with slave labour. Captive slaves, unless liberally supplied with partners, do not make for multiplication, while under the best circumstances the slave womb may not be very pro-ductive. Thus to satisfy the demand for more and more helots, slave-trading and slave-raiding were now developed, and produced that Mediterranean terror, which, revived under the western Corsairs amid Christian tears, lasted till the rooting up of Algiers by the British the year after the victory of Waterloo. Hume has described the process adopted by what were really pirates as the " systematically prosecuted hunting of man."

Perhaps the greatest misuse of all of the slave systems in Rome was the cult of the gladiators, slaves encouraged and trained to fight each other or be slaughtered in dozens by a bravo, to satisfy the lust of the public for blood and excitement, and who were often whipped into the arena. Delos was the great market, but though slaves were brought there from Gaul and Spain and North Africa, it was the Asiatic countries bordering the Levant that furnished the greater portion of *les misérables*. There were also certain additions to the slave population by the action of Roman penal laws against Romans. Certain offences carried liability for slave status for life or for periods, and we shall see this system obtaining in England when cavaliers and Highland rebels served slave sentences in Virginia. A creditor in the Roman Empire could sell his debtor, though the law—often disregarded—forbade them being put in chains. Debtors sentenced as slaves to their creditors were said to be *addicti* to them.

As the days of the Empire grew longer, however, we see happily not only a human consciousness evolving as regarding slave-holding, but a general tendency towards emancipation. Many laws were passed, largely in the interests of humanity, controlling the slave status. It is Blair who writes that in latter days no Roman slave " need despair of becoming both a freeman and a citizen," in fact Blair considers at any rate the later form of slavery superior on the human side to anything obtaining in Greece. Manumission as defined by the laws was of two main kinds, complete and lesser. Of the greater, *manumissio justa*, there were four methods of release : *i.e.* by *adoption*, which was a rare occurrence ; by *testament* ; by *census*, seldom used ; and by *vindicta*, the usual form so far as man's lifetime was concerned, when a master liberated his slave by saying before a magistrate " *liber esto*," " Be a free man," when the Lictor clinched the gift of freedom by a blow, the last to be endured.

The *manumissio minus justa*, which seems but to have

been partially legal if recognized at all, was carried out by a formal letter from the owner, by merely pronouncing words of freedom, or by putting the cap of liberty—the *pileus*—on the slave's head, and stating the particular amount of freedom conferred. In A.D. 19 a law, *lex Junia Norbana*, was passed giving such freemen the same status as the Roman colonist. A slave thus freed usually only freed his family, and legally, if not in practice, remained a slave till his death, and he could not dispose of his *peculium*. A man freed by this " lesser " freedom remained his master's client.

A full freedman usually took his master's name, owing him deference (*obsequium*) and aid (*officium*). Conditions might be annexed to the freedom, and their neglect might bring about re-enslavement. During the last century B.C. the number of conditions of this kind becoming too burdensome, they were considerably limited. It often occurred indeed that an owner who freed his slave might gain considerably. The slave bought his freedom from his *peculium* or savings, and the master would get another slave with a portion of this purchase price ; at the same time he gained a supporter or client. A freedman's natural heir could inherit only half his property, half being the property of his patron, *viz.* his former owner. If a freedman died intestate and without natural heirs, his property went to his patron. Freedmen and their sons had certain civil disabilities, and it was not till the third generation that the slave family became entirely Roman (*ingenui*). As regards the amount of a slave's *peculium*, Cicero states that a diligent slave saved enough for his freedom in five years. It is not to be wondered at, therefore, that manumissions were frequent and that Augustus had to pass laws limiting the number of manumissions lest the State be swamped with freed slaves. The *lex Furia Caninia*, passed about A.D. 7, forbade the freeing by testament by any owner of more than a hundred, however great his *familia*.

It was under the Empire indeed that Roman citizenship became a world-wide matter, and the freeing of slaves largely contributed to this universality of race. Freedmen now filled many of the lesser offices of State, and in the army. Great proconsuls even had slave descent, while the talents of the cultured of the conquered nations enriched the commonwealth. Horace was the son of a freedman, Livius Andronicus, Terence, and many another of literary reputation had been slaves.

The possession of a woman slave did indeed give her owner right over her body. But unions between freedmen and slave women, and between slaves and freedwomen, were ruthlessly repressed, as hitherto. While the children of the slaves were slaves and not legitimate, legislation later allowed for the recognition of *contubernium* as something resembling marriage in the case of subsequent freedom.

The rape of a virgin, freedwoman or slave, was severely punished by law.

If a slave for any reason was returned to the seller, any of his family, parents, brothers, and folk of his *contubernium*, *personae contubernio conjunctae*, went too. It was also held that in giving effect to testaments, families were not to be separated, a proviso never established in Christian and civilized America.

When Christianity spread in the Empire, slavery was such a part of the warp and weft of society that there could naturally be no uprising against it. Christianity dealt with the spiritual and not with temporal status, and indeed it was to the slave population, and all the poor and oppressed, that Christianity brought peace and the certainty of personal value before God. Its spread surely conduced to that treatment and amelioration of outlook towards slavery in the Empire referred to, that was at any rate leading the rougher form of slavery to serfdom and ultimately to emancipation. Under a Christian Empire many a further

27

amelioration of slave status ensued, and slaves accepted for the Ministry automatically became free. Under Christian Rome freedmen were recognized as full citizens, though the right of patronage still remained, without which the incentive to manumission would have been reduced.

During the latter days of the Republic and the generation of the Empire, it will be obvious how great was the need for industrial labour, as well as in the large estates now devoid of Roman peasantry. Huge, highly equipped armies and fleets demanded a supply of munitions and arms almost as large as armies to-day ; vast factories and wealthy and efficient contractors were essential, and thus the output of equipment for the Legions became the work of vast slave organizations. Whether these industrial slaves were better treated and herded we do not know, the story of the comparative comfort of the domestic slave and the harsh treatment of the agricultural slaves, in their estate barracoons, having alone come down to us. But it is not hard to realize how the vast interchanging of races that the system engendered produced a fabric ready to fall into rags when the wilder Teutonic races destroyed the divine prestige contained in the very word " Rome."

The cessation of conquest put an end to the most legitimate source of slavery recruitment and produced a shortage of slave labour. This shortage encouraged the preservation and the self-production of slaves among the owners. The slave became more and more a part of the family, a poor relation, and owners rarely now sold. Manumission tended to produce a race of freed labourers, much as in the West Indies in modern times. More and more during the second century A.D., as Gibbon shows us, were the posts of the intelligentsia filled by freedmen, and teaching, learning, medicine, and secretarial posts were entrusted to them. Art, painting, and literature gained from the produce of slaves, so that the gifts of the mind under the Empire were more products of a system than the gifts of a race. The freed artisans began to compete with factories employing slave labour, forming associations for the purpose. On the land the evil days were steadily melting as freedmen became tenants, paying a share of their produce as rent.

The internal system of Rome was almost entirely recast by Diocletian. Professions, arts, and crafts became largely hereditary, and some resemblance to the Indian caste system arose, less the indissoluble blend with religion of the Aryan bonds. It has been said that this system, while sacrificing individual freedom, made for stability and order, and also lessened the gap between free and slave life! In the countryside the rural slaves were gradually merged into the body of the *coloni*, free persons originally who took land on lease, but who gradually developed into a body *adscripti glebae*, that is, inscribed on the roll, personally free, but detained on the land by reason of debt. They paid a portion of their produce, gave some labour on their landlord's domains, and became much as the Saxon peasantry before the Black Death. In the constitution of Constantine we find that the *adscripti* were recognized as permanently attached to the land. If one abandoned his holding he was brought back and punished. Anyone who employed such had to restore him and pay a penalty. The children of a union between persons of a different *colonia* were divided among the respective *domini*. Late laws still further bound the *adscripti* ; but the system produced security and content, though a *dominus* had some power of chastisement. It was considered a great advance on the *familia rustica*, the family of rural slaves. This existed alongside a system of predial rural slaves, under overseers, but these had their own home and villages, and gradually merged in the *coloni* and *adscripti*. In a system where there was a place for everyone and everyone in his place, and where food must be grown by someone, this life of serfdom was a not inhumane development from slavery, and a useful half-way house to better things. In A.D. 377 a law of Valentinian forbade the sale of even these predial slaves, and intermarriage between them and the *adscripti* was permitted. Slavery in Rome was, at long last, at an end.

THE SERVILE WARS

Mention, however, has not yet been made of one of the dangers of so vast a slave system, that of rebellion, though allusion has been made to precautions of distribution. There were actually several cruel and disastrous servile wars during the history of the Republic, though not, it would seem, in the days of the Emperors. Even before the Roman slaves broke out, Carthage was nearly brought to the dust in the year 238 B.C., when her slave mercenaries, an early version of Mameluke and Janissary, rebelled as actual troops in arms, and were with difficulty vanquished. The first servile war of Roman history broke out in Sicily in 134 B.C., when slaves, goaded by the ill-usage of their patrician landlords, burst into rebellion, and committed much destruction, indulging in those atrocities to which a submerged community in rebellion always seems impelled. The fact that many lesser freemen joined the slaves shows that the discontent was economic as well as servile. The slaves had defeated the praetors and also the Consul Fulvius Flaccus and gained many successes, and continued in arms for close on two years, and it was not till the Consul P. Rupilius with large reinforcements arrived that the rebellion was put down ; and put down it was, with all the horror and atrocity that a servile rebellion always provokes. Slaves and rebellions are a contradiction in terms ! A second servile war broke out also in Sicily thirty years later and was suppressed by the Consul M. Aquilius in 101 B.C.

After another thirty years, however, a far greater servile danger arose, when a number of gladiators under Spartacus broke from their school at Capua (B.C. 72), roused the slaves and trained them, and inflicted a long series of military defeats on the Romans. The gladiators, naturally a trained and daring nucleus, formed a formidable basis for a servile rebellion, and the Romans were now experiencing a fierce nemesis for their heartless gladiator policy that put human beings to kill each other to make a Roman holiday. It was Crassus himself who finally trampled out the rebellion with a cruelty only approached by the excesses of the rebels themselves.

Before even the servile rebellions, and for long after, the countryside was infested with cut-purses and highwaymen recruited from runaway slaves.

CHAPTER THREE

Slavery and Serfdom in Early Europe

★

Slavery among the Teuton Races—Serfdom—Slavery and Serfdom in the British Isles—Slavery in Saxon Times.

★

SLAVERY AMONG THE TEUTON RACES

WHEN the Teuton races from the great German rivers started their moves, north, south, and west, they came as a deluge that swamped mighty Rome, rotten with its slave system. They too, however, were as ruthless slave owners as the Romans, but lacking the civilization which made cruelty refined, they were by so much the better masters. Vandals, Goths, Burgunds, Visi-Goths, and Saxons or Englishmen, there was nothing they did not know about enslaving their weaker neighbours or their prisoners of war. Indeed the word " slave " is but " Slav " from the numbers of the great Slav people taken in war, who formed the bulk of the slave population in Teuton hands.

But the savage Teutons had ideas of mercy, for it was the custom among them to encourage their slaves to become leaders and freemen, and this had indeed some resemblance to that system which produced the slave kings of Ghuzni and Delhi. They even selected from their martial slaves, who distinguished themselves, husbands for their daughters, and thus refreshed their blood and varied the dynasty.

Kingsley, who was all Teuton in heart as Carlyle was all Prussian, tells us in *The Forest Children* of how the great clans, when Rome had become the slave of her own slaves

32

and the end was nigh, called forth from the Rome they had conquered—from the unholy sink of the city—the Teuton young folk, even as Hitler would call in his Nazis, to lead laborious lives. In January 295 the Emperor Theodosius died, and ere many months were past the Goths were in Arnio, and Alaric's hordes swarmed round the city and offered the new emperor terms. The Goth demanded " All your gold, all your silver, the best of your precious things, all your barbarian slaves." It is said that he got 40,000 Teuton slaves from Rome, adding them forthwith to his army, which now numbered 100,000 men.

Where the Teuton and their hangers-on finally settled, there they seemed to have started the beginnings of the feudal system, which was but putting into definite shape the ancient custom of the tribes ; and wherever they settled the various people evolved laws that had a very distinct basic resemblance to each other. The laws and customs of them all have been largely preserved among the Saxons and Angles even to this day, whilst they have been lost by the others. All of them in turn, as they settled in their new rich lands, produced an easement of the slave conditions ; but, while raising some slaves to serfdom and villeinage and gradual absorption, they were equally ready to make new ones.

The Lombard laws were fairly typical of the trend of Teutonic thought, took some ken of the condition of slavery, and may be quoted as a sample. They were collected and published in writing by King Lothair in A.D. 643, and in them provisions were made for three classes of slaves. First a superior class, called *Aldius* and *Aldia*, who probably corresponded to the *Liti* of Tacitus, who seemed to be hereditary half-freemen holding farms under their master, and who thus resembled the serf of later days. They may have been some of the old half-free Roman *coloni* found on the land when the Lombards took

C 33

possession. They were probably too cunning farmers to be wiped out and were worth keeping and using. The other two classes among the Lombards were *servus massarius* --farm slaves, and *servus doctus*—the educated house slave.

The *Aldius* could marry a freewoman, but the marriage of a slave to a freewoman was punishable by death. If an *Aldius* married an *Aldia* or a freewoman, the children had the status of the father, but if he married a slave woman, the children followed the mother and were the slaves of the lord. This again emphasizes the stain with which the status of slavery branded a human being—however desirable an entity and however highly born before being captured.

SERFDOM

The story of serfdom is one of extreme interest in the study of the development of the world, and is a condition which in some form seems to have existed throughout the populated area from early times, both contemporary with and after the slave-holding periods. It has remained to our own day, and its origin and condition are also a matter for considerable controversy, which is perhaps due to the varying conditions that obtained in different parts of the known world. Serfdom is not slavery, in that speaking generally the serf was bound to the land, and went with it. He was a " bound " tiller, who was compelled by the condition of its existence to live on the land, till the owner's land for so many days in the week, and for the remainder was free to work on his own holding. A serf could not be sold as an unattached slave. The owner of the soil had no rights over the person of the serf, male or female, save in such customs as *jus premiae noctis*, or *le droit du seigneur* in certain lands, which was a custom to improve the serf strain rather than the satisfying of a *libido* for the estate virgins. In fact the damsel might demand the service of the lord, so that her eldest son might have a cultured strain and a

chance of higher things.   The well-bred appearance of some
of the peasantry in certain parts of France to this day would
seem to show that the right was both demanded and exercised.   With the same idea we read that the Nair priests on
the west of India were required to sweeten the ruler's brides.

The serf, though usually predial—that is to say attached
to the soil—was not always so, as there are records of
domestic serfs.   To this day in India, in old-world parts
of Rajputana, there is an hereditary domestic serfdom,
subject to no legal compulsion however, in which certain
castes gladly serve, in hereditary menial or semi-menial
capacities, the same family.

For the origins of serfdom, as of slavery, one must look
to wars, with this difference, that it would seem that serfs
were usually folk of conquered races, while slaves were
actual prisoners of war.   A conquering people want land
to own and control, but not necessarily to colonize ;   as
hewers of wood, and drawers of water, as ploughmen and
herdsmen, the inhabitants of a conquered land may remain.
Indeed it would seem that it has been the rule of the world
that less powerful or less developed races go down before
the more powerful or the more virile but not necessarily
the more civilized.   In very early times Anthropoids may
have been enslaved or enserfed by more developed folk,
but even when we had come to what, for want of a more
embracing term, we call neolithic man, the men of the
new Stone Age, we constantly see, so far as the signs can
be read, ruder races going down before the more accomplished and developed.

Through the ages, too, has the indigent or debt-ridden
freeman sold himself into bondage for the sake of sustenance
for himself and family, a system as modern as it is old.

We know a good deal of the story of serfdom in Ancient
Greece and Rome, and in the former the story of conquered
inferior tribes holds good.   In the confines of Greece and

Macedonia were conquered, less-developed tribes, who had not been enslaved, but merely enserfed. In Crete and on the Asiatic mainland the same conditions obtained, and the Helots of Sparta, another subject race, were described by Polluxas as of a status between freemen and slaves, which exactly describes serfdom, allowing for the fact that in various climes and times serfdom more nearly approached freedom or slavedom, as the case might be.

In Asia, on the great estates of the Seleucids, there were many conquered folk allowed to live on as serfs. In Rome, many of the slaves born or captured were gradually settled in those two well-known conditions referred to, one the *adscripti* or serfs, and the other the free *coloni* who owned their own small-holding and owed no service therefor. Their status was very definitely prescribed by law in the later days of Rome.

In almost all the lands over which Rome held sway, due to the system that had grown up long before serfdom was formally established, the ruling classes, being often an overlay from a conquering race, held the subject races in some form of serfdom that was not necessarily harsh.

The Germanic tribes who swarmed in as Rome left had a very similar system. They rarely worked their slaves, but gave them land exacting tribute, and thus made them serfs. The Roman *coloni* and settled slaves, and the German servile peasants merged eventually, and we have the serfdom of the Middle Ages born of a meeting of debased freedom on the one hand, with a lightened slavery on the other. However, in France there was a quite definite separation of serfs who belonged to their lords (but could not be sold away from the land), and the villein, who could only be compelled to give a certain number of days' work and other services and outside that was a free agent. In more modern times, as conditions improved and changed, an important factor was the desire of landlords to get tenantry,

36

to till their lands, and attract labour from elsewhere, and thus villeinage slowly died.

Curiously enough Russia, where serfdom lasted longer and where war slaves were held, had a free peasantry till modern times. Peasants whose debts were paid could always move. But gradually we see a debt-bondage growing up, with debt so heavy, especially on Crown lands, that the peasant was seldom free, and became a serf for life, and in time a hereditary one. In the early days of the nineteenth century there were half-hearted attempts to free the serfs in Russia, but it was not till 1861, when the strain of the Crimean War had broken up the *ancien régime*, that the Tzar Alexander, of his own initiative, succeeded in abolishing the serfs to the number of some 15,000,000. The peasants were given a portion of the land, owners were compensated, and the recipients paid the State a hire-purchase rent till the debt was liquidated. It is the descendants of Alexander's small-holders, and those whose lands have increased as the years have rolled on, who have incurred the vials of Soviet wrath and legislation.

SLAVERY AND SERFDOM IN THE BRITISH ISLES

Slavery and serfdom had a long history in the British Isles before the Saxons came, set far deep in the mists of time, through the long days of the Bronze Age period, and all the waves of invaders and settlers that we have seen, enslaving those they conquered. In Ireland perhaps this has been even most pronounced, when Celt impinged on Formorian and Firbolg. In Ireland, indeed, it is quite possible that the underlying bitterness that can get uppermost in the Irish character is an inherent memory-complex of ancient enslaving of the non-Celtic races by Celt, rather than of the Anglo-Norman conquest and the rule of the Anglo-Saxon. But it will be new to those who are not familiar with our history to know that till the beginning of the seventeenth century in Scotland, serfs wore metal collars, riveted on, with their owner's name. Again, so late as 1744, children were being kidnapped in Aberdeenshire to sell as slaves to the growing Virginia plantations, which were hard put to get labour before the African slave trade developed. Indeed it was not till 1775 that the serfdom which still held in Scotland for salters and colliers was abolished by Act of Parliament, and as that Act proved insufficient to end the condition, another was necessary in 1799 to complete it, more than ten years *after* the Houses of Parliament had passed a resolution condemning even the African slave trade !

Before tracing in more detail slavery and serfdom in our own land, which followed indeed the same story of war and conquest just referred to, it might be helpful to glance at our " pre-history " outline of invasions and settlements so far as we know them. We are beginning to know a good deal more of our racial antecedents, as the spade, the study of pottery, and the workings of the deductive brain take us deeper into the past. It seems that some race came in on the old flint-using neolithic man, and may have absorbed or enserfed him. Whether the long Bronze Age meant more than one race, or whether it meant the progressive civilization of one folk that produced an Avebury and a Stonehenge, we do not know. But we do know that there came in the earlier days of the first millennium B.C. the first Celtic or Aryan invasion, which must have swept away the Bronze Age, possibly an Iberian, civilization, before a ruder, more virile seizer of other folk's land. There is no need to think that the Goidelic Celts massacred the Iberians, they took what land and women they wanted and no doubt enslaved and enserfed the remainder. Years later came the second invasion of those Brythons who wore breeks, *saccos quos bulgas vocant.* They drove the earlier Celts north-west and westward, but those Goidels who

38

stayed, or the Iberian serfs they left, were no doubt ruled, enserfed, and absorbed by the Brythons. Indeed slaves were a British export before the Romans came. Rome came in for four hundred years to rule, to educate, and to civilize, but not to abolish slavery ; and then came Saxon savagery to destroy the Roman-British civilization, to conquer and re-enserf the folk that Rome had blended as one, and who no doubt themselves held slaves and serfs.

This serfdom is undoubtedly the ultimate development from the slavery caused by this constant impinging of bronze on stone, and iron on bronze, and hardness on softness, by peoples to whom *vae victis* meant slaughter or slavery. To the Saxon and Dane, the Romano-Iberic-Celtic *mélange* no doubt went into serfdom with its own serfs by its side.

Such systems as these take long to eradicate, and since they include the mingling of earlier and weaker races, tend to leave subconscious memories and instincts that taint mentalities under even a modern system.

The successive enslaving and enserfments that the English had continued and enlarged followed much the same course with the coming of the Norman, so that as Iberian had gone down before Celt, and Celt before Saxon, so did the latter, the English, go down in their turn, and the serfdom of mediaeval times evolve alongside a dominion of newer making. The Anglo-Saxon churl must have meant a man of a much-mingled strain, in which the Oriental and African settlers from the Legions and their Auxiliaries must have added traits of their own. But to this day among the infinite variety of cross-breeds do we see now and again some clean-cut Pict, Dane, Celt, or Saxon appear among us, whose ancestors may have been through the mill of slavery.

SLAVERY IN SAXON TIMES

After so general a review of the *mélange* that makes up the British mass, we may perhaps look a little more closely

39

at the coming of the Saxon, who should be more accurately called the Englishman, since that is the name by which Saxon, Angle, and Jute were called by their neighbours.

It has just been said that the Englishmen had heard, in common with all Germania, the surprised cry " Rome falls," and set themselves a-moving. After years of piracy along the coast, when Romo-Britons had neglected their " moat " and the *classis Britannica* had been allowed to weaken, the English were coming to stay, and their slave-raiding was turning to slave-owning, and slave-trading with the Irish and merchants who traded their British slaves south for them.

The Teuton races, democratic freemen as they all were, were inveterate slave holders and slave makers even when they gave advancement and freedom to the better ones. Freedom went with land, and a " landless " man was almost a slave, and as contemptible as a " masterless " man in feudal times. The Englishmen's custom, as already explained, followed the lines of all the German races.

But to be free yourself was one thing, to cherish freedom for all mankind quite another. The English, like the other Teutons, kept slaves of the lesser breeds and brought their slaves to Britain with them. Possibly with land going a-begging they freed the best of the slaves they brought over, replacing them with the captured Briton. The slaves the English actually brought with them may have included many serfs of the type of the lesser Roman *coloni*, who would soon have been settled on land, and set to clearing more forest. Not long after the subjugation of the British, the English of the various independent kingdoms started their own internecine wars and enslaved their fellow-Teutons, whatever the captive's rank, and it was this that brought fair-haired English child slaves to Rome, and produced the famous " non Angli sed angeli " story. The State, under the Heptarchy and after, made no stand against this long-accepted slave-morality, but to its credit the early Church of both northern and southern missions set its face towards at least the amelioration of slave conditions. Archbishop Theodore refused Christian burial to all kidnappers, and forbade, under pain of the Church's ban, all sale of children over the age of seven. Ecqberht of York went further, and forbade *all* sales of children and kinsmen. The murder of a slave by lord or mistress, no crime in the eyes of the State, became a sin for which the Church at least exacted penance.

The slave now began to be attached to the land, and could only be sold with it, thus adding to the number of serfs, and could even purchase his own freedom, while King Aethelstan brought slaves into the system of the freeman's responsibility for the prevention of crime, then as now the duty of the English people.

But the Church, as she got more and more into the saddle, was not content with penances and excommunication. She herself set examples which Wilfrid inaugurated by freeing 250 serfs attached to his estate at Selsey. The clever clergy taught that to manumit slaves by will was a deed that would help the Christian soul at death. At the Synod of Hertford the bishops bound themselves to free at their decease serfs on their estates who had been reduced to serfdom by want or crime, the year of death taking the place of the year of Jubilee. Slaves were usually set free before the altar or in the church porch, and the Gospel Book bore, written on its margins, the record of emancipation. Another method was for a slave's lord to set him at cross-roads and let him go wherever he listed. When emancipation became fashionable, a slave's master would take him by the hands, in full shire meeting, and give him the lance and sword of a freeman. And so the good work went on, steadily, and it was now, no doubt, that serfdom began to turn to villeinage, in which state a man held land of his lord, but was only compelled to work a certain number of days on his lord's land, and was otherwise free. As in the song of *The Farmer's Boy*, " the rest of your time's your own ! " but it was better than that in the song. So set among us was villeinage that some of its provisions remain as customs to this day in Copyhold, but the law of heriot, whereby the estate of a deceased holder gave a horse to the Lord of the Manor, probably only referred to returning the war equipment of a mounted man-at-arms given to freemen.

Early in the days of its activities, the Church had secured Sundays and holy days as days of rest for slaves.

Britain and Ireland were sea-girt lands, with a constant wash of sea-borne conquerors and of immigrants, and the overseas slave trade was one of the national businesses from long before the Christian era to the nineteenth century. Nor Rome, nor Cranmer, nor Calvin, nor reformer could stamp the habit out, and just as Bristol shared with Liverpool and London the greater portion of the negro trade and was largely organized to that end, so do we find that in the tenth century, Bristowe—as its earlier name ran—was extremely busy in shipping slaves to Ireland. Ireland long before the Norman days was an inexhaustible recipient. The Danes, both of the old and new settlements, were slave makers and also slave carriers, in their rôle of the northern world's ocean traders. We read in *Anglia Sacra* (p. 258) of how good Bishop Wulfstan prevailed, or partly prevailed, on Bristol " to drop that barbarous custom, which neither the love of God nor the King could prevail upon them to lay aside."

Bristol was the mart for slaves from all over England, and there we may be sure, new captures, tiresome children and unsatisfactory domestic slaves were sent. In fact the fear of being sold off to Ireland no doubt kept farm and domestic slaves fairly amenable. The *Anglia Sacra* also states that Bristowe was particularly the mart for young women, whom they took care " to put into such a state as to inhance their value " as of a mare sold " in foal," but it might be thought that such conditioning would have been left to the purchaser. That it should be recorded that a slave girl *enceinte* was specially marketable, is but another remarkable illustration of the physiological taint that the slave incurred merely from his or her status. Is it to be wondered at, therefore, that Christianity, bringing back the lost sense of personal value, should have spread so rapidly among the slave strata of Rome ?

It is not to be expected that the Danish Kingdom of England would have done anything but enhance the country's desire to hold and trade slaves, nor that the Normans would have set any stern face against the custom. The manorial feudal system that they developed, however, militated against the condition, when every man had to be related to land holding ; though we cannot doubt that the great houses certainly had a class of landless servant, who with no stake in the country save with his master, was very little removed from the slaves of earlier generations. The serfdom that had grown to villeinage was of course existent, and the increase of population did produce a free even though landless cottar, until the upset of the Black Death loosened all bonds in the desire " for life and escape." How complete an agency the Black Death was is a matter of some controversy.

But apparently in all times of upheaval there was a tendency of some revival of servitude for the beaten side, and this became most marked in the succession of the wars and upheavals of the Stuart days,[1] when Bristol once more flourished as a slave market.

[1] *Vide* Chapter V.

CHAPTER FOUR

The Slave Kings and Armies of Islam

★

*The Spread of Islam—The Slave Kings of Central Asia—The Slave
Dynasty of Delhi—The Janissaries—The Mamelukes—The Enslaving
Ottoman—The Harem Slave.*

★

THE SPREAD OF ISLAM

AN entirely new and more ruthless phenomenon now
appeared, with an even fiercer facet of slavery, in the rise
of Islam, " The Faith of the Submission," from its matrix
in the potholes of the Arabian desert.   Born of the truth
of Judaism and the folly of the Jewish-Christian enmity,
it seized the Arab imagination and their age-old belief in
the omnipotent El, and it rushed across Asia and along the
remnants of the dead Roman Empire in North Africa like
the roar of a forest fire.   Conquering all in their path, the
virile Arabs made the women of the Middle East their own,
and in a couple of generations had bred hosts of Moslems
to feed their fanatical forces.   So much was this the case
that ere long the Arab Empire, organized with unexpected
efficiency, was one of the largest that the submissive world
has ever seen.   With it, all ancient orders were upheaved.
The Arab stream mingled with that of Turk and Tartar
and Afghan in Central Asia, and as the years rolled on the
Turkish hordes adopted Islam, save those in South Russia,
who turned to Judaism, and produced the Russian " flat-
nosed " Jew of our day.   The Arab leaders set up kingdoms
and principalities all over Persia and Central Asia, and

44

with it all went a vast and cruel slave system far more severe than ever contemplated or enjoined by the Prophet. To serve that system, a ruthless, inhuman race of slave merchants for slave goods of all kinds arose. As the eastern Arab and Turkish leaders and princes grew more wealthy and more luxurious, the trade in slave beauty became one of the most organized systems known to us. Races, subject or avaricious, where beauty adorned their women, were fiercely exploited. Since the East is prolific, parents could satisfy the slave merchant by selling their surplus daughters when raiding was inexpedient.

The Arab conquerors and colonists in Central Asia and the Arabian principalities maintained hosts of women and owned large numbers of men slaves, and among them was engendered that terrible doctrine that a slave womb could only produce slaves, which maintains to this day. The principle of slave armies and slave soldiers, brought up to arms from youth and even bred therefor, was established. So much was this so that the whole structure of Moslem life and outlook has been tainted by it, and can hardly escape from its ethnological evils. From this habit, developed and organized under the Turks, as Turk succeeded to Arab in the hegemony of the Moslem world, arose several strange by-products of slavery. Slave forces became all-powerful, and slave children were snatched from parents and brought up by the rulers for military purposes in military seminaries, of whom some rose to great power. They eventually formed groups that not only controlled the thrones, but filled them from among their numbers by election, which meant the dominance of the stronger among them. Examples are to be seen in great slave rulers in Ghuzni, whose names ending in " *tegin* " [1] denotes slave origin, and the slave dynasties of Delhi. Classic instances of slave fraternities dominating as landowners and rulers

---

[1] E.g. *Alptegin, Sabakhtegin.*

are those of the Mamelukes in Egypt, and as a highly trained dominating army, the Janissaries of the Ottoman Sultans, who carried the Ottoman banners to the Danube and the walls of Vienna, only to fall at long last before the military genius of Prince Eugene.

THE SLAVE KINGS OF CENTRAL ASIA

As the centuries of Arab conquest rolled on, the central Arab Empire faded, and indeed it was the rising power of various Turkish groups and branches, and the dying out of the original fire that had spread the Arab conquests, that marked the next stage. Great independent, or but nominally dependent, principalities grew up in Central Asia, with Islam as their dominating faith, but since Turki race and language differs so entirely from Arab, there was only the common bond of Islam between them, and for a long time not even that.

It is essential to realize in thinking of this succession of Turk to Arab that from the great civilization of Islam, with the universal acceptance of Arabic and the Arabic Qoran as the ecclesiastical language, a universal way of life and civilization arose, similar to a great extent to the universality of the Mediaeval Church and the Latin tongue. Indeed Hinduism was but a similar and earlier attempt to unite countries and races. When the last of the Turkish races worked their havoc, they came as Pagan, not yet in the Moslem fold.

Arab and Turk had, however, intensely in common, the slave habit and system. The Arab governors and the princes, as the Turks first came to them, found that they made magnificent soldiers. The first to rise to fame was a Turkish commander-in-chief in Khorassan, one Alptegin, whose suffix " tegin " already mentioned denoted his slave origin. Alptegin, after a quarrel with Arab authority,

46

retired to the mountains of Ghuzni, and there founded a kingdom of his own in the tenth century. He was succeeded by a slave, Sabakhtegin, who had married his daughter. This slave king had received a *sannad* [1] from the Arab ruler at Bagdad as independent king, though it suited him to acknowledge the Samanid ruler's authority of Transoxania. Ere long, in defending the Samanids against a new Turkish horde, in what was the first Turkish invasion of the Arab Empire, his services were rewarded with the Governorship of Khorassan, and this started the State of Ghuzni, which under the famous Mahmud and his successors became the Kingdom, nay, almost the Empire, of Ghuzni and the rule of Northern India. It will be noticed that in the case of these Afghanistani and Indian slave kings there is an attempt at times to set up a dynasty, but often the slave king's sons are quite unfit to succeed to turbulent one-man thrones, and that another slave, by *coup d'état*, by election, or by group support, soon succeeds. But in the case of Ghuzni, a dynasty was actually able to survive.

In 999 Sabakhtegin died, and was succeeded by a thrice-competent son, Mahmud, "Mahmud of Ghuzni," so famous in Moslem song as *Sultan Mahmud Ghăznăvi*. Sabakhtegin had made his peace with the Ilek Khans of Turkestan, with whom his father's wars in support of the Caliph's power at Bagdad had been fought, and agreed that the Khans should be supreme in the valley and basin of the Jaxartes if held. The Khans, however, had seized Bokhara, which ended the Samanid house, while eventually Mahmud came to terms with them, whereby the larger bulk of the Samanid territory fell to him and he was supreme up to the Oxus, which gave him time to pursue his plans of Indian conquest. Eventually he was recognized by the Caliph as supreme ruler of the East.

[1] *Sannad*=warrant, or title-roll.

To him, known as the " Idol-breaker," the invasion of Hindu India was a holy war. Twelve times he crossed the Indus, penetrating far down the Ganges, destroying the ornate temples, setting up in some sort " The Faith of the Submission," and eventually establishing his governors in Lahore, though conversion rather than dominion seemed to be his ruling principle.

He was remarkable as a patron of learning and letters as well as a conqueror, and it was for him that the Persian poet Firdausi wrote the *Shahnama*, the Book of Kings, and the architects and builders of his time strove to make mountain Ghuzni a place of beauty, both in mosques and castles as well as in palaces.

This slave-bred Turk did really establish a dynasty, and dying in 1030 his son Masud succeeded, and spent ten years in holding what he had got and staving off a fresh inroad of pagan Turks, this time the confederation of the Ghuz, from whom sprang Seljuk, the founder of the ruie of the Seljuk Turks in Persia and Bagdad.

The dynasty of Mahmud of Ghuzni lasted with stormy successions till 1135, and it was to some extent a non-slave dynasty ruled by his descendants, till finally it fell before another Turkish conqueror from the small State of Ghor in the hills near Kandahar, who signalled his victory by destroying the beautiful Ghuzni. The Ghuznavid Sultans survived a while in Lahore, but ere long fell before the all-conquering Ghorids, who between the years of 1175 and 1194 became masters of Hindustan.

In this short outline of the various facets which slave customs imposed on the East, it was not till 1202, when the second Ghorid sultan died without effective family succession, that the phenomenon of the slave kings of Delhi—often referred to as " The Slaves " in Indian histories—arose, and something resembling the Mamelukes' rule in Egypt came into being. But although Sabakhtegin's

son, the *Sultan Mahmud Ghăznăvi*, had succeeded in
establishing a family dynasty which lasted several generations, and their Ghorid successors one that endured from
father to son for two reigns, yet during all this period
provincial governors and military leaders were almost all
slaves trained for war, and to some extent for administration
and in personal devotion to the master, in the schools and
systems already briefly described. Indeed it seems that in
the constant succession of world-stormers that the times
and evolving races of Asia were putting forth, this system
alone gave any promise of faithful service. Even that faith
often enough but hung on the prestige and relentlessness of
the leader, slave or otherwise, of the hour.

The Slave Dynasty of Delhi

In the year 1206 the second Ghorid sultan was murdered,
when his great slave servant, a Turk, Qutb-ud-Din Aibuk,
the " Moon Lord," was governor of the Punjab. To him
the succession, since no Ghorid of importance remained,
to the throne of Ghuzni and Ghor, of Lahore, and Delhi
fell almost automatically. With his succession the real
Islamic rule of India may be said to have commenced,
although ten years earlier one Muhammad Ibn Bakhtiyar,
a slave of the Ghorid Sultan, of the Turco-Afghan race of
the Khalij, had made himself Governor of Bengal, nominally
on behalf of the Ghorid.

Delhi itself has many relics of the dour stately erections
of the " slave " period and the art of the Turkish builders,
including the great Minar that is known to modern sight-
seers as " The Qutb." Qutb-ud-Din had for years been
the virtual ruler of Delhi, but did not long survive his
succession to the Sultanate. But it was these twin slaves
of the Ghorid, Qutb and Ibn Bakhtiyar, who had brought
Islam to the bulk of India. There was no son of Qutb-ud-

D   49

Din who could possibly succeed, and the latter's death was followed by great disorder till his slave Altamish, more correctly Il Tutmish, the "World-grasper," seized the throne with the support and concurrence of the bulk of the "slave" leaders and Turks of Delhi. Altamish reigned for twenty-five years and added Sinde to Delhi, and also secured that Ibn Bakhtiyar's Bengal should recognize the Delhi rule by appropriate rendering of revenue. The Caliph of Bagdad, still nominally head of all Moslem countries, now recognized India as a province of the Islamic world control that once was the Arab Empire, and gave his licence for the first time to Altamish as the Islamic head. Altamish died in 1235, with no male descendant who could hold the sceptre. For a short while his supporters placed his daughter Razia on the throne, the only woman, it has been said, till Queen Victoria, to sit on the Delhi throne. But a woman on the throne of Delhi was more than Islam could stand, nor indeed could any woman long ride the Turco-Afghan whirl that lay beneath the throne. Even marriage could not save her, and the Turkish slaves who held the real power saw that she was murdered within three years. Finally a third son of Altamish was tried, and he nominally held the throne for twenty years, while his great slave minister Balban held the reins of government. Here there was enacted the well-known Asiatic farce of the Mayor of the Place, the puppet throne and powerful minister, which is permanently illustrated for us in the Persian game of chess, where the feeble king is defended by the powerful Queen, who in eastern nomenclature has the correct title and name of *Vizier* or Prime Minister.

So slave-born Balban was really the third slave king for those twenty years, while his puppet Nasir-ud-Din buried himself in learning and lent Balban his signet. Balban was a strange character. Of noble Turkish birth from

Turkestan, he was carried into slavery as a lad by marauders and sold in India. The story runs that Altamish, selecting slaves—many required as catamites—from lads brought before him, ignored the ill-favoured and dwarfish Balban. The latter called out to the Sultan, asking for whom had he bought the slaves. " For myself," snapped out the Sultan. " Then buy me for the sake of God," cried Balban, and this Altamish good-humouredly did. Balban ruled as *Vizier* for twenty years, always making much of his fellow-slaves who were in power, and when Nasir died he passed to undisputed succession and ruled India for another twenty-two years. Balban, as an old man, still retained fire enough to put down with probably necessary ruthless-ness an insurrection by another slave Tugril, but it was with the constant inroads of the new pagan horror of the rising Mongols that he was most concerned. Ousted tribes flocked to Delhi for shelter. His favourite son who might have succeeded was killed fighting the terror, and Balban died of the shock in 1186. A useless grandson proved a failure and was murdered. Turmoil and bloodshed thus ended the slave dynasties, and the Khaliji faction placed one of their number on the throne, and founded for a while a genuine non-slave line, though it has just been said how Ibn Bakhtiyar Khaliji, first Moslem ruler of Bengal, was himself one of the Ghorid slaves.

So this strange method of succession at Delhi came to an end, after eighty years, though it was really but one of those dynasties which with the short exception of the Lodis were all Turks, whether Ghuznavide, Ghorid, Slave, or Khaliji, or even the Sayyad, which was only nominally Arab, down to Chagatai or Mogul. To those who moralize on race and leadership let it be borne in mind that, whether it was Mogul at Delhi, Manchu at Pekin, Ottoman on the Bosphorus, or Khajjar at Teheran, this strange Turkish or Tartar folk, whose matrix was the almond eye of the

Mongol, supplied the rulers for the whole of Asia. It was not till the final fading of the Mogul name in 1857 that the tradition left even India, while it did not quit the world till after the war of 1914. Further, it is to be remembered that it was based from the Bosphorus to the Pacific on the old conception, following perhaps on the tradition of Rome, of slave soldiers, chiefs, and kings. To those who would palliate the institution, it might perhaps be said that the Turkish rule of slave selection was perhaps but a rude world's form of university.

THE JANISSARIES

The Janissaries, the men of the *Yeni Seri* [1] or new model army of the Ottoman Sultan, were definitely an organized disciplined force on slave lines, the only " regular force " in the Turkish army. This force was undoubtedly the source of most of the power and military success of the House of Ottoman.

The Janissaries owe their inception to the great Murad (Murad I, 1360–1389), who for twenty-four years of his military career, during which he led his armies, never suffered a reverse. He recruited a " regular army " of standing corps from his Christian prisoners of war, and he maintained it on the slave lines already well known in Central Asia. One thousand Christian lads yearly, of the ages of ten to twelve, were conscripted from the Christian children of the conquered portion of the Byzantine Empire, and only those of exceptional physique and health were taken.

Forcible conversion to Islam followed, with, of course, circumcision ; and receiving Moslem names they were trained—and trained very thoroughly—under the eyes of Murad himself. For six years this training continued,

[1] Turkish *Yeni Tcheri*, new soldiers.

when they were drafted into the special army, which after a few years attained the strength of 12,000 and eventually ran to 40,000 men. All intensely trained to arms, supremely athletic, their imagination captured by the Sultan from whom alone came advancement, the character of unusual individuals developed remarkably. Discipline was severe and great prowess was demanded, and the troops thus formed were trained, after the western modes that had descended from the Romans, to march, to fight, to use the new firearms, in addition to bow and spear and scimitar. Their regiment was their home, they were allowed to acquire no property, everything belonged to the unit. It was the desire, the wise desire, of the Sultan to have at his beck men entirely devoted to his cause and with no sort of ties with the world of the homely virtues. So long as the Sultan was a man of great character, ruthlessness, and wisdom to temper it, so long could this conception serve their imperial purpose. So long in fact as " Amurath to Amurath succeeds . . .," so long as a Murad succeeds a Murad, and his hand can keep his head. Unfortunately Amurath did not always succeed, and a succession of feeble Sultans made the Janissaries the arbiters of the throne and intolerable to all men of vision and moderation.

Of the Janissaries in their prime Sir Edward Piers has written :

" Take a number of children from the most intelligent portion of the community ; choose them for their strength and intelligence, instruct them carefully in the art of fighting, bring them up under strict military discipline, teach them to forget their parents, childhood, friends, saturate them with the knowledge that all their hope in life depends on their position in the regiment, make peace irksome and war a delight, with the hope of promotion and relaxation from the hardship and restraints

53

of the barrack, the result will be a weapon in the hands of a leader such as the world has rarely seen. Such a weapon was the army of the Janissaries.''

Much indeed of the reputation of the Janissaries for ruthlessness in Europe came from the excesses and massacres of prisoners carried out by them, whom the Sultan, not even at times so great a ruler as Solyman the Magnificent, could not restrain. But in the slow progress towards Vienna and the Danube, that only Eugene's military skill and power of leadership could withstand, and from which he rescued Europe, it was the Janissaries who were the only real disciplined bloc that the West had to meet.

As the generations rolled on, the slave basis of the Janissaries was modified and Moslem lads were admitted. But the lawlessness of the later days was but increased by this under the weaker rulers, and though the history of the greatness of the Turkish Empire is the history of the Janissaries, yet the era of the slave armies and their tradition was nearing the inevitable end. Long and famous had been the strong, ruthless, cruel and at last intolerable domination. Equally ruthless was the *dénouement*.

A Sultan with something of the old spirit had emerged from the Cage on the Bosphorus, and in 1826 Mahmud II took vengeance for the humiliation he and his predecessors had undergone at their hands. Faced with the great rival to Turkey that had arisen in Egypt in the person of Ibrahim, the son of Mehemet Ali, Mahmud had determined to put the armies of Turkey on a modern footing. All the force of reaction, especially the Janissaries, opposed his plans. Strong in the possession of a new force of artillery, he struck on the 11th June 1826, when a *firman* was issued incorporating the Janissaries in his new infantry. Those in Constantinople marched in a body to the Palace in repetition of their old habit of compelling their masters. But they had met their match. Unfurling against them the sacred Ottoman banner, Mahmud pounded them in the streets with the guns of his new artillery, and drove them back to their barracks. There the Imperial guns did their task; no quarter was given, and the old force that had grown too turbulent was destroyed by gun-fire or in the burning barracks. In Constantinople 4000 were killed, and Mahmud carried out the liquidation equally thoroughly in all the other cantonments. The Janissaries were no more, and the name of the once famous force disappeared from the Turkish army list.

Thus ended one of the great and infamous offsprings of the Islamic slave system.

In Egypt a few years earlier a similar purge of a slave-born oligarchy in its decadent remnant had been carried out by means cruel, treacherous, but no doubt necessary. The nemesis of years had fallen.

The Mamelukes

This other great slave emanation, more familiar by name to the travelling public to-day than the Janissaries, whose liquidation just referred to took place a few years before the latter, was that of the Mamelukes. That is a term derived from the Arabic word for slaves, and they were an older organization than even the Janissaries, but not as in later inception born of a levy of Christian boys, but from the Turkish and Circassian slaves bought from Gengis Khan by the rulers of Egypt. They date from so far back as 1240, and were but another form of the slave forces and slave cadet service referred to as a feature of the Moslem domination of Asia. Like the Janissaries they ere long made themselves an overriding power in the State, even placing one of their number on the throne of Egypt ere many years had passed, and continued to do so by election and intrigue till Egypt became a Turkish province in 1517, when the conquering Turkish Beys who now ruled the land took them into their pay. From 1240 onwards till the days of Mehemet Ali in the early nineteenth century, the story of the Mamelukes is the story of Egypt : land-owning, overriding, controlling, and in the aspects of military value, deteriorating. In 1798 under the broiling sun of the desert they galloped round the perspiring columns of Napoleon's infantry, causing intense difficulty in supplies and water, but were defeated at the Battle of the Pyramids. Thence they withdrew up the Nile to Nubia, whence as French and then British left Egypt they returned to resume their now effete power.

Their end was as the end of the Janissaries and to come sooner. A strong man had arisen, nominally Governor of Egypt under the Turks, who were able to reassert their power. Mehemet Ali, the Albanian, the first Khedive of Egypt, had no intention of leaving a Mameluke tradition with any germ of recovery. On the 1st of March 1911 they, with their retinues, were decoyed to a feast at the citadel in Cairo, and there massacred—the eventual fate of all Praetorian Guards. To this day visitors are shown in the citadel the Mameluke's leap, where one on a magnificent Arab jumped the great sunken road that leads down from the inner citadel over the defiles into which they had been decoyed. The Mameluke tradition now but remains as an instance of the strange conditions and byways to which the slave spirit and its emanations have led lands and nations. In the case of Egypt many centuries of astounding drama and upheaval lie behind this story of slave turned master.

The Enslaving Ottoman

Turkey, the Ottoman Empire, which included of course in name at least most of Arabia, was the most inveterate and ruthless slave holder. In the wideflung conquests made by Ottoman Sultans, all Christians and other non-Moslems were sold as slaves to the number of many thousands. Four-fifths of the proceeds of the sale of slaves went to the soldiery, one-fifth to the Sultan. Loot and plunder and the sale of slaves was the one object of the Ottoman campaigns. In 1393 the Sultan Bayazid invaded the northern half of Bulgaria and carried away numerous slaves. A similar fate followed on in Hungary and wherever the Turkish Army was victorious.

In the first half of the fifteenth century the Greek Emperor had sold Salonika to the Venetians. The Sultan, Murad II, refused to recognize the right of the Emperor to sell it, so low had Rome now fallen. He led an army against the place in the year 1430, carried it by assault, and annexed it. He flattered himself that he had acted with great clemency in not permitting a general massacre, but contented himself with selling the Greek inhabitants into slavery. So large was the number and so great the proportion of girls among them, that even a good-looking girl fetched no more than the price of a pair of boots.

In 1570 when the Grand Vizier Sokolli, who was the virtual ruler of the Ottoman Empire, took Nicosia, the capital of Cyprus, after a seven weeks' siege, 30,000 inhabitants were massacred. Thousands of Christian women took their own lives to escape the ruthless lust of the victorious Turkish soldiery, and 2000 of the better-looking children of both sexes were sent to the slave markets at Istamboul. It was the same siege at which Kara Mustapha the Turkish commander flayed alive the Venetian commander, to whom he promised safe conduct, for some imaginary insult. From Nicosia the Turk marched on to Famagusta, which fell, with the reputed massacre of 50,000, and the usual selling into slavery of all who were young and comely.

The great defeat of the Turks at Lepanto will be mentioned in the next chapter, where 15,000 Christian slaves were released from the banked galleys. Many volumes might be written of all the Turks have done through the ages in selling the Christian world to slavery, and we may pass on to a typical Turkish threat which failed, though the victories of Hunyadi and Prince Eugene had killed their reputation on the Danube as a world menace. Between 1821 and 1824 the Greeks were engaged in the most desperate of their many struggles against their Turkish conquerors. The Sultan, who had been much impressed with the army on a western model that his vassal Mehemet Ali had formed in Egypt, invited him to bring his fleet and his army to help subdue the Greeks. Mehemet Ali sailed with a convoy of 10,000 infantry and 1000 cavalry, landed at Navarino and defeated the Greeks heavily, capturing the whole of the Morea. The Greek Army was on the point of being destroyed, Mehemet Ali threatening to remove the whole Greek population and sell them as slaves, replacing them with Arabs and Egyptians. It was a typical threat of the slave-making mind, and would no doubt have been carried out had not the Allied fleets, led by the British, destroyed the whole Turko-Egyptian fleet at Navarino, and thus compelled the withdrawal of the Egyptian Army whence it had come, while a French army shouldered the Turkish troops out of Greek territory.

During all the earlier days of the nineteenth century, slavery continued unabashed throughout Turkey, from the imported or bred African to the Circassian and other comely girls for the harems of the wealthy, the latter the established custom since the Ottoman came as conquerors to Hellespont. The British policy of saving Turkey from Russia, however important in the upholding of the balance of power, brought much opposition on account of the

Turkish attitude towards slavery, and protests were made by the Anti-Slavery Society that the Turkish flag should cover slave dhows bringing slaves from the Sudan. In 1857 the Porte had made promises to Lord Stratford de Redcliffe, in the general clearing up after the Crimea, in which Britain had made so many sacrifices for Turkey, but like most other Turkish promises they were but words. Again, in 1880, Britain entered into a convention with Turkey for the suppression of the slave trade which was equally disappointing. Turkey was a party to the Brussels Act of 1890 and the Berlin conferences, both of which aimed at the suppression of slavery. The first result of the Berlin conferences was the unfortunate affair of the Congo Free State. Since the Young Turk movement, the series of unfortunate wars in which Turkey was involved prior to the World War, and the regeneration of the Turkey of to-day shorn of its slave-holding Arabia, slavery at long last has faded out, leaving in all slave-holding states a strange and unavoidable tail of sequelae in the warp and weft of the people.

In the matter of women perhaps the Turkish harem, especially that of the Sultan, has through the ages shown that side of the slave system in its most developed form ; and though the sighs and the miseries are happily gone, let us hope for ever, its methods are still of academic interest.

THE HAREM SLAVE

The life of a female slave in Turkey was perhaps the most typical example of the Turkish attitude to slaves. The more important Pashas and nobles had a large female establishment, in which there might or might not be four legal wives. The rest would be slave women. The leading example was, of course, the Sultan's establishment, the hareem, to give it its proper phonetic spelling. Abdul

Hamid had a thousand women slaves. No Turkish Sultan ever had a legal wife, but the women he liked and chose became *hanun effendi*. Any slave, any of the odalisques, which means women of the chamber, might become a *hanun effendi*, the baton lay in the knapsack of the humblest! The mother of the recognized heir to the throne would be *bash hanun effendi*, or chief lady. The Sultan's mother, the Valida Sultana, would be in command of all the establishment of the harem. Any of the odalisques who bore a son to the Sultan would be a *hanun effendi*, and even any who shared his couch would receive *daira*, an endowment of some kind.

The palace establishment of the " deprived " was considerable, black slave eunuchs, normally called *kizlar aghasi*, " masters of the maids," in reality *daru sé adal aga*, " lords of the abode of bliss," guarded the inside. The outer doors were in charge of white eunuchs, known as *kapu aghasi*, " lords of the Gate."

There was some measure of recognition in the sanctity of womanhood in Turkish households, in that any slave who entered into sexual relation with her master became of importance and was entitled to maintenance ever afterwards.

CHAPTER FIVE

The Corsairs of the Mediterranean and the Barbary States

★

The Decay of the Pax Romanis—The Barbary States and the Rise of the Corsairs—The Coming of the Turk—El Magnifico and Barbarossa—The Battle of Lepanto—Of Morocco—The Later Days of the Barbary States and Pirates—The British Extirpation of Algiers—Some Stories of the Rovers.

★

THE DECAY OF THE PAX ROMANIS

WITH the fall of the Roman Empire of the West came an end to the security to trade which the Roman fleets had long secured. With the fall of the Empire of the East the masterless men of the Mediterranean took to piracy on the high sea and the profitable life of promiscuous slave-raiding.

To end the cultured life of that centre of the later Roman civilization and home of Early Christianity—the Romanized territory of North Africa—came, in the seventh century, the great Arab floods that the urge of Islam had set loose on the remnants of the older civilizations. Egypt and North Africa were submerged, and partly Arabicized, while Moor and Berber accepted the stimulating doctrines of the Prophet. To such effect and with such *éclat* did this come about, that to this day there is the western Caliph still holding sway and influence, when the usurping [1] Turkish Caliph of the East has faded from men's memory. The

---

[1] " Usurping," since the Caliphate should be in the Prophet's tribe, and the Ottoman Sultan became " Caliph " by very doubtful means.

61

Sultan of Morocco is still Caliph, " The Successor," to the Moslems of western Africa.

The semi-independent Moslem ruler of North Africa, who soon broke loose from Bagdad, fostered or failed to control piracy and slave-raiding in the middle and western Mediterranean. The trading city-states of the northern Mediterranean littoral—Venice, Genoa, and the like—were constantly engaged in struggles against these torments of the Inland Sea.

Many were the Europeans of all nations who for centuries long languished as slaves in the west of North Africa, in the hands of what eventually were known as the Barbary States, Algiers, Tunis, Tripoli, and Barka. Not only were captured crews enslaved, but their passengers of both sexes and all ages, while in addition slave-raiding on the coasts of Europe was a very lucrative occupation. Indeed many a ravished beauty from some Mediterranean sea-coast town or village ended her days in no less seclusion than the harem of the Sultan of Constantinople, since the pirates took their wares to the best markets.

It will be remembered how Defoe tells what was probably his own story in the earlier pages of *Robinson Crusoe*.

" Eyeless in Gaza at the mill with slaves," as the incomparable line from Milton has it, was too often the fate of a Christian sailor. Many Christian slaves indeed secured their masters' favour, often by accepting unprintable indignities, rising thereby to as great fame and influence as some of the Central Asian " slaves " whose story has already been outlined. Indeed the corsairs, Barbarossa and Piali, whose adventures will follow, were Europeans by birth, and this rise of converted Christians is a constant feature in the Turkish service from earliest times, even as recently as the Crimean War. Beyram Pasha, so famed for the defence of Silistria, was a Briton ; Kméty Pasha, in the defence of Kars, was an Austrian; while Omar Pasha, the Commander-in-Chief of the Turkish Army acting with the Allies in the Crimea, was also an Austrian.

THE BARBARY STATES AND THE RISE OF THE CORSAIRS

The overrunning of what was known in Roman times as Mauritania, the country of the Moors, by the Arab spate whose overflow into Central Asia has also been related, has just been outlined. The principal inhabitants of Mauritania were the people still known as the Berbers, and the term Barbary is but a derivative. Indeed it is said that it is from them that our and the Roman word " barbarian " have their origin, and the *hoi barbaroi* of the Greek were none other than the people of the coasts, then, as of later years, known for their evil reputation at sea as well as their fierce fighting spirit on land. When that astounding phenomenon, the Arab Empire of Bagdad, that had overrun so much of the world in so short a time, began to lose its momentum and the unity of purpose that had characterized its enterprises, the Mauritanian or Barbary States survived under Arab or half-Arab rulers of varying capacity.

The States beside Morocco itself were Algiers, Tunis, Tripoli, and Barka, nearest to Egypt as aforesaid.

With the coming of the Turk, whether Moslem or Pagan, to the Levant littoral, there was little likely to be any mitigation of the Mediterranean slave-trading and slave-raiding. Indeed there came about in the early sixteenth century a combination of the power of the corsairs with that of the Ottoman Turk, which condemned the Christian folks of Europe to slavery by the tens of thousands. It was calculated at one time that there were 30,000 Christian slaves held in Tunis alone. For the best part of a century the Barbary States had been part of the empire

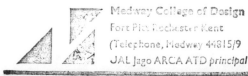

of the Sultans of Constantinople and gained prestige thereby. Their corsair navies, and those of the independent corsairs who had settled themselves in their ports, were an adjunct of the Turkish Navy.

It had been the custom of the corsairs to put their galleys to sea in fleets of twenty, with an " admiral " in charge of each. This honoured term of " Admiral " is but the Arabic commencement of a title " Lord of the Sea," *Amir al Bahr*, and it simply means " Lord of," and is thus a horse without a carriage ! It was these independent fleets often combining into large groups that swept the Mediterranean, a terror and a nightmare to all good Christian folk on the sea and those within reach of the sea, and it was they who joined forces with the Turk and placed the Barbary States under the Sultan's dominion. It should be understood that the corsairs, so called, stand for more than one category. They were sometimes the actual chiefs, themselves leading their own navies, or they were the chiefs' admirals working under, or against, their lords' orders, while they were at times independent pirate " admirals " like the Sali rovers, who had settled themselves in, and dominated, a port that did not belong to them as a base for their nefarious operations.

The tangled remnant of civilized trade that survived the collapse of Rome was sorely harried by the corsairs, even when they were kept at times in some sort of suppression by the power of Venice, of Spain, and of the Pope himself ; but out of it all there finally arose the Turkish naval power, which combined with the Barbary States to make the Mediterranean for long periods at a time little better than a Moslem lake and a slave factory.

When the western powers themselves took to enslaving the people of Africa in the seventeenth century, had they brought their operations to the north coast of Africa rather than the west, there would at least have been some sense

64

of justice in revenge for the long years of Christian slavery at African hands.

In the year 1520 Selim, the ninth Ottoman Sultan, was succeeded by his son Solyman, to use the popular spelling, who was to be known to history as Solyman the Magnificent (El Magnifico),[1] and who ruled for forty-six years. Under Solyman not only was the Turkish dominion extended far into Europe, but a navy was formed that for a while practically dominated not only the Levant but the whole Mediterranean. Selim, Solyman's father, had done much for his navy, and Solyman continued the policy of making the high seas his own. But strive as the Turkish admirals could, they were out-sailed by the pirate corsairs of the Barbary coasts. As good Moslems there was every reason for the corsairs becoming good Turks, and Solyman invited many of them to join his navy and sweep the southern seas. He gave high appointments to many of them, making them *Amir al Bahr*, "Lord of," of his fleets, and eventually as related swept them for a while into the Ottoman Empire.

El Magnifico and Barbarossa

The first and most distinguished of the Turkish corsair admirals was Khair ud Din, better known as Barbarossa,[2] one of four brothers of Greek descent born in Mitylene, who in early life took to Islam and then, under cover of commerce, to piracy as a profession. Two of his brothers lost their lives in this family business, and he became the terror of the whole unpoliced Mediterranean. As he gathered strength and ships he made war on his own account, seized the Barbary State of Algiers, making it his own, whence he devastated the coast of Europe, his name

---

[1] El Magnifico was his name to all Europe. To Turkey he was "The Law Giver," a tribute to his organizing power.

[2] Barbarossa＝Redbeard.

becoming a household word of terror in the cities of the West. As he found that to maintain himself in Algiers against the civilized world was beyond his powers, he recognized the sovereignty and received the support of Turkey.

His development of Algiers was a matter of some political acumen as well as Islamic sympathy, for he brought 70,000 Moors out of Spain on his ships and settled them in Algiers. The neighbour state of Tunis was in the effete hands of one Muley Hasan, the twenty-second successor in the long dynasty of the Arab Beni Hafis. This slave-raiding pirate had little to recommend him. He had the traditional ruthlessness without the character to profit by it.

He had killed forty-three out of his forty-four brothers on his succession—in the East you either slay, blind, or incarcerate your brothers [1]—but was now chiefly intent on collecting a harem of four hundred catamite boys, proceeds of his slave raids. The suppressing of such infamy seemed an excellent excuse for El Magnifico to obtain control over Tunis, and he deputed Barbarossa to capture the place from the decadent Dey.

This he was able to do with little difficulty, but Muley Hasan appealed for help to the Spanish Emperor Charles V. Charles had not the least sympathy with one of the slave plagues of Europe such as the Dey of Tunis, but still less with the arch-pirate and slave-holder Barbarossa. He arrived and drove forth Barbarossa, who put up a fine defence against a far superior force. The defeated corsair retired to the interior, and Tunis became a Spanish possession. Not only did Charles V disregard Muley Hasan, which he but deserved, but although coming nominally as the ally of the Tunisians, who incidentally

[1] That is to say half-brothers by many mothers; full brothers often had a better fate and could be trusted.

gave no help to Barbarossa, the Spaniard permitted his soldiers to pillage the place and murder 30,000 of the inhabitants. No more ruthless or terrible sack had ever been carried out, even in the annals of Arab and Turkish outrage. The only excuse that justice might allege is the ruthless holding of male and female Christian slaves snatched both from ship and shore by Tunisian corsairs for generations. However that may have been, the Dons surpassed themselves in Christian massacre! Muley Hasan, however, was reinstated in his ruined Tunis, and remained a ruler under Spanish protection, definitely detached from Turkey.

Shortly after, the Sultan, knowing well the story of his prowess at sea and his fine defence of Tunis against the Spanish, summoned Barbarossa to Constantinople and made him Grand Admiral of the Turkish fleet. In 1538, while head of the Turkish Navy, he, with a hundred and seven war vessels and galleys, defeated the combined fleets of Spain, Venice, and the Pope, off Prevesa. The allied ships totalled one hundred and thirty, under the command of the famous and almost invincible Venetian, Admiral Andrea Doria, several of whose vessels the Turks captured or destroyed. Barbarossa then went with the Sultan to the misadventure at Corfu, which the Venetians stoutly defended, but in the course of this war succeeded in taking all the numerous Venetian islands in the Aegean with the exception of Crete. The remarkable career of this sea pirate turned admiral closed with his death at Constantinople in 1546.

There were, however, plenty more of his kidney in the pirate navies of the Barbary States, who succeeded to service with the Turks and upheld the corsair reputation as sailors and pirates. The most distinguished among them was one Dragut or Torghut, a Croat turned Moslem, who, once a Turkish subject, had turned freebooter. Like

Barbarossa, Dragut had carried consternation in his pillaging and kidnapping of slaves on the Spanish coast. Everything was fish to his net, and even after he had entered the Turkish service he pillaged the Sultan's allies with impunity.

Finally summoned to Constantinople to account for some unlicensed captures of Venetian vessels, Dragut, who knew better than that, took to the coast of Morocco and there set up as a pirate slave-chief on his own. But Draguts are hard to come by, and finally El Magnifico invited him to return, offering to make him Governor of Tripoli if he could take it from the Knights of St. John. Accepting reinstatement, Dragut did as required, and duly became Governor of Tripoli ; losing his life, however, in the abortive attack on Malta in 1565.

Equally renowned in the Turkish Navy was another renegade Turk, Piali, who had originally left Turkish territory also for the life of the corsair. Invited by Solyman to join the Turkish service, he became commander-in-chief of the Turkish Navy. He commanded their fleet in the same unsuccessful attempt on Malta in which Dragut lost his life. An earlier exploit was his defeat of Andrea Doria at the head of Spanish, Venetian, and Papal fleets which were attempting to retake Tripoli, and also captured for the Turks the district of Oran, on the coast of Africa beyond Algiers.

In 1568 Sokolli, the competent vizier of the Sultan, determined to recapture Tunis, placing the expedition under Ouloudj Pasha, a renegade Italian corsair pirate and magnificent seaman who had followed Barbarossa and Piali in serving the Sultan. Ouloudj had been made Dey of Algiers, and in this capacity now took the town of Tunis. The Spanish garrison, however, took refuge in the citadel, which they held for another six years.

With Algiers and Tunis now under the aegis of the Sultan, it is not to be wondered at that the corsair fleets

RESCUED ZANZIBAR SLAVES

A group rescued by a British cruiser in 1893.

became more and more daring and the outcry of the raided more and more persistent.

With Tunis back in Moslem hands, it once again became a centre home of piracy, and filled to the edge with Christian slaves. Indeed in the seventeenth century this was estimated at 20,000 in Tunis alone. So real, indeed, was this danger that continued so long, that Martin Luther composed a hand-book for Protestant soldiers and sailors who fell into Moslem hands, and it was because of the frequency with which sailors of all countries as well as passengers and dwellers by the sea were captured, that the prayer in the Litany was written specially : " That it may please thee to have mercy on all prisoners and captives. *We beseech thee to hear us, Good Lord.*"

The demand of the Turkish Pasha for Christian beauty stimulated the kidnapping of girls, while the corsairs supplied their best captures to the harems of the Sultans.

THE BATTLE OF LEPANTO (1570)

In the years that followed the death of Solyman in 1546 the Turkish grip on the Mediterranean had grown more intense, and the capture of Cyprus by the army under Mustapha Pasha, with the foresworn destruction of the Venetian troops who had surrendered on terms, together with the flaying alive of the Venetian Commander in the brave Bragadine referred to, had seriously alarmed Europe. After the capture 2000 Christian children of both sexes were, as already related, sold as slaves. The reaction was fanned by the Pope, and in 1570 he entered into an alliance with Spain and Venice to oppose the growing naval supremacy which the corsairs were conferring on Turkey. Next year a vast fleet assembled at Messina under young Don John of Austria, who though only twenty-four years of age had already shown great military capacity in expelling the Moorish power from Spain. The fleet consisted of two hundred galleys and six powerful galleasses heavily armed. The personnel consisted of 80,000 soldiers and rowers ; half the ships and personnel were found by Spain, one-third by Venice, and one-sixth from the Papal resources. The Duke of Parma, who was afterwards to command the great Armada, commanded the Spanish fleet. This expedition, unfortunately, was too late to save Cyprus or the sack of Famagusta and Nicosia referred to in the preceding chapter, and the slave holocaust of the children. To oppose it the Turks assembled in the Gulf of Lepanto a far greater fleet of two hundred and ninety galleys, with 120,000 soldiers and rowers. They, however, lacked any galleasses, the over-mastering battleships of the period.

The Turkish supreme command was in the hands of the young *Capitan*, Pasha Ali, of no great experience, with the experienced corsair, Admiral Ouloudj, as his second. The Turkish fleet was by no means fully trained, and needed pulling together. Ouloudj pleaded for time, but this the impetuosity of the *Capitan* would not allow. In both fleets the rowers were galley slaves chained to the oars, with the lash as the equivalent of more fuel and drive. The Turkish galleys were rowed by Christian slaves, the Christian fleet by convicts. In both cases the admirals had promised, as was the custom, freedom after victory.

What it was like in the rowers' banks when the great galleys went into action, the men chained to their seats, you may realize for one brief moment if you read Kipling's *The Finest Story in the World*, told with that verve and understanding that few can attain for us. Recent films have also given one or two magnificent presentments. It may be remembered that when galleys were rammed and sunk or burned, it was not often that the task-masters slipped the master chain, and rowers went down with galley or burned in its inferno.

On 5th October 1571 battle between Cross and Crescent
was joined, and then was fought one of the biggest fights
ever seen in the Mediterranean. The two fleets met in the
Gulf of Lepanto on a fair day, the Christian fleet drawn up
in a crescent, the Venetians on the left, the galleasses like
great redoubts stationed at intervals in the line, a very
different array from the great Armada that the Spanish
commander was yet to lead. Galleys were the better
fighting vessels in a fair sea. Don Juan, the Christian
commander, was in the centre in the *Real*, the *Capitan* in
the *Sultana*. Whatever the Turkish commander lacked in
knowledge he made up in courage, and as the two fleets
closed he rowed straight for the *Real*, the Turkish vessels
raked by the heavy armaments of the galleasses as they
approached. As the *Sultana* came alongside the *Real*
another Spanish galley ranged on the other side, and with
the three locked together Spanish soldiers poured on to the
Turk with sword and boarding-pike. A desperate struggle
stamped over the bloody dead and the *Capitan* was killed.
To the annoyance of Don Juan, Pasha Ali's head was cut
off and set on the main-mast of the Spanish flagship. It
was instantly noticed and the combatants were encouraged
and dispirited accordingly. Along the line the Christian
galleys rammed or boarded their adversaries, the long rows
of oars being smashed and ripped by the steel prows of the
rammers as the rowers tried to back away before the broken
oars crushed and maimed them. Ouloudj, the old corsair
admiral, had been more successful in leading the Turkish
right wing, outmanœuvring the Venetians and succeeding
in sinking fifteen galleys that were detached from the main
body. When he had realized that the Turkish main fleet
was defeated he succeeded in breaking through the Christian
line with forty of his own galleys and escaping. Except for
this detachment of Ouloudj, the whole of the Turkish fleet
to the number of two hundred and sixty-six was captured

or sunk, 56,000 Turks being killed, and 15,000 Christian slave rowers were released, though many more must have gone down with the galleys.

It was an astounding victory, never witnessed since Actium (B.C. 41), nor, it has been said, was there such another till Nelson destroyed the French fleet off the mouths of the Nile.

But it is one thing to win a great victory, another to have rulers and alliances that can reap the fruits thereof. The fleets of the victors dispersed, to be fêted in their ports and share in the unimplemented *Te Deums* of praise. All the sculptors and artists of civilization set about commemoration, but the Turks were left alone to recoup their losses. Ouloudj with his remnant collected other stray fugitives and managed to reach Constantinople with eighty galleys, where he was joined by the corsair admiral Piali.

Of Morocco

The story of Morocco from the days of the Romans and the coming of Islam is far too long to attempt an outline here, even in view of its terrible slave past. Morocco lived a fierce and complicated life of its own, entirely careless of human life and mercy, inexorable as a slave holder, being among the principal customers for the merchandise of pirate states both in men and women. It did not concern itself very deeply with the Barbary States themselves, which were, however, at times under its control. It had permitted, in the sixteenth century, rovers to establish themselves at Sali opposite Rabat on the Atlantic coast who outshone even Algiers and Tunis in their piracy and slave-trading. The Sali rovers were long execrated, and like the corsairs of the Algerine coast were even capturing ships in the English Channel. Despite Morocco's menace to Christian liberty, most of the Powers had commercial treaties with its rulers.

So far back as 1551 Master Thomas Wyndham proceeded as a trade emissary to the kingdoms of Morocco and Barbary, and very shortly after Queen Elizabeth appointed Mr. Edmund Morgan as envoy to the court of " Maruecos and Fessi." Portugal had long started on her endeavour to secure footings on the coast of North Africa, and acquired Ceuta as early as 1414. Fifty years later she had acquired a slice of northern Morocco, and in the next century her seamen established forts at the seaports of Mazagan, Saffi, Agadir, and Azzamour. About 1640 she also acquired Tangier, which with Bombay came to Britain as part of the Dowry of Charles II's Portuguese queen.

The British occupation of Tangier lasted from 1662 to 1684, twenty-two years in all, and when it was lightly abandoned the accompanying loss of prestige *vis-à-vis* Morocco and the Barbary States was considerable.

In 1664 Morocco fell under the rule of one Sultan Er Rascheed, who rescued it from anarchy by his own force of character, but inaugurated a regime of relentless cruelty and piracy on the seas. A still worse and more pitiless tyrant succeeded him in one Moklai Ismail. He was a ruthless executioner of all opponents and law-breakers, his executioners always being by his side, and his sentence translated to them by the simplest gestures. It is related, however, that Maestre John, a Catalonian slave, had acquired a strange influence over him, and frequently interceded successfully for Christian slaves and victims. In his harem of 2000 women was one Englishwoman, captured at the age of fifteen and made, it was said, to turn Moslem by having her feet placed in boiling oil as a persuader. Six hundred sons of his grew up to be old enough to ride. He had a foreign legion of European renegades and released slaves as well as a standing army of blacks.

The Sali rovers as well as the Barbary corsairs filled his bagnios, and though those who accepted Islam were well

73

treated, they could rarely escape, while those who refused to be converted were treated with the utmost cruelty and frequently tortured. The Sali rovers themselves were not always *personae gratae*, and had their settlements bombarded and sufficiently pruned to grow the stronger.

Several devoted Catholic Orders spent their time in efforts of all kinds to release Christian prisoners. Europe retaliated by enslaving Moors, and there is an entry on record of Moorish women sold at Marseilles.

So when in 1830 the French set themselves on their great imperial mission in the domination of North Africa, there was a large measure of poetic justice in this, and Morocco would justify far harder treatment than ever it has received. It is interesting to note that the French Foreign Legion is but the adaptation on modern lines of the old Moroccan conception of corps of renegade Europeans, and it is probable that some of these were among the first to stand in the ranks of the French form of the Varanger Guard.

The Later Days of the Barbary States

The failure of the Christian Powers to take advantage of their decisive victory must be considered responsible for the many years of slavery in the Barbary States that were to ensue. Ouloudj was now the *Capitan Pasha* or Commander-in-Chief of the Turkish Navy, and with Piali the corsair set about to rebuild the fleet under the directions of Sokolli, the Turkish vizier, who with the other Turkish ministers was determined to rebuild, cost what it may. One hundred and sixty galleys and eight of the largest size galleasses were put down. In 1573 Venice made peace with the Sultan, and in October of that year Don John led a Spanish fleet alone to recover Tunis, which he did all the more readily since the citadel, as related, had never left Spanish hands. But 8000 Spaniards were left as a garrison, and next year Ouloudj was sent with two hundred and sixty galleys and his new galleasses with 40,000 soldiers to make short work of the Spaniards. The coastal States now remained part of the Turkish Empire till the middle of the seventeenth century, when the failing power of Turkey induced them to fall away. Constantinople in its effeteness had long been posting inept court favourites to various governorships in these States, so that the troops and sailors themselves had to elect their own leaders, and very soon the even nominal attachment to the Porte died away. That did not, however, produce any diminution of their activities, while post-Reformation wars and quarrels prevented Christendom from combining against the common pest. The Deys of the Barbary States elected by the Janissaries or other Ottoman soldiers were for a while submitted to the Sultan for an approval that was but nominal. Independence was achieved, and the States now stood before the world as pirates and little else. The bagnios of Algiers and Tunis were still full of captured crews, while their slave merchants still specialized in raided female beauty for the markets of Constantinople and for the harems of the Sultans.

Not only were the coasts of Italy, France, and Spain their hunting-grounds, but their galleys and brigs had appeared off the coasts of England and Ireland. The waning of their connection with Turkey, however, allowed of attacks by the European Powers on the pirate nests without such being considered as affronting the still powerful Turk. Vessels of war were now powerful things, and in 1617 a French fleet under Admiral Beaulieu defeated the Algerine pirate fleet, consisting of forty vessels of three hundred to four hundred tons, destroying most of them. Between 1615 and 1620 the Barbary rovers had captured four hundred British vessels, and in the latter year a British fleet under Sir Richard Mansel also beat up Algiers, without, however, the success that had attended the French attack. A Cromwellian fleet under Admiral Blake was to do much better thirty years later. Exasperated by the unabashed piracy which took such toll on all and sundry, the Protector ordered both Tunis and Algiers to be dealt with handsomely. Blake bombarded Tunis and destroyed a considerable portion of the corsair fleet, and thence moved on to Algiers, where great consternation reigned. All slaves and prisoners of British birth were forthwith disgorged without a struggle, and the pirates began to think twice before English vessels who showed their flag were molested. In none of these operations was the Porte even notified, showing how apart the Barbary States were considered, and indeed how by casting off their allegiance to the Porte the States were but digging their own graves. Some faint Turkish feeling must, however, have been existent, for in 1663 we see King Charles' Restoration Government making a treaty with the Sultan that permitted of his dealing with the Algerines whenever he wished. Indeed it was the need for keeping those gentry in order and keeping the rovers off the route to India and the Cape that brought about the British occupation of Tangier, which was so heedlessly brought to an end at a later date. The British Navy in the years that followed was constantly engaged, although not very successfully, against the pirates. The number of English slaves, however, in the Barbary States seems to have much diminished. The fear of the rovers is a constant theme in the old journals of travellers and the logs of vessels. But in the later years of the seventeenth century and during the eighteenth century, the pirate curse was so world-wide that the misdeeds of the corsairs was only a portion of that piracy and slavery which was largely put down by British energy.

Now and again corsair fleets still co-operated with Turkish fleets in the Levant, but by way of alliance rather than as a feudal or subject service, and the two principal

SUDANESE SLAVE GIRLS IN CAIRO RESCUE HOME (1889)

States—Algiers and Tunis—maintained their independence and persevered in their rape of civilization. At Tunis a Greek Dey succeeded in starting a dynasty which lasted in creaking form till 1881, when France annexed the decaying remnant. Algiers was finally put out of its misery in 1830 by a French expedition of conquest, but as during the Napoleonic Wars the policing of the high seas had slackened, and the pirates had raised their heads, Lord Exmouth in the year after Waterloo led a fleet, accompanied by the vessels of the Dutch fleet, to exterminate all pirate and armed vessels of the Dey of Algiers. As it is so near to our own times, only a few years before the reign of Queen Victoria, some outline of this operation in the extermination of this slave-raiding curse, which the enmities of Christendom had allowed to exist for a thousand years, will not be out of place. But it is not beside the point here to remark that though for a century the misdeeds of the pirates and their raids for slaves on the coast of southern Europe had been challenged and ended, yet all the while the ships of their most Christian majesties were busily engaged in inflicting worse cruelties and horrors on the unfortunate blacks of the west of Africa. And this story of slavery is the worst of them all.

THE BRITISH EXTIRPATION OF ALGIERS

This is how the British fleet under Lord Exmouth practically drew the teeth of the last of the rovers and paved the way for the French conquest in 1830.

With the long tally of offences during the preoccupation of the Napoleonic Wars the rovers' cups were full to overflowing. In 1816 Lord Exmouth led a fleet of eleven British vessels, including four battleships, into the Mediterranean, making the Dey of Algiers deliver up 1792 Christian slaves, and then appeared before Algiers itself aided by a

Dutch squadron of five warships, demanding the release of all Christian slaves and the rendition of the Algerine war fleet which was a menace to civilization. This fleet consisted of four frigates of 44 guns, five corvettes of from 24 to 30 guns each, and a flotilla of 30 gunboats and mortar ketches. As the Dey of Algiers proved recalcitrant and had collected a large force of Turks, Moors, and Janissaries, the British fleet stood in to engage the forts and Algerine ships, and a very fierce engagement ensued, which reflects very great credit on the courage and resolution of the pirates. The forts were all heavily armed and well supplied with ammunition, as were also the pirate war vessels. After several hours' bombardment, in which no fewer than 10,148 shots were fired by the Allied fleets, the British and Dutch stood out to anchor out of range and away from the burning vessels. The Allied fleets lost 141 men killed and 742 wounded, of which the British share was 128 and 690, and the Dutch 13 and 52 respectively. The whole of the pirate fleet was destroyed and 1200 Christian slaves released, a total freed of close on 3000. The action was rewarded with the Naval General Service Medal with a clasp "Algiers." Piracy and slave-raiding in the Mediterranean was now definitely ended, and the long centuries of outrages avenged. Fourteen years later the country was taken over by the French and formed the first possession of their now vast African Empire. With it civilization in North Africa began to recover after the long ages since Roman North Africa went down before the barbarians.

SOME STORIES OF THE ROVERS

There are stories enough of the corsairs, the Sali rovers, and, to our shame, Christian abettors and copyists to fill many books, and a few may be noted here. For instance, at times mild young Englishmen and others would turn rover and slaver. One, Sir Francis Verney, having quarrelled with a masterful wife and his mother-in-law, and squandered his fortune, went cruising from Algiers and " turned Turk." He was, however, captured by the Sicilian anti-rovers, and put to the galleys for two years, which curbed his naughty spirit. In 1615 the Scottish traveller Lithgow found " the sometime great English gallant " dying in the hospital of St. Mary of Pity at Messina. One Sunday, ten years before the coming of the Armada, Ilfracombe was held to ransom by Sali rovers, when all the inhabitants were in church. But among the rovers and slavers were many Englishmen, for it is on record that Mr. Nutt, the Mayor of Dartmouth, and several other notables, were concerned with the plunder of a Colchester ship at Torbay ! Sir John Elliott, Vice-Admiral of Devon, and Mr. Nutt both went to prison for the escapade. The story of Admiral Morison's cruise round the British Isles to destroy rovers, and his many astounding adventures are hardly credible. At Sinclair Castle he found one of his own boatswain's mates, turned pirate, and being entertained by the Earl of Caithness. The Admiral, carrying a gallows on his ship, entered Broadhaven in Ireland by the subterfuge of pretending he was the well-known pirate, Captain Mainwaring. He was heartily received by an English and Scottish receiver of stolen goods, and an English schoolmaster.

In the belief that he was Mainwaring he was entertained by Mr. Cormac, the gentleman of that place, his wife, and three handsome daughters, whose desire was to hear of their sweethearts and receive " their tokens " ! The Admiral gave them all a handsome telling-off at the foot of the gallows, only hanging, however, a twice-pardoned pirate captain.

It was to build ships to root out the Sali and other rovers and defend British shipping that Charles I fell foul of his people over ship-money, the non-maritime counties caring

79

little for what happened to the shipping of the coastal ports.

The last recorded case of Moorish piracy and slave-raiding in British waters took place in the Thames so recently as 1817; but in 1898 a Spanish vessel was seized by Riffian pirates off the north coast of Africa.

The most romantic of all the countless stories is perhaps the following : In 1785 a French ship outward bound to Martinique foundered in the Bay of Biscay, but her passengers and crew were rescued by a Spanish ship. The Spaniard was then captured by a Barbary corsair. Among the passengers was a young lady of a French family of good standing, a contemporary and school friend of the future Empress Josephine. A negro maid revealed her rank, whereon the pirate sent her to the suzerain, the Sultan of Turkey, whose favourite odalisque she became.

From behind the veil she watched empires going up in flames before the arms of Buonaparte, who had now married Josephine. Perhaps through her influence Turkey now, despite the British alliance, came into the French orbit even after Trafalgar ! But by 1812 the French favourite had become Queen-mother (Valide Sultana) and the real power behind the throne. Furious at the divorcement of Josephine, her influence was now the other way. She succeeded in inducing the Sultan to make peace with Russia, of whose forces a large portion had been neutralized by a Turkish army. Thus released, this Russian force moved fast on Napoleon's flank to turn his retreat to a rout—one more example of the strange side-issues of a slave system.

PART II

WEST AFRICAN SLAVERY AND ITS AFTERMATH

F

CHAPTER SIX

The Commencement of the African
Slave Trade

★

*The Origin of the Negro Slave Trade—The English enter the Trade—
White Slavery in the Plantations of Virginia—The Development of the
British Slave Trade—The English Shippers of Black Slaves.*

★

THE ORIGIN OF THE NEGRO SLAVE TRADE

WE now come to the blackest of all the slave stories of
the world : the merciless exploitation of millions of negroes
from West Africa, not as forced or indentured labour, the
price perhaps of world development, but as sheer un-
mitigated slave-holding and slave-kidnapping in its worst
and most ruthless form. Further, it was a system regardless
of human life or human rights and amenities, and so
heedlessly wasteful that millions lost their lives in the mere
process of acquisition and transit. We should not think
well of a live-cattle trade which lost one beast *en route* for
every steer landed. Yet this is what the African slave
trade meant, as indulged in by the civilized Christian folk
of the West with their vast priesthood and churches to the
glory of the Prince of Peace. It has been described as a
" monstrous aberration," and it was an aberration under
no control.

The story commenced in a curiously simple way, much
as the invasion of London by the gull followed the innocent
voyage of discovery of two gulls thirty years ago !

It seems that in 1442, when that well-known Portuguese explorer, Prince Henry " The Navigator," was examining the West African coast, he directed one of his officers who had captured some Moors to carry them back to their own country. · The Moors presented him in return with some gold dust and ten " blacks." Both the gold and the labourers seemed a desirable acquisition, and the Portuguese forthwith established forts and settlements on the African coast to put more of these desirable commodities into their hands. The negroes were then of value for work in Portugal itself, and thence were imported into Spain. The Colonial slave trade seems to have originated with the introduction into the new colonies in South America of the Spanish-bred descendants of these negroes. In 1502 one Nicolas de Ovando was sent as Governor to Haiti, and while there received definite instructions as to the proper treatment of the inhabitants of that island, and was also allowed to take some of these Spanish negroes with him as labourers. These were held in Spain as slaves, the product of slave parents, largely in Seville, and were good Catholics in religion. Next year, however, we find Ovando reporting that there were already many negroes there in Haiti, whence does not transpire, and desiring that no more be sent. However, we read that seven years later King Fernando ordered more to be sent for the working of mines. The importation of the blacks was not quite the beginning of the modern slave story, for as early as 1494 Christopher Columbus had proposed to exchange South American Indians against livestock, and had actually sent home 500 Caribs, Indians taken in war, to be sold as slaves in Seville. Queen Isabella had originally approved, but learning that the Indians were a quiet and docile race, ordered further inquiry to be made into what the rights of their acquisition were. Their return to America was eventually ordered. The Bishop of Chiapa, Bartholemy de las Casas, was by no means satisfied with the treatment of the inhabitants of Haiti in the matter of their labour. He finally recommended that the demand for labour that could work in the climate should be met by allowing Spanish colonists to import up to ten negroes, especially for mine work. However well-intentioned the bishop's recommendations were, they were undoubtedly responsible for the initiation of the West African slave trade, for to meet the plans he had suggested, the King had given authority to one of his favourites to obtain and import 4000 negroes annually. Such a demand could only be met from some source that could raid the African hinterland, the Spanish contractors obtaining their requirements from the Portuguese, who in their turn went to African chiefs who enslaved their own people, the actual purchasers being a firm of Genoese merchants who bought the concession from the royal favourite. The trade in negroes, not appearing to the consciences of the age as evil, naturally appealed to the business instincts of the Genoese, and soon to all other venturesome folk who could command the necessary capital and had no scruples about a traffic that none seemed to deem infernal.

THE ENGLISH ENTER THE TRADE

It was not to be expected that trader-England with a slaving instinct behind her would long remain outside so enterprising and lucrative a business, and the honour, or the obliquy, of being the first British slave trader belongs to Sir John Hawkins. Hawkins' father had long been interested in the Guinea trade, and had visited that coast three or four times in the ordinary ventures of the day for gold and ivory. It was his son who, in the latter half of the sixteenth century, took to a serious trade in what was at first but a side-line, and on his third voyage took to the West Indies 400 slaves whom he sold for about £25 a head.

Queen Elizabeth encouraged the African trade, though not necessarily that of the subsidiary traffic in negroes, and indeed at first the English looked askance at the human cargo. As late as 1620 we read of a Captain Jobson up the Gambia searching for a Barbary merchant taken by the Portuguese who refused the offer of negroes, saying that the English were a people who " did not buy or sell one another [this was before Cromwell had sold cavaliers and Irishry] or any that hath our own shapes." When told that other white men did so, he replied that " they were another kind of people different from us."

Indeed it was not till after the Restoration that the trade was seriously considered in England, when in 1663 an African company arose with a charter containing a reference to slaves.

Indeed the rest of maritime Europe had come into the negro trade, since England elected to follow John Hawkins' enterprising lead. It was then a mere matter of trade or merchandise, and about 1600 the Dutch took it up, followed by the French, Danes, Swedes, Brandenbergers, and finally the English. The trade was supported by King Charles, and since the Crown approved and Holy Writ had given its sanction, the British merchants—especially those of Bristol, who had made money over the trade to the British plantations of Cromwell's Royalist and Irish prisoners—took it up. How the slave-trading instinct was inherent in Bristol has already been related, and the harsh measures of the Parliamentary Government found no difficulty in reviving it.

It must be remembered that there were no American or West Indian Colonies in British hands in Queen Elizabeth's reign, and it was only later that the first definite settler came into being. Further there was no demand for black labour in the North American coast at the commencement of settlement. The growing English slave trade was confined to business with the Spanish-American colonies. In the early days of the seventeenth century, however, there was an outbreak of the black-labour disease in Virginia, when in 1620 a Dutch slave ship arrived at Jamestown and sold part of her cargo to the tobacco-planters of the colony.

The demand for blacks grew slowly at first, but as the plantation increased the demand for negro labour rose too. Before, however, following the great development of the British share in the horror, we may glance at the astounding story of the white slave labour in Virginia, and later in the Carolines, which to some extent postponed the demand for negroes.

White Slavery in the Plantations of Virginia

The instinct for slavery came out once again as the best way of disposing of political enemies, and again a better alternative than slaughter, when England came to the duress of the Civil War and the risings in which the Stuart dynasty faded away. The growing prosperity of the American colonies of the Elizabethan founding soon demanded labour for plantations, and after the " Crowning Mercy " of Worcester it was old Oliver and the Council of State who sent many hundreds of Royalists to be sold as slaves in Bristol. Happily, perhaps, many who purchased them were of Royalist sympathies, and entreated them generously. There were many, however, who exacted many pounds of flesh. It was perhaps a better end than the piking which followed the onset of the trumpets at Drogheda. In 1615 there were no bowels of compassion for Irishry, who perhaps in their massacres of English and Protestant had forfeited any claim for such. At any rate the Council of State ordered the Governor of Waterford to deliver to three Bristol merchants, whose names are specified, as many Irish prisoners as they might require as slaves, to be carried to the West Indies.

87

Because this was a game that successive parties could equally compete in as they came into power, Roman Catholics, Royalists, Quakers, and other non-juring communities, all went the way to the Bristol slave mart. The trade was not confined to supplying Virginia and the Carolinas, but to such places of death as Jamaica, Barbados, and other British islands where planters needed men. After the Monmouth Rebellion the same fate was ordained for many Somerset lads by Jeffreys, who, cruel though he was, was but applying a cruel law, and it was the Crown and the Council that ordered stern treatment.

But when rebellion and religious schisms were not, the needs of the planters still continued ; and when Royalists and Quakers were not available, the kidnappers were quite capable of seizing boys and girls, and even men and women, for sale across the seas.

It is to his credit that Judge Jeffreys at Bristol, in 1685, made a violent charge to the Grand Jury on the subject of kidnapping, and then bade the mayor, clad in his robes of office, probably a worthy slave-trading merchant, " leave the bench and stand as a criminal at the bar," calling him a " kidnapping knave " and fined him £1000. He further bound six aldermen to appear before the King's Bench on a similar charge, and for a while this spread fear and dismay among the worthy slavers, and it may be counted as righteousness to Jeffreys, whose memory so sorely needs something on the other side.

The kidnapping which Jeffreys tried to suppress lasted, as already mentioned, till 1744, and it is surprising that this curse of the old Danish pirate and of the corsairs should be endemic among ourselves till such recent years. It certainly shows how deep-rooted and instinctive was the desire to trade in flesh and blood, and how eagerly Bristol and Liverpool rose to the industry of slavery.

During the reign of Charles II kidnapping had attained

indeed to considerable heights and was winked at by authority, while some of it was mitigated into indentured labour of a rigorous type ; and we shall see how exactly the same sort of thing was being carried out later by the French in obtaining labour for Reunion from the Pacific Islands. As there were Royalists, Quakers, Catholics, and Non-Conformists among the colonists in America, there was opportunity for settling labourers whose indentures were over, and societies to this end existed, as well as for purchasing and liberating the unfortunates who were slaves. We see the indentured system coming as a punishment when Highlanders and other Jacobites were sold for a period to the plantation after 1715 and 1745, including mutinous soldiery. Scottish societies in America endeavoured to look after the Highlanders and to settle them on release, and much of the sturdy stock in the States may be traced to this particular form of settler. Unfortunately the practice of sending criminals to the plantations produced the undesirable leaven that its direct child, our transportation system, introduced into Canada and Australia. The convict ships were the direct descendants of the slave ships, although of course reasonably well conducted. Transportation, like work in the galleys, not in itself undesirable provided it be properly organized, was a poorer way indeed of starting overseas dominions than the enslaving of Quaker and Royalist and Highlander for his political doings. It is also not edifying to think how comparatively short a period separates British plantations from Russian labour camps ; at any rate in principle.

It may well be imagined that an underlying complex born of this slave descent may have induced the bitterness that lay behind some of the support accorded to the American leaders in the War of Independence. Among the many stories of the period told by Captain Hugh Crowe of Liverpool, is one of Irish slaves in the market at Charlestown being chaffed by negro slaves, who pretended they would buy them, crying " Och, Masters ! Och, jewels ! Don't let them blackamoors buy us at all, at all ! "

THE DEVELOPMENT OF THE BRITISH SLAVE TRADE

The aloof attitude of the good Captain Jobson up the Gambia River did not long prevail. The great expansion and development of sugar and tobacco plantations shouted for labour, and after all, white men could not be expected to come under rebellion duress every day. Nor could kidnappers obtain sufficient numbers.

From the day that the Dutch ship first sold slaves in Charlestown the appetite grew, and seventy years after the number of black slaves in Virginia alone had risen to the astonishing figure of 200,000.

The first rush for the African coast over, the development of its trade went on for some time in the hands of exclusive companies, tempered by interlopers, which aroused bitter opposition in Bristol. And ere long the trade, so far as our country was concerned, fell into the hands of reputable companies who knew how to organize, and whose slave cargoes, despite the fear of risings under which the crews often worked and which occasionally occurred, even to the destruction of all the slaver's crew, was conducted on more humane lines than the rapscallions of Portugal could be trusted to do. It is also well to remember that the partaking of Sweden, Brandenbergers, etc., in the trade, had nothing to do with colonial possession, but was only a matter of getting a share in a lucrative business.

Assuming for the moment, as many not unworthy statesmen with the conscience of the period declared, that the development of the world did demand and justify a compulsory migration from West Africa to the Americas, a trade properly conducted and adequately supervised might have a colourable justification. If that were so, the only way to securing its proper conduct was by chartered companies under the strictest supervision. In any case the world, even if it cared, was not competent to supervise and organize such a trade on humanitarian lines, and nothing of the sort was ever attempted. The trade became a scramble among many worthy people, who, however, had to employ all that was inhuman and unscrupulous among the nations, which in England became possible when an Act of William and Mary threw it open to all and sundry. With this Act went all hopes of any control worthy of the name. The African company, which had been the principal licensed traders before this Act continued to exist, was encouraged by large Parliamentary grants, entirely justifiable perhaps when we consider the importance to Britain of African trade in general.

The contract for supplying the Spanish colonies with slaves had finally been given by Spain to the Dutch, from whom it passed to the French. By the Treaty of Utrecht, however, this right was transferred under a Spanish *assiento* from France to England. The right ran comfortably, for all save the victims, for thirty years, when the Government of Philip V announced his intention of denouncing the *assiento*. This raised an astounding protest in England, not, however, to be wondered at when we realize the extent to which British labour of all kinds and British interests were involved. So great was the feeling that Walpole was constrained to declare war, but in palliation it should be remembered that the Spanish denunciation had no connection with any shame or reluctance to continue the trade, but was merely the usual flouting of British interests in favour of others whenever the former's disarmament and pacifist tendencies seemed to make her safe so to flout! The importance of the trade to the British—and many most worthy and amiable folk drew their income from such investments—will be understood from the available figures. Between 1680 and 1700, twenty short years, 300,000 negroes were exported by the British. Of these the African company was responsible for 140,000 ; and other traders, all British, 160,000. It was a sorry record, but nothing to that to come, for between 1700 and 1786, to the island of Jamaica alone (British since 1655) the total was 610,000. It was further estimated that for the period of 106 years since 1680 the total of British-run slaves was 2,130,000, or an average of over 20,000 a year. This trade reached its height just before the American Rebellion or War of Independence ; Liverpool was the leading port, but London, Bristol, and Lancaster took a fair share of fitting out the slavers. The total number of slave ships in being was 192, carrying in one trip over 47,000 slaves. During the war the trade naturally dwindled, but on its termination soon recovered.

It was necessary to have stations on the African coast, which incidentally conducted other trade and thus could unblushingly assume the title of " Factories." In 1791 there were, it is recorded, 40 on the west coast—15 Dutch, 14 English, and the others French, Portuguese, and Danish. About this year the figures of slaves exported show how predominant was the British share in the trade, viz. 38,000 ; compared with French 20,000, Dutch 4000, Danish 2000, Portuguese 10,000.

It might occur to a modern mind that the last people to share in and profit by the kidnapping of their own folk, which alone made the trade possible, would be the African chiefs themselves. Yet they were the principal and govern-ing accessories, egged on by the European agents, dazzled by the wealth and luxuries that the trade put into their hands. For two centuries did they and their armed retainers carry on a fierce and relentless destruction of neighbouring tribes and then gradually extended their operations further afield. Their methods consisted almost entirely of surrounding villages at night—a method holding good into the twentieth century—massacring the old people, keeping perhaps many of the women and bringing the males and some of the women down to the slave barracoons, as the Portuguese called the sheds of collection that were dotted down the coast. Over and above the loss of life in these raids and before embarkation on the slave ships, the loss was great in transit. In brief, the relevant figures of loss were for the Jamaica trade as follows: In actual transit $12\frac{1}{2}$ per cent., in harbour and before sale $4\frac{1}{2}$ per cent., with about a third more in the seasoning. It was thus obvious that for every slave becoming efficient another lost his life, and including shore and raid losses before being put on the sea, the tally of human life was a good deal bigger. At all times in the slave trade, the fact that the number of female slaves was far less than the male produced inhuman conditions, and even for such women as there were, fertility suffered from all the disadvantages known to accompany polyandry. The Jamaica figures are so reliable that they may again be taken as illustration. In 1640 there were 40,000 slaves in the island, and up till 1820 the number imported was 800,000, yet in that actual year the slave population was but 340,000. In 1798 the male slaves exceeded the female by 30,000. The well-known fertility of the negro races had never a chance to have full play till Virginia started its policy of breeding slaves under favourable conditions for the North American market.

With many people in England making large fortunes in the trade, the facts connected with it became, as the years rolled on, well enough known, and many folk began to be concerned at the horrors revealed.

Long before the forceful Granville Sharp and Buxton became prime movers in the abolition of the trade itself and in the emancipation of slaves already held, or the great Lord Palmerston arose to back them, there were humane and prominent men voicing their growing dissatisfaction. The denouncers increased and waxed vociferous, both in prose and verse. So early as 1671 the Quakers expressed grave doubts. Ninety years later they expelled from their body any who took part in the slave trade. In Pennsylvania, the Quaker settlement in the Americas, the brethren also voiced their horror ; in 1774 they even decided to expel any of their members who held slaves and refused to emancipate them.

THE ENGLISH SHIPPERS OF BLACK SLAVES

In examining the story it will strike the impartial reader that the abolitionists did undoubtedly over-colour, not their argument against a soul-destroying condition, but their accounts of the cruel conditions under which slaves were carried in British ships. Once the trade got into reputable hands, British business instincts soon realized the advantage of bringing cattle to market in good condition. The need for profit produced the necessity for crowding in the small ships of the period, but the good ships of Bristol and Liverpool were far better as a rule than the slavers of Portugal and America. The abolitionists, in their desire to rouse our consciences, let their enthusiasm outrun the truth, or the exceptions were quoted as the rule. This overstating, not of the objections to slavery, but to the treatment of the slaves *en route*, roused the fury of the quite respectable firms in London, Bristol, and Liverpool, who made their money from a trade which many had endeavoured to conduct with some order, and only a few voices in the wilderness had as yet condemned as wrong.

Equally overcoloured were the statements of the apologists who produced stories of happy slaves dancing and singing with joy at the prospects of their new lives. It might also be stated that slaves, not barbarously entreated, but horribly crowded, with their memories of lost homes blunted, *would* have danced with joy at the prospects of sunshine and land and room to move ! So, as Mr. C. M. MacInnes writes in his quite commanding book, *England and Slavery*, to form a correct judgment on this matter one must walk midway between the " Scylla of the abolitionist exaggeration and the Charybdis of apologist extenuation." He is in no sort an apologist himself, having the greatest horror of the whole business, but as an historian is concerned for accuracy, and quotes many letters to show that many companies and captains managed the actual business none too badly so far as the matter of humane treatment went. He specially quotes from the instruction of a London firm to one of its captains, showing the general desire of good people and also of good business men to deliver their merchandise, whether slaves or ivory, in good condition.

Towards the end of the British trade the actual carrying became almost an art, and Captain Hugh Crowe, who took the last slaver out of Liverpool, had made many voyages without losing a slave. Slaves whom he had carried would come aboard to greet him years after, in memory of his kindness and good reputation, and there were many like him.

MacInnes is at pains to quote scales of rations, messing arrangements, etc. Such are only what one would expect, but so much has been said otherwise that really belongs to Portuguese and American running, that it is something to be able to reflect that an inhuman trade was usually, when in British hands, reasonably well conducted. For instance, Sir William Young describes two ships which he visited at Barbados in 1791. The *Pilgrim* of Bristol, with 370 Eboes from Bony.

" Were in the best possible order ; she was six feet in height between decks, without shelves or double tier in the men's apartments, and as clean as a Dutch cabinet. We visited every part of the ship ; in the hospital there was not one sick, and the slaves mustered on deck were to all appearance and uniformly, not only with clear skins, but with their eyes bright and every mark of health. . . . The *Pilgrim* had not a scent that could offend, and indeed much sweeter than I could have supposed possible, in a crowd of any people of the same number, in any climate." On the other hand he also saw the *Anne* with 210 Gold Coast negroes, which he reported to be crowded, unhealthy, filthy, and unhappy, with only 3 feet 6 inches between decks.

It is also on record that not unnaturally some slaves fretted themselves to the bone, even as a nervous hog can lose a stone in half an hour's lorry run ; while at times slaves from the interior would not eat, poor wretches, because they thought they were being fattened for a cannibal feast !

CHAPTER SEVEN

Great Britain and Slavery

★

Great Britain and Abolition—The Awakening—Abolition and Emancipation—The Arising Difficulties of Abolition—The Drama of Toussaint L'Ouverture—Conditions in the British West Indies—Abolition and the Treaty of Paris—Portugal, Brazil, and the Slave Trade—Emancipation in all British Lands.

★

GREAT BRITAIN AND ABOLITION

DESPITE the heavy guilt of Britain's share in the earlier slavery in her colonies, and the share of the country generally in the lucrative business of slave-trading, the whole credit of stirring the world to abolition and emancipation undoubtedly stands gloriously to our credit. It cannot be said that it stands, in the origin of our consciousness, to our people as a whole, or our Government, but to a small coterie of enthusiasts who in the last quarter of the eighteenth century threw their whole heart into the extinction, not indeed of slave-holding—for complete " emancipation " was yet far off down the coming years, and unhappily is still so—but of the execrable slave trade from West Africa and all its horrible concomitants. Slavery was a recognized condition ; slave provision had long been a business ; British enterprise, like that of many nations, had long been engaged ; but it is safe to say that few of those who ventured their money in what was a profitable trade had any real idea of what it all meant. The national conscience, never so far stirred, was roused, despite a sometimes justifiable opposition to the methods and language of the abolitionist, and soon decided in anger and shame that Britain should no longer have a prominent share in so inhuman an institution.

The Awakening

England had long been the home of kindliness, and despite many of our rough and inhuman customs, the modern tag of the music-hall song, " You can't do that there 'ere," so expressive of the British social outlook, which had its expression even in the cruel repression of the Stuart risings, already held sway. During the eighteenth century many factors were stirring the national conscience in many directions, especially as our beneficent imperialism was developing. The principles of John Wesley the Anglican were spreading to all grades, and the national character was moving towards a tender conscience, which young folk of to-day like to call Victorianism.

Our share in the infamous slave traffic was being brought home to the man in the street, which meant the trader and the lesser professional classes.

The wars with France in North America, and the unfortunate struggle of the Colonial Rebellion, meant that a far wider number of the middle-class British were familiar with the slavery of North America. Its attractive paternal side, where happy slaves served kindly masters, which alone made the system bearable, was known to many; but with it came the knowledge of the other side—the bad masters and the tragedy of the sales, especially death sales, which often separated families. The coercion of the recalcitrant, which is a necessary accompaniment of even the best slave system, and the horror of the outside replenishment, were far more widely known.

The first anti-slavery blow in Britain was struck far back in 1772, when the father of abolitionism, Granville Sharp

(1735–1813), obtained from Lord Mansfield the epoch-making decision, that whenever a slave touched British soil he was free.[1] A Durham-born man, he was for some years an employé of the Ordnance Service, but was also a well-known writer and pamphleteer on subjects which covered a wide range of philosophy and humanism. In 1787, in association with Clarkson, he succeeded in founding the " Association for the Abolition of Negro Slavery." That very year an attempt was made to restart in Africa negroes who had come to London, working and starving in many capacities, in docks and long-shore craft, furnishing big drummers to the Army, pugilists to the ring, and pages for ladies of fashion. Four hundred of the poorer of them were sent to found a settlement at Sierra Leone.

Earnestly and eagerly did Granville Sharp develop their cause, taken up also strenuously by the more famous Wilberforce of undying memory (1759–1833), who brought his enthusiasm, as the young Member of Parliament for Hull, to the great purpose. From 1787 onwards he led the growing Parliamentary group of abolitionists, with the general support of Pitt. It was not till 1807, however, that he was able to get his Bill of Abolition made law, although on three occasions—in 1789, 1791, and in 1804—the House of Commons passed resolutions condemning the slave trade. They were such strenuous times of war and danger with the whole world in upheaval, that even the initial success achieved at this date (1807) is to be marvelled at. From that year any form of slave-trading was illegal in Great Britain. But to pass such a law for Britain was but the beginning of the trouble, for half the world was still engaged in the trade, and many interests were involved, by no means all unworthy or disreputable. Many a worthy

[1] At this time there were about 20,000 slaves in England, largely servants of retired planters. The Mansfield decision made them free to leave their masters, as they wished.

person derives his or her whole support from such a source as property that has become, from circumstances entirely beyond their control, slum ; and so it was with slave-trading.

The leaders of great movements of this kind in this country have many small followers, whose enthusiasms lead to blind abuse of all connected with the system that they condemn, and thus engender, not unnaturally, bitter opposition from others than the actual vested interests. Abuses which are part of a long-recognized system take long to remedy, and their suppression develops and explores unexpected ramifications, and so it proved to be in the matter of abolition.

From abolition on paper of the British trade to actual effectiveness was a long road. Other Governments had to be led to follow suit, the Napoleonic Wars demanded all Britain's energies, and other European Governments had much to concern them. Even when all Governments are agreed to something more than lip-service they are still far removed from effective action. Nowhere is that more recognized than in those beneficent activities which, even alone, make a League of Nations worth while. A Government may pass anti-drug ordinances, it may even earnestly desire to give effect to such, but either the probity or the efficiency of its police and customs services may be quite inadequate to implement the law !

And so it was with the slave trade. The abolitionists were now, with the passing of the British law, eager to proceed, and did eventually proceed, to the entirely separate though allied question of emancipation, which is a different story.

There was now to arise the great reformer and humanist, Thomas Fowell Buxton (1786–1845), who so eagerly led crusades against many of the social evils and prison horrors of the day, and who in 1824 threw himself—at the instance of

Wilberforce—into the second anti-slavery phase, " emancipation," as well as keeping alive the fires of abolition.

ABOLITION AND EMANCIPATION

Every science and almost every activity must develop its
own vocabulary of new or specialized expressions, and it is
interesting to note those in use when the campaign against
slavery took practical form. The state of slavery had two
great facets, and indeed has them still, viz. slave-trading
(the supply of the slave from the various available sources
which were of themselves legion) and slave-holding. You
may kill the slave trade as our fathers saw, and you have
then to deal with the slave holders.

This was the great problem of the statesman of a century
ago. Humanity would agree to abolish the trade ; economy
was not so certain as to the question of existing slave
property, on which in some cases the food of the world
depended. The two problems were in any case almost
distinct in the early nineteenth century, as indeed they are
to this day. We hope, for instance, that the Abyssinian
matrix of slave-trading has now been destroyed, but the
slave-holding of Arabia is not necessarily doomed thereby
so long as the slave womb is fertile and the slave gives
birth to a legal slave.

In the early days of Wilberforce, Buxton, and the great
movement, " abolition " meant the ending of the actual
trade from West Africa, while " emancipation " meant the
freeing of all slaves. The latter meant still more : that the
interests of many worthy people and great industries would
be threatened, and the whole world stirred in antagonism,
unless the matter went with great wisdom and judgment.

As the generations passed, however, the term " abolition "
was applied also, logically enough, to slave-holding, and in
the United States " abolitionist " meant the protagonist of
the abolishing of the slave-holding. The larger phrase

absorbed the older term " emancipation," so that the " abolitionists " of the days of Abraham Lincoln were the " emancipators " of an earlier diction.

The first great struggle, as the conscience of kindly England was slowly stirred to a full realization of the horror long existing outside their ken in an Africa that was really dark, continued for years, and when it at last resulted in the final international agreement to abolish the slave export from Africa the battle had been but a quarter won. The chief responsibility for the enforcement of abolition fell to the British Navy. The astounding number of unexpected angles, effects, and influences which arose in the process, as well as the *sequelae* of the emancipation of the slaves in the British Empire, which clashed with the accepted and usually admirable British conception of the sanctity of " property," must be considered. There are many tales of badly administered methods of compensation which left sore hearts behind, and there was much that made the path of righteous men needlessly rough as regards both abolition and emancipation.

THE ARISING DIFFICULTIES OF ABOLITION

Before, however, we can proceed to the prolonged struggle for emancipation, there are many strange corners to explore in the various unforeseen and practical difficulties that arose over the abolition of the African trade over a period of fifty years. Not only are they of considerable historical interest of their own, but they have an enduring and practical interest in that they have recurred on a small scale in the eternal watch and ward that still goes on, to prevent, or at any rate minimize, the slave trade that Arab or Levantine still conduct between the east of Africa and the Arabian mainland.

So many British people made large profits from the slave trade from the west of Africa, that it was not surprising that after the passing of the Act of 1807 many interests shifted their centres of operation to non-abolitionist countries and ran their business under alien flags. It is obvious enough that unless all the principal nations agreed on abolition, and declared all slaves on shipboard as prize and all slave-running analogous to piracy, interference with non-abolitionist ships was an act of war.

When Great Britain became abolitionist in 1807 the great world was torn with the Napoleonic Wars and too busy to take serious action. The penalties imposed by Great Britain will be referred to later.

The situation as regards Spain was a curious one, for as already related the trade had long been denied to Spaniards themselves, but this prohibition did not preclude purchase of slaves from others less scrupulous. Up till 1713 the French made the profit denied to Spaniards, while after that year the trade went into British hands, largely owing to British naval superiority during the many wars with France. In 1789 Spain, in justice to her own people since slavery was not yet abhorrent to civilization, removed her embargo on their joining in the actual trade. It is said that during the ensuing fifteen years more slaves were run into Cuba than during the previous two hundred years.[1] For fifteen years the annual average was 5840, but for the last four years it rose 8600. But Spain was at war with Britain from 1796 to 1802, and this meant, as Mathieson explains,[2] that the actual transporting of the slaves belonging to Spanish slave traders was carried out under the neutral American flag.

THE DRAMA OF TOUSSAINT L'OUVERTURE

The outbreak of the French Revolution gave rise to some enthusiastic ineptitudes in the matter of the emancipation of slaves in French Dominions. The island of Hispaniola

---

[1] Humboldt, *Ile de Cuba* (1826), i. p. 169.   [2] *Great Britain and the Slave Trade.*

had been entirely Spanish, but before the Revolution France had gained possession of the south-western half and named it S. Domingo.

When the National Assembly hammered out its "Declaration of the Rights of Man," slave-holding was obviously a direct negation thereof, but it was not till 1794 that the total abolition of slavery was carried in the Assembly—a quite impossible step to take at one stride. The news of the Edict of Abolition created chaos in the colony, where in addition to the negroes there was a considerable population of mixed blood, with political aspirations above their immediate capacities. Ten years of squabbling, quarrelling, and warfare, continued with murder and rapine, to which French revolutionary troops sent to compel the liberation but added.

Eventually there arose a figure who attained some fame at the time and has since been given a niche in history's temple, partly from the extravaganza which the fashions of France and the Directoire exercised in his appearance. Toussaint L'Ouverture was a negro slave, said to be a son of a chief in Africa, who had acquired some education and *savoir faire* and with it had adopted his romantic name. He was at last able to get some measure of control in S. Domingo, and in 1801 issued the following proclamation (*Times*):

"Citizens. It is with great satisfaction I inform you that I have taken possession of the Spanish part of the island in the name of the French Republic . . . the measure of prudence and humanity I have taken prevented the effusion of blood, and with very little loss I have put myself in possession of the whole island. After the first attack persuasion was the only means I made use of. My undertaking has been crowned with success. Health and fraternal amity.

Signed. The General-in-Chief,

Toussaint L'Ouverture."

He had undoubtedly got turmoil and chaos in hand, organized government, disciplined an army, and showed very considerable qualities. How long he could have managed this large territory, for large it was, and what could have been his relation to France, or what could have been made of him by sympathetic treatment, we shall never know. He did not appeal to Buonaparte, who was restoring France, as a desirable asset, but only as "a rebellious slave." He sent his draft of a constitution to the First Consul, in which at any rate the sentiments were the highest. Buonaparte would not accept him, sent an expedition, captured him by treachery it was said, and sent him to a fortress on the Jura where he died of neglect.

How far this remarkable man, apparently a pure negro, could have made good, and managed his island which the madness of the General Assembly had thrown into disorder and massacre, we shall never know. At any rate L'Ouverture had brought some order out of chaos and showed great gifts. His end was a cruel and unnecessary tragedy, and his life and character has long been something of an enigma.

Buonaparte was too concerned with other matters to prosecute to a successful conclusion a return to the pre-Revolution condition, and Santo Domingo became a republic in 1804. The Spanish Haiti half became a republic in 1844. The quarrels of the two, and the negroid ineptitude displayed, are exercising the neighbours of the two republics in this year of grace, 1937 and 1938.

Conditions in the British West Indies

It is not unfair to say that the British slavery in the West Indies was in many ways the most rigorous of any under our countrymen, and the reason is not far to seek. Even at the time of emancipation the white population of all the islands was not more than 65,000, scattered among many islands, while the slave population numbered 400,000 in Jamaica alone.

The result of this was that with the gradual increase of the slave population the fears of the whites against risings and outrage grew, and not without reason. There had been several risings in the past, ruthlessly suppressed, but marked in the opening by outrages. So early as 1791, for instance, there were in Jamaica 250,000 slaves, with 10,000 free negroes and 1400 maroons, as against 30,000 whites. In 1809 in Barbados there were 15,000 whites and 69,000 blacks. The memory of the earlier rising and outrages lay no doubt at the bottom of Governor Eyre's severities in the rising in Jamaica in 1834, at which such an uproar was raised, and for which he was censured by public opinion, but exonerated by the official inquiry, which dubbed his measures wise and justified. In view of the known horrors of previous rebellions this no doubt was so. In his younger days he had made his reputation as a protector of aborigines in Australia, and it was the horrors of another servile rebellion on the eve of emancipation that must have prompted his actions.

It will be realized how different was the position in Virginia, where, though the black population was very large, considerable numbers of a more virile settler than the West Indian planter, accustomed to war, could be assembled at short notice.

But even with this fear of a servile rebellion, the account of the treatment of the slaves in everyday life reads strangely and unnecessarily barbarous. Slaves would be harnessed and driven by the whip, flogged ruthlessly by a special estates flogger; even women were beaten on the bare buttock in the fields as a matter of routine for any dallying, beaten too with a lash that stripped flesh from the person. When emancipation came to the islands the conditions that obtained there made the transition all the more difficult.

ABOLITION AND THE TREATY OF PARIS

It has been pointed out how preoccupied was Europe in great upheavals in the year that the British abolition became law. That year, 1807, had seen the final crushing of Prussia at Friedland, where Napoleon beat Russia and the portion of the Prussian Army that had survived the defeat at Jena the year before. It had seen, too, the final defeat of Russia at Eylau and the subsequent Treaty of Tilsit. Spain was no longer at war with Britain, but was overrun by French armies, and its Government peripatetic. The Portuguese Government had fled to Brazil from Europe to escape from Napoleon's columns, and all this meant small hope of international action on any of the humanities yet awhile. The alliance between Spain and England to expel the French from the Peninsula was incidentally a god-send to the slave traders. The United States followed Britain in making the slave trade illegal, a considerable step forward considering the stage of their development and their great slave interest. But the slave traders of the States were many, wealthy, and resourceful, and the British alliance with Spain rendered the Spanish flag immune. There were also many British subjects as lawless and daring as the slave traders of the United States. Although the British penalties on the traders were £100 for every slave carried and confiscation of ships and cargo, it was said that the success of only one venture in three was exceedingly profitable ; and the excitement of running the cruiser blockade appealed to many, especially as privateering had come to an end. In 1811, however, Great Britain made the slave-trading penalty transportation, and that very soon put an end to the defiance of their laws by British subjects. In 1820 slave-trading was made piracy and a capital crime in the United States, so much was public opinion advancing in its ethics. The British Parliament followed suit in 1824, though British share in the blockade-running did not actually now call for the greater penalty. It so remained, however, till 1837, when transportation again became the maximum.

The four years from 1807 till 1811 practically saw the end of all British slaving enterprise, but by no means ended the trouble, nor approached thereto. However righteous the British had become, the world rendered little more than lip-service to the humane intention of their laws.

It has been explained that it was not till 1789 that Spain officially opened the trade to her own subjects, who surely then made great use of it. It had been urged in England that, in return for our support and protection, she should have been compelled to follow our lead in slavery! But Nelson had finished her fleet and her hands were terribly full. A similar charge lay against Portugal, but her Government had fled to Brazil for fear of the French. Mathieson relates that Canning told the House in this connection, that had our Government been refugee in Jamaica it was not likely that we should have been abolishing the slave trade at this period!

During these great wars Sweden alone (1813) followed our example in prohibiting the trade to her nationals, though Denmark had done so as early as 1802. That such remote seafaring states should even have found such declaration necessary shows how every nation possessing capital and ships would have its venture in what was then one of the most profitable of trades. The morality of the proceeding apparently entered the heads of no one among them.

The ending of Napoleon in 1814 seemed a great occasion on which to summon the world to reconsider its attitude and to make humanity its own. Hardly had the first Treaty of Paris been signed in 1814 when Holland followed Britain with a declaration of abolition. Bourbon

France agreed to support Britain in advocating abolition, but gave herself five years grace, for with Senegal and Goree —her African colonies seized during the war—restored to her, a period of profitable slave-trading lay ahead.

Wellington, fast emerging from military leadership to world statesmanship, was always abolitionist, but he was not prepared to plunge the world back into war to please the unmeasured haste of our enthusiastic humanists, any more than in our days Baldwin would face war with Italy for the League's sake. Time must be allowed to bear its share in the benevolence. Thus we find him writing to Castlereagh in 1814 from Paris that he had laid the addresses of both Houses of Parliament before the King, who said " that he would be happy to do anything he could . . . but that he must attend to the wishes . . . of his own people . . . that many years had elapsed and much discussion . . . before the opinions in England had been brought to the state of unanimity. . . ."

At Vienna, when the Congress of the Powers was sitting, the abolitionists looked for some definite pronouncement, but had to content themselves with the pious declaration of February 1915, to the effect that while their desire was for total and universal abolition each power must reserve the right to fix its own time. Considering the complex issues involved, this provision is not to be wondered at or objected to, especially as the declaration was a quite definite enuncia- tion of the general principles that guided them all in their detestation of the principles of the system.

But a new upheaval was to change the outlook. Buona- parte had escaped from Elba and was once more dictator of France. To placate England he suppressed the new-born traffic, so long closed by the British Navy and restored by the Bourbons, and under the Second Restoration of the Legitimists after Waterloo it was not renewed. The vested interests, however, to which Wellington had agreed were too strong, and France persisted for many years in a trade officially illegal but actually countenanced by authority, high as well as inferior, till in 1824 the British Government told France that her flag " covered the villains of all nations."

By the second " Treaty of Paris " in November 1815 Britain and France both engaged to prohibit the slave traffic without restriction, in their dominions, and the French laxity in observing their undertaking is the best illustration of the force of Wellington's warning just quoted, and also shows that popular Governments, nay any Government, cannot long fly in the face of the wishes—good and even evil—of the people. If it cannot lead it must follow. We shall see the same trouble in the case of Saudi Arabia to-day.

From 1815 right up to 1831—the whole period of the restored legitimist Bourbon rule—many slave ships sailed annually from French ports to run the blockade of the British cruisers in carrying slaves from West Africa to the West Indies—a sorry business. How the cessation of war in 1814 complicated that blockade, so far as our cruisers were concerned, with the disappearance of the right of search will be referred to. At this stage it will be as well to realize, too, how the position of Portugal, as an African as well as a South American possessionist, with a perversely slave-trading clique, complicated the problem.

PORTUGAL, BRAZIL, AND THE SLAVE TRADE

From much earlier times than the abolitionist movement Portugal had acquired sovereignty on the west coast of Africa south of the Congo, and owned the South American colony of Brazil. In shipping her own African people as slaves to her colonies, her legal—and to some extent her moral—position was on a different footing from that of adventurers who bought from negro and half-Arab chiefs and raiders to sell in any market. So far back as 1810 Portugal had entered into an undertaking not to engage in the trade outside her own territories, in the case of parts of Africa in which other powers had abandoned their trade. The latest qualification rendered her undertaking somewhat non-committal, since France, Spain, and Portugal had not renounced their trade. Still on paper it was a step in advance, that pointed a way to follow.

But here inherent dishonesty of intention, or perhaps in the power of execution, arose. At the mouth of the Rio Grande stood an island, Bissao, described " as of no earthly value except for the purpose of the slave trade." Formerly a few Portuguese slaves were shipped from there. Now it became the emporium of all the scrupulous international slave-trading gang. Slaves from all the country round were seized and brought to the island, and thence under the agreement slave ships sailed openly for the Brazils, while the British cruisers looked on helpless. It was indeed a rough road on which the enterprise of British humanity had embarked !

The situation after the Napoleonic Wars was thus a peculiarly difficult one. The United States had prohibited the import of slaves, but her well-equipped traders were continuing the trade elsewhere.

France had prohibited the trade nominally only, and was allowing, as just related, every sort of irregularity and filibustering from her shores. Portugal's position was peculiar, and a cover for roguery and evasion. North America was providing clippers to outsail any British cruiser. The watch and ward under sail of the long slave coast of Africa was almost impossible, and naval opinion was divided between the merits of the comparatively healthy but less effective open sea patrol, and the deadly though occasionally exciting inland patrol along the swampy coasts.

British policy, stimulated by the enthusiasts of the Anti-

Slave Societies, aimed at three things, apart from the different principle of emancipation.

1. That all Powers should proclaim the slave trade as illegal.

2. That they should insist that their nationals and preventive services should observe their own laws ; a difficulty, as already stated, evident enough in modern days as regards white slavery and drug traffic.

3. That all nations should declare slave-trading as one of the forms of piracy.

The enumeration of even these three points alone had complications, the problem was growing, especially since peace had automatically limited the right to search. But where the carrying of slaves was declared piracy, there the cruisers of all nations, and particularly those of Britain, would know how to act.

As it was, because the British cruisers exceeded their powers in capturing and condemning ships of Portugal, that country was given an indemnity early in 1815 of £300,000. Later, in return for agreeing not to chase slaves north of the Equator, she was also released from repayment of the greater part of a loan of £600,000 received from Britain. Two years later, indeed, she put some limitation on the Brazil trade, and even agreed to treat with us ere long for abolition.

Another paper victory came in 1817, when Spain promised to give up her trade between Africa and the West Indies, and to abrogate it altogether by 1820. Agreement as regards right of search was arrived at that greatly pleased the British Parliament. Two courts were set up to adjudicate on slaver prizes, and one at Sierra Leone, with a mixed tribunal.

But once again the inadequacy of lip-service was seen. It is true that the right of search, properly carried out, did mean the death of the trade, but—— !

WILLIAM WILBERFORCE

1759–1833

The dodges of the evader were legion. In the first place, as yet no ship could be deemed a slaver, and therefore a prize, unless she actually had slaves on board. Slaves would be assembled on shore awaiting the slave ship, which only embarked slaves at night when a favourable wind would give the slaver a good start. The chance of escape was well in the slaver's favour, and often those of acquittal if captured. Further, the treaty only provided for the confiscation and not destruction of condemned ships, which were then sold to another slave trader. The British treaty-draftsmen may have been very obtuse, or the Spaniards singularly " slim," for the slave trade still went on merrily. In 1831 and 1833, however, when the Legitimist *régime* in Paris had given place to that of Louis Philippe, genuine progress was made. All doors were really closed for France, the French cruisers began to do their duty with energy, French and British could search ships with each other's flag, and what really mattered was that captured slavers could now be broken up. Denmark, Sardinia, and Sweden all took the same course. Spain alone remained intractable.

In 1832, however, a more liberal and human form of Government—at any rate in theory—arose in Spain also, and received British support. A treaty was signed introducing the rule enjoining the breaking-up of all condemned slave ships, and also creating severe penalties for participation by Spaniards in the trade. Unfortunately Spain did not implement her good intentions with the same zeal as France displayed in wiping out her prolonged turpitude, and this brings us to the need for a reference to the Cuba slave trade, at last in peril of its existence.

Another queer contradiction had grown up during these years. The British activities had made slaves scarcer and therefore more valuable, and this incited traders to run the risks for the sake of the enhanced profits ; so much so that people said, with some truth, that attempted abolition had but increased the trade and added to the miseries of the blacks. So long as it was necessary to have slaves on board to be liable to penalty, slavers when pursued cast their slaves overboard; sometimes to clear their decks, sometimes to induce the pursuer to stop and attempt rescue.

Also it is curious that still these stock-riders took no care to bring their stock to market in good condition, or even save them from dying *en route*. In the Brazils huge reconditioning establishments were needed before the human stock could fetch any decent market price.

The fact that for thirty years and more Great Britain had been paying for a large cruiser establishment to maintain a movement that did not command success, raised in the Commons, in the parties, a very strong parliamentary protest.

EMANCIPATION IN ALL BRITISH LANDS

As soon as the theory of abolition was firmly established as the law of England, which had been put into very definite if not yet successful practice, the abolitionists of the trade became both emancipators and abolitionists *in toto*, feeling that they could now come into the open as the protagonists of the removal of slavery, lock, stock, and barrel, from the world. With a British Government and public now fully sympathetic, it was actually possible to undertake the emancipation of all slaves in the British Empire. But slave-holding, as already emphasized, was no crime either against law or ethics, since Holy Writ contained rules for its better regulation! The policy of cultivation by slave labour had been enjoined and encouraged by the State. There could be no question, therefore, of destroying private property by emancipation pure and simple. The only plea for that could be universal maltreatment of slaves by owners, making them worthy of such punishment. Therefore when Parliament passed the Emancipation Act they provided £20,000,000 for compensation of owners, exactly as to-day we buy out coal royalties, tithes, and such-like.

Between the Act of Abolition and the Act of Emancipation a quarter of a century had elapsed, which should have given the planters in the West Indies plenty of time to set their house in order—be it remembered that the plantations of North America had long since ceased to be British. The West Indies, therefore, were the principal spots in which the Act would have effect, and it was said that they had done little useful to put their concerns in a condition to compete with any competitive situation, whether as regards labour or the trading conditions that were coming. Emancipation, with sugar so heavily protected that the poor in England could not buy it, produced a scarcity that raised prices and increased for a while the shock of the change. But a nemesis was coming in the shape of free trade, which, together with the rise of the American cotton trade, left the erstwhile all-important West Indies high and dry, with their plantations suffering from overcropping, in the non-competitive slave-labour conditions under which they had thrived.

The actual distribution of the twenty millions compensation was no easy matter, as may well be imagined, and produced both hardship and dishonesties.

South Africa, among the colonies in which slaves were held, produced a trouble peculiarly its own. The distribution of compensation to the slave-owning Boer farmers was no doubt equitably carried out, but farmers lay far afield and communications were long. It was one thing to get a treasury order, quite another to know how to encash it ; and traders were sharp enough to buy up—often at ridiculous prices—the ill-omened yellow slips which the backwoodsmen did not understand.

The farmer got then far less than the face value of his order ; content for the moment to get hard cash instead of paper, yet soon bitterly to realize the small amount his slaves apparently meant in money.

It was a typical bureaucratic mistake to issue certificates rather than distribute cash, and it was one of the principal causes that prompted the Dutch to make the " Great trek," and escape from bureaucracy and a Government they did not understand, and which did not understand them. What that trek meant and the bitterness that lay behind has had amazing results in British history.

The statesmen of England were alive to the great break in production and prosperity that might result if the slaves were entirely freed at the first start, and enacted that the emancipation should be followed by twelve years of apprenticeship before the slave could be fully free. That was a very proper provision of a half-way house in which the slaves became *adscripti glebae*, properly paid and treated, but not free to leave their master. Twelve years, however, was too long, and was reduced to seven, but even that was excessive. It did not give the slave a sufficiently proximate date to cheer him, and many of the planters, though they had drawn their compensation, did not play the game with the apprentices ; nor was the official machinery for working the apprenticeship efficient enough—conditions were unhappy, and ere long the period was reduced and finally abolished, chiefly at the instance of the Society in London.

CHAPTER EIGHT

The Progress of Abolition and Emancipation

*

The Problem of the Freed Slave—The Sierra Leone Settlement—The Various Societies—The Niger Expedition of 1839—The British Navy and the West African Trade—The Parliamentary Uprising against Coercion.

*

THE PROBLEM OF THE FREED SLAVE

THE upsetting of a world system must bring new and unexpected problems. Slaves are at least fed, and freed slaves, unless there is a large labour demand which they are qualified to fill at hand, may easily starve. The moment the Navy found itself with captured slaves on its hands, the disposal of their freight presented a great problem, and required a far better administrative system to deal with it than the world was capable of devising. There were negroes in London, largely freedmen whom the zeal of anti-slavery enthusiasts had rescued. Negroes as labourers without their families were obviously undesirable ; the strange facts, still observable; of the sex attraction of the negro for the less restrained among white women made their presence in our slums undesirable. As Chinese fathers are now, so were negro fathers then. It is to be remembered that the very bitterness of the lynching of negroes in the southern States to this day for offences against women, lies in the fact that the offenders have often but given way to provocation. The disposal of the poorer

117

negroes in London, many indeed of his own liberation, attracted the attention of Granville Sharp, and they were started off to a new settlement just established at Sierra Leone, whose story will be related. This was started before even England had passed her Abolition Laws.

But the real disposal trouble came when the British cruisers of the slavery patrol caught slave ships. Not only did terrible losses in slaves occur at sea, but inadequate arrangement for their establishment on land produced many troubles. No doubt the abolitionists hoped that slaves thus released could be repatriated, but experience showed that this was hardly possible. Many had come from villages raided and burnt, and if sent back would only be captured again and sold. Many had been months in the barracoons, where slaves were collected and could not describe their place of origin.

The loss at sea of confiscated slaves occurred in the following unavoidable happenings. They would be in ships making east for the Americas, and when rescued it took weeks to beat up against adverse winds from the right of Biafra, where they were for the most part captured, to Sierra Leone. They were terribly badly accommodated and died like flies, despite the kindly treatment that was accorded them. The British cruisers were not fitted with medical personnel and drugs for such a purpose.

It had not occurred to them at home that adequately equipped floating depots were needed for such work; indeed at one time captured slavers were cleaned and kept as tenders to cruisers, though but ill adapted and with little of what we should now consider adequate establishment and equipment. In any case floating depots could ill keep pace with a chase.

Between 1808 and 1844 negroes taken from condemned slavers were all settled in Sierra Leone, at the expense of that colony of about £10,000 per annum. This gave a faint basis to the complaint of Cuba and Brazil, that we merely stole their slaves for our own purposes ! The settled ex-slaves, however, were by no means a satisfactory population, and the population was also becoming excessive ; so that after 1844 they were, on the recommendation of the Select Committee on the West Coast of Africa, offered employment in the West Indies and settlement there as free labourers. Under Government auspices free labour from Sierra Leone had already migrated to the West Indies. Under the circumstances, it was not unnatural to put some pressure on the ex-slaves by saying that if they stayed in Sierra Leone they would have to rely on themselves alone ; nor was this unreasonable, in view of the fact that those who would not go soon picked up jobs, lodged and fed as unpaid apprentices, even in Sierra Leone.

France and America elected to scoff at our intentions, but as they had done so little themselves to implement their own undertaking to put down the trade, Great Britain was not greatly concerned at their attitude. Nevertheless the fact that we were developing the African coast settlements with the freed slaves gave some colour to their accusations, despite the fact that we had originally inaugurated African development as a method of starting an economic life which would in itself kill the exporting of natives at the interior.

It was the undoubted fact that as the years passed, the work of our cruisers, by making slaves scarce, enhanced the slave price and made the value of the cargo that escaped so very great that the whole trade was stimulated. Further, the mortality in the trade exceeded the numbers we were able to capture and release, which was a paradox that did not escape the notice and derision of the opponents of our coercive system. The heavy losses among the unfortunate cargoes of the captured slavers, both those taken on the coast and those brought back from the coast of Brazil in their pestilent ships, was one of the leading cards in the parliamentary explosion of the forties.

THE SIERRA LEONE SETTLEMENT

The colony of Sierra Leone is intimately connected with the British suppression of the slave trade, and, as a colony, may indeed be said to owe its origin to the suppression of slavery. It was discovered so far back as 1462 by Pedro de Sintro the Portuguese, and probably received its name from him on account of the resemblance of the hills above to a lion. Portuguese influence had gone when, as already mentioned, the philanthropic abolitionists sought to found a home there in 1787 with Granville Sharp's 400 poor negroes from London, and 60 Europeans, as a beginning of a land for the rescued or emancipated negro victims of the slave trade. Next year the Timni chief Nembana sold a strip of territory to the British, who thus acquired the best harbour on the coast. (The planting of rescued Africans from Africa was not its only purpose.) An early raid by a chief injured by white slavers brought the settlement to an end, the survivors being collected and established two miles off. In 1792, however, the colonists returned to the site, which was rebuilt and called " Freetown." Of the Portuguese times none remained save a few families who claimed to have Portuguese blood in their veins. For six years from 1793 Zachary Macaulay was the administrator, piloting the settlement through a raid and pillage by the French in 1794. As yet the British Abolition Act had not been passed, and Sierra Leone was only required for escaped or otherwise freed slaves. For instance in 1792, Lieut. J. Clarkson, R.N., brought over 1100 ex-slaves from Nova Scotia, largely negroes who had served in the British Army or Navy during the American rebellion.

The general development of Sierra Leone, which had no status as a colony, was in the hands of a Chartered Company, which was chiefly the machine of philanthropists rather than of financial speculators and pioneers, and the benevolent development of the African coast was its principal objective. But it cannot be said that either Granville Sharp's London negroes or Clarkson's contribution from Nova Scotia were at all happy material on which to found a new self-supporting settlement or sustain a dividend-paying company. Nor were these whose only language was English at all acceptable to the Africans of the neighbourhood, since only among western people does the black skin seem to cover any congruity. The freed slave settlers had come from many areas, and were quite unrecognizable by the Sierra Leone tribes. They nominally came as Christians, but it was not till 1804 that the Church Missionary Society took them under its benevolent wing. The climate did not make for good administration, for the period 1792–1814 saw eighteen different Governors, and by the 1st January 1808 the Chartered Company gladly hauled down its flag to give way to that of the Crown, which had made Sierra Leone a colony. By this time the more dependable of the negroes had settled down as traders or in some sort of a profession. The 1st January 1808 was, however, the date of the coming into effect of the British Act of Abolition, and, although under considerable difficulties, the development of the colony to receive the freight of captured slavers now began. Some were met, as explained, by inviting the later freedmen to go to the West Indies. The prolonged years of cruiser activity naturally brought much business to Freetown and contributed to the employment of those liberated, and thus the new colony, with its merciful if none too logical objective, gradually emerged through frontier difficulties, annexation, and small wars, to the prosperous settlement and Crown Colony of to-day.

THE VARIOUS SOCIETIES

Some more detailed mention of the societies that brought about abolition and emancipation is overdue. When some sense, however fanciful, of injustice or grievance is aroused in England, the formation of a society forms the usual incubator of the cure. Often has and does this society overlap or impinge on the activities of another society round the corner, of which the first society has no ken. That is our custom, from which great results have come, although at times the existence or formation of societies may seem to the facetious almost a cult for the propagation of secretaries, honorary or otherwise. The number of our societies is legion, and the good they do is probably inverse to the number of societies dealing with the same subject.

True to our national custom, the first act of those aware of the turpitude of the slave trade and the slave condition in all colonies, was to form a Society for the Abolition of the Slave Trade so early as 1787, which was the constant instigator, goad, and remembrancer in the matter of abolition, with Granville Sharp as the first chairman.

The anti-slavery societies, however, soon became one powerful influential body. In 1804 was formed the African Institution, a society which also brought powerful influence to bear. Its object was not trade or profit but to promote a knowledge of West Africa and stimulate industry and civilization among the coast negroes. Its activities will be referred to later. Out of this admirable institution was formed in 1823 the first Anti-Slavery Society, whose object was the abolition of slavery itself, viz. emancipation in extension of the original programme of the 1787 society, which dealt with the abolition of the horrible trade ex-Africa. Its journal was the *Anti-Slavery Reporter*, edited by the Zachary Macaulay aforesaid (father of Lord Macaulay), who had been the administrator of Sierra Leone from 1793 to 1799.

These original societies had branches or were in touch with similar local societies in Britain and elsewhere, many of which were children of the Quakers, the Society of Friends, always to the fore in the cause of humanity.

In 1837 was formed by Fowell Buxton the corollary of the Abolition Society, viz. that of the Aborigines Protection Society, whose object was the protection of the undeveloped races against the exploiting by white people in the great upheaval of world development which had begun with the discovery of the Americas. This body had as weary a hill to climb as the Abolition Society, and almost as many wrongs to put right.

In 1839 the original Abolition Society blossomed into a wider role with the more complete title of the British and Foreign Anti-Slavery Society. The two societies then continued with unabated zeal their astounding work in the world, and when abolition and emancipation, all through the nineteenth century, came to full fruition in all civilized countries, the protection of aborigines became, not the more insistent problem but, of equal importance. Its spheres of action at any rate had roots among the opinion of all the humane and civilized people of the world. It was not therefore to be wondered at that the two great societies decided in the twentieth century that their power and influence would be enhanced by amalgamation, and any overlapping of energies and aims avoided. A little over a quarter of a century ago (at the time of writing this), viz. on 1st July 1909, the amalgamation, fusion, and marriage took place under the combined name of the Anti-Slavery and Aborigines Protection Society. Since then the work done has been immense, both in the activities of abolition and emancipation, as well as that of protection. With the expanding of industrial needs and the narrowing of the world's confines, fresh giants arise to be slain, just as the older horrors have been felled to earth. Indeed it is to the astounding prevalence of slavery in the twentieth century that these societies are still directing their energies, which,

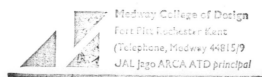

despite the unified direction from the League of Nations, cannot, for many a weary year yet, disappear from this unfortunate world.

To convince a world that can hardly credit it, let it be said here and now that there are still several millions of genuine slaves on this globe with no hope of freedom before them. To rouse public opinion once more is still the society's principal task.

Some passing mention has already been made of the African Institution, formed in 1807 as a means of furthering knowledge of and civilization in the west coast of Africa, and stimulating industry. Its object was not profit, but to act as remembrancer of coast affairs and scandals to the Government and public. The defunct Sierra Leone Chartered Company had similar objects included in its platform, and by so much it was the successor to the higher aims of that body. It was sending out seeds, silkworms, and eggs, and it was also educating children. In 1809 we find it reported the swarms of slavers flying falsely the Spanish flag in the hope of escaping our cruisers. By 1826 so much of the Institution's objects were in process of being achieved that it was dissolved, though in 1839 the abortive African Society that was formed to explore and civilize the Niger revived its good objects. It was distinctly one of these bodies to which we owe the peaceful and highly developed condition of, at any rate the British portion, the west coast settlements to-day.

THE NIGER EXPEDITION OF 1839

With the Niger holding the position that it does to-day in African development and trade, it is interesting to note an attempt just under a century ago to open it up to trade and primarily to anti-slavery operations, a very definite offshoot of the activities of anti-slavery champions of the

time. It has already been told how the old African Institution, formed to promote the amelioration and civilization of the slave coast, made development of industry for
the sake of the people one of their objectives.

That institution had faded away as the times changed,
but in 1839 it was resuscitated by Buxton, under the name
of a Society for the Extinction of the Slave Trade and the
Civilization of Africa. Both the old institution and the new
society disavowed any intention of being associated with
commerce, but somewhat naively announced that if any
chiefs offered concessions that could be humanely worked
another company might be formed to exploit the concession.

The society had its opponents, both those who deprecated
interference with individual enterprise, and competition
with those who had already put steamers on the river, and
those who pointed out that none of our African settlements
had contributed by reason of their commerce and prosperity
greatly to lessening the slave trade. However, Government
in July 1839 accepted the proposal for a Niger expedition,
and voted £60,000 for the building of an outfit of three
steamers for an expedition aimed at establishing factories
and entering into commercial relations with the various
chiefs. At this period we were active in many river enterprises, and had just sent Chesney off to the Euphrates with
steamers carried in parts across Syria. Prince Albert
naturally took the chair at the first public meeting of the
society, and Buxton collected enough money to form a
company to be known as the Model Farm Society. The
City of Liverpool had sent out an expedition in 1832, but
only eight of its forty-seven members ever returned. The
climatic conditions and the matter of the right time to go
were not considered, and for these reasons disappointment
was likely. A good deal of delay and breakdowns occurred ;
at last, however, it got under weigh, concluded certain
treaties, acquired some land for a model farm, and then

proceeded to die from every sort of tropical disease. Six months were spent recruiting the expedition at the none too suitable Fernando Po, and though the surviving commissioners with the expedition were prepared to start again, it was recalled, all save one steamer, which was to be manned with kroomen and go to look for one Carr, the manager, left on the model farm. Carr had disappeared, however, and the steamers' crew took to crime and lawlessness. That was the end of it, and the whole expedition returned, leaving one-third of their quota of 145 behind them, while only 9 of the survivors regained their health. It was a poor result, and a little more knowledge and common sense might easily have helped it to fare better. The African Society did not survive such a fiasco, and was dissolved in January 1843.

The British Navy and the West African Trade

It was one thing—even if a big thing—for enthusiasts and statesmen to pass Anti-slavery Acts, Laws, and Regulations, but quite another to get them carried out. However much other Powers might render lip-service to the cause, there was only one agency that could carry it out or could be trusted to carry it out, and that was the British Navy. The unfortunate Navy, freed from the cares and exertions of the Napoleonic Wars, was now condemned to long years of watch and ward on the dreary African coasts, whose only advantage, at any rate from the officers' point of view, was that it was better than the half-pay list of the post-Napoleonic Admiralty and Treasury. So for years the British cruiser patrol proceeded slowly to stamp out all slave-running, with vessels equipped not with the speed of steam, but with sail, and handicapped by the lack of modern signalling devices.

For fifty-odd years the cruiser service went on, hated by the officers, who often broke down under the strain, not altogether disliked by the men who enjoyed the excitement of a chase and appreciated the chance of prize-money for captured slaves.

The slave-runners were at times in desperate hands, and many a small cruiser had a desperate fight with a heavily armed slaver and determined crew.

The service was prolonged over so many years, that naturally there were controversies within the Navy itself as to how to conduct the patrol. There were great protagonists of the "inshore patrol," and the seizing of the slave barracoons, even when the law did not help. The inshore patrol undoubtedly was the most effective, and the zealous wanted power, and sometimes snatched it, to raid the slave-dealing chiefs up the rivers and behind the swamps. It was, however, a devastating service, especially in the medical and dietary knowledge of the period, to the health of all concerned. The distant patrol meant much improved health, though few of the officers supported Commodore Hotham as regards its efficiency. In fact the work in the open sea demanded really fast cruisers, and the constant construction of these was financially difficult, while the illicit Yankee traders openly built the fastest clippers the shipyards could produce.

The various difficulties that the Navy had to face in incomplete treaties and laws have been alluded to, and it was not till "equipment," even without slaves, branded a ship as a slaver, that the Navy was satisfied with the conditions it had to interpret.

During these years it is not too much to say that the only thing that stood between the negro and his slave fate was the British Navy. Between 1810 and 1846, 116,862 slaves had been liberated from captured slave ships (*Parliamentary Papers*, 1847–48), and from a parliamentary return of 1845 a fourth of the British Navy was employed on the coasts of Africa, Cuba, and Brazil, viz. 56 vessels of 886 guns and over 9000 men. Of this " Preventive " or " African " squadron, however, 36 was the actual number said to have been actually at sea at the same time (Madden, p. 218).

There are many stories of the vicissitudes and adventures that befell the ships of the patrol during these fifty years ; stories of fierce encounters, long chases, cast-overboard slaves, raids in the swamps, and law cases when international lawyers sued naval officers for action taken on their iniquitous clients outside the law.

The naval records of this period are full of incidents of the slaver clearing. So early as 1816 the *Queen Charlotte*, a colonial schooner of the Crown, was specially equipped for the chase of slavers, and it was not long before she saw the rough side of the service. On 11th March she engaged the *Louis*, a French slaver from the West Indies. The *Louis* resisted search and was not captured till three of her own crew and as many as twelve of the *Charlotte* had lost their lives. The war with France being over, the British action was *ultra vires*, however morally justified.

All through the succeeding years British ships were constantly engaged with the desperadoes who a century earlier would have been pirates.[1] Even so late as 1861 Lord Palmerston reported that the naval casualties in action on the patrol had totalled 34. The prisoners on board a captured slaver sometimes rose, as in the case of the Brazilian *Felicidade*, from which it was not possible to remove the captured crew, and which was in charge of a midshipman and a crew of nine seamen. The prisoners rebelled, killed nearly all their guards, and made off with the ship, although when subsequently recaptured a British Court declared it had no jurisdiction to punish the murderers.

[1] The pirates, of whom many histories have been written, sold as slaves those of their captures who were not made to " walk the plank."

THOMAS FOWELL BUXTON

1786–1845

Hundreds of officers achieved distinction through the years, and foremost among the prominent names are Commodore Hotham, Captains Denham and Matson. Many were the stories of the bluejackets' kindness to captured slaves. Conspicuous is the human story of the cruiser *Rifleman*, a steam frigate which on 28th June 1849 had sighted an apparent slaver moving up the coast. Giving chase, the quarry ran ashore, and she was found lying on the beach, abandoned by her crew, her decks crowded with slaves and the seas breaking over her. Two midshipmen, Pocock and Beckett, were placed aboard of her to try and prevent the slaves from being washed off, and Hitching, the second master, was sent aboard her with a fresh crew. The wind increased during the night, but in the morning the *Rifleman* closed in and got a hawser aboard. Along this, at great risk to their own lives, the three officers passed the slaves one by one to the cruiser in a cradle. The work, tedious and fatiguing, took a whole day, and when it was over every seaman received charge of three of the chilled and frightened slaves to be nursed and restored : 127 were rescued thus.

The coming of steam put the cruisers on better terms with the traders for a short while, but the Yankee filibusters engaged in the Cuban piracy built faster steamers than the British Navy, whose vessels were made to fight as well as chase.

The Parliamentary Uprising against Coercion

But however devoted the service of the cruisers, the fact was patent to the parties that for thirty years the Navy had patrolled the slave coast to its own intense discomfort, without destroying the slave trade. That was an immense disappointment to the abolitionists and all humane folk in the world. Not only had it failed to abolish it, owing largely to the apathy of other powers, as related ; but it

I   129

had, as also explained, driven the trade to develop itself on better lines—better that is as regards evasion of the blockade. It was almost as the quarrel between guns and armour ; better armour produced better guns ; piercing projectiles produced better armour ! The slave cruisers were evaded by the fast clippers, who to compensate for their risks packed their cargoes like ducks in a crate, with no provisions of any kind for sanitation. Loss of life was terrible ; the slaves, now largely boys, lay in an eighteen-inch space between them and the next layer, and could only turn on their boards if all turned together. So high was the price, however, that the years of repression had produced, that the trade was more worth while than ever, and capital of a kind was more freely used. When the ships were old they were often burnt after a voyage, being so unutterably foul that no one would clean them.

So a strong conviction was growing up in many quarters that we were doing no real good by our efforts, and were at any rate on wrong lines. To this movement of objection flocked all those interests in England that still supported slavery and suffered from abolition. Rife also was the accusation that by making trading convention with slaving countries we were encouraging the trade. This was specially so in the case of Brazil, with whom we had a sugar convention.

A not unnatural side-issue was the desire of the slave owners who had lost their slaves to see others lose theirs ; in other words, our planters in the West Indies, whose slaves had been emancipated now for nearly a generation, had no use for slave countries which entered into competition, such as Cuba and Brazil. And all the while the slave states of the United States held their slaves, in many ways humanely enough, and " said nuffin'."

The British cruiser patrol had begun soon after the passing of our abolition laws in 1807–1814—and had been effective since 1814—and it was now 1840, and still the trade succeeded in surviving! It was not surprising that the nation and Parliament were uneasy. However necessary the sugar conventions, it was said that when the news of their establishment reached Havana the prices of slaves rose 15 to 20 per cent. The pros and cons on the sugar controversy, however, are beyond the scope of this work. Free-trade and protectionist theories, abolitionist, and anti-abolitionist, and the problem of feeding the growing industrial population all shared in the question, and with it ran also the problems of the comparatively new idea of indentured labour which had its own series of problems, anomalies, and evils that might not be far removed from slavery.

The orthodox abolitionists were now in for a bad time. The world could not be organized to put sufficient pressure on Cuba and Brazil to stop slave-trading, and this British naval patrol had lasted thirty years and the end did not seem to be in sight, while relaxation only meant more slave-running without restriction. In 1845 a Member of Parliament, Mr.—afterwards Sir—William Hutt raised the whole point in the House. He quite recognized the disinterested objects of the nation, and applauded them in trying to put a stop to the trade, in spite of the demands for economy, which he said had been " fiercely long demanded by the nation with no uncertain voice." He described the thirty-odd years of attempted suppression thus : " The utmost latitude, one might almost say licentiousness, of means—public money to any extent—naval armaments watching every shore and every sea where a slave ship could be seen or suspected—courts of special judicature in half of inter-tropical regions of the globe—diplomatic influence and agency such as perhaps this country never before concentrated on any public object." It was a very effective indictment so far as it went, and he continued to allude to the conditions under which the modern slavers worked—indeed atrocious enough—and even went so far as to assert —which was but faintly true—that before we interfered the traders went about their work humanely and with due regard to delivering their cargo in a marketable state. He even asserted that before we started the trade had been conducted with conspicuous regard to good handling. He was a telling speaker and ended one of his periods by saying : " Whenever I perpetrate knowingly and recklessly cruelty and bloodshed in the name of humanity and religion, denounce me as a hypocrite and a villain." The tragedy was that there was enough truth in the indictment to make a strong if mistaken case. Others thought, not unjustly from one point of view, that Spain and Brazil had been very badly treated by this strange way of interfering with their affairs. This was not a right argument, though again we can well see that there was something in it. Had we been a more logical people, and not so tired of war or in such haste to disarm, we could have forced these States to accept abolition after 1815. Against this it may, of course, be urged that the peccant nations could not compel their own public opinion, however much they desired to do so, and thus this ill-winded pirn had to be fought out on the floors of the British Commons and Lords.

The argument, however, did produce figures and statistics which we may look back on with satisfaction. It was true that from 1842 to 1845 20,000 slaves had gone to Brazil, but on the average this was far less than in 1839 ; while in 1845 importation into Cuba had fallen to 1300. In 1847 one British cruiser alone was taking slavers at the rate of three or four a week. The controversy was stimulated by retired naval officers who did not agree with the official methods raising the usual controversies as to the most effective methods of conducting the blockade. The discussions also produced some horrible statistics as to how the trade was now conducted, and it was stated that three months' recuperation in special depots was necessary in Brazil before the slaves could be sold.

The years of this prolonged controversy produced all sorts of strange opinions from prominent people : Carlyle questioning the morality of a policy which could put the whole world in such a turmoil, and the great John Bright, Member for Manchester, the city which was most interested, was not able to speak with any decided voice. For several years select committees of both Lords and Commons sat on the subject, and it was the final report of the Lords that settled the matter. The Government of the day were strong and supported the coercionists, *viz.* those affirming the efficacy of the naval blockade and desiring its continuance, and therefore it was maintained, on better lines no doubt from the ideas elicited. Mr. Gladstone, curiously enough, was against the interference with the trade, and even said " that it was not an ordinance of Providence that the Government of one nation shall correct the morals of another." In this Mr. Gladstone missed the point, since the argument was against the right to raid and buy rather than to hold and breed, but he did make an effective point that while we released each year 5000 or 6000 slaves, we were responsible for the death of 8000 or 9000, presumably by the rigours that the blockade forced on the runners.

CHAPTER NINE

The Later Slavery of Portugal, Spain, and Brazil

*

*The Problem of Portugal and Brazil—The Astounding Slave Story
of Cuba—Emancipation in Cuba.*

*

THE PROBLEM OF PORTUGAL AND BRAZIL

THE eventual success of Parliament's defence of the coercion
policy did not change the slave situation but stimulated the
employment of better cruisers. Reference has already been
made to the peculiar position of Portugal and Brazil,
especially when under one Crown, *viz.* the actual possession
of slave-bearing territory on the west coast south of the
Equator, and slave-requiring colonies in the Brazils, and
how after the Napoleonic Wars a treaty had been concluded
in 1815 confining all trading to that between her own
dominions in Africa and Brazil. How that treaty was
evaded has also been described.

When in 1825 Brazil finally separated from Portugal,
England—who had assisted the former to gain her independence—insisted on a treaty more stringent, on paper,
than that concluded with Portugal in 1826. The latter
undertook to make the slave trade piracy for her subjects
by March 1830. This step she did not however take, but
in 1831 made partial observation of her treaty by passing
an Act which empowered the punishment of slave traders

and the confiscation of their vessels. But the terms of her treaty of 1815, properly observed, should have put an end to her slave traders when the Brazils became independent. She had now no interest in Brazil, and had agreed in 1815 only to permit the slave trade within her dominions, now non-existent.

In 1835 England endeavoured to force her into a treaty similar to that just made with Spain. It was about this time that the great Lord Palmerston began to make the anti-slavery cause his own, and the behaviour of Portugal very properly stirred him to great wrath. He publicly stated that she had not conformed to one single restriction which her own treaties on the subject imposed, and he further declared that all along the coast of Africa, in the debarred lands north of the Line as well as in the permissive south, she was still kidnapping and shipping negroes. And these are his actual words : " The ships of Portugal now prowl about the ocean, pandering to the cruisers of other nations, and when her own ships are not sufficiently numerous for the purpose, her flag is lent as a shield to protect the misdeeds of foreign pirates." Even strong words like these from England's traditional strong man did not produce action or expedite agreement. Ten years earlier, as already related, it had been necessary to address similar words to France. In 1839 negotiations finally broke down, and Palmerston introduced his Bill which provided for the condemnation in the special courts of all ships equipped with slave fittings, and even special water and provisions on board ; thus escaping from the hitherto crippling provisions that to make the vessels liable there must be slaves on board as well.

Further, since there were no Portuguese colonies holding slaves, the trade would be held illegal by us whether the cargo came from north or south of the Line. We were getting on, and there was now to be some chance for our cruisers, so many years already on their beat, to make their action effective. The majority of the illegal Spanish ships who traded under the Portuguese flag were driven to seek another. In the cause of humanity it will be noticed that the British Parliament had passed an Act controlling another Power, and intended to enforce its Act by force of arms ! Strange, illegal, yet humane though effected by arms ! The trade with Brazil could now be attacked, and the hearts of the abolitionists were greatly cheered—but, a very big but remained. Brazil was an independent Power, her ships and those of the United States were deeply implicated, and to the United States were transferred those foreign vessels now driven from the Portuguese flag's protection.

What an ill road it was to follow ! What a depressing condition our cruisers still had to face !

With the Spanish Treaty signed, and the coercive Act against Portugal and practically against Brazil on her Statute Book, England was at last in a position to really get on all fours with the slave ships for the first time for certainly twenty years. These treaties and acts did not in the least compel any loyalty or activity from their signatories, but it gave the British cruisers legal status before the slave-prize courts in their more searching activities. There still remained the roguery of the United States and the protection her interested flag was to give to the slavers of Portugal, Spain, and Brazil.

But Britain was not satisfied with the Portuguese status of 1839—and three years later, by a treaty of 1842, Portugal did actually declare the slave trade piracy and agreed to all measures for its suppression, and the British Act of 1839 so far as Portuguese vessels were concerned, was repealed. The Brazilian Government on achieving independence had agreed to the Act of 1817, and the activities of the courts enacted that they should cease in 1845. This made it necessary for Britain to pass an Act, as she had done for

Portugal, saying what Brazil should or should not do. Traders, however, preferred to be tried by the Admiralty Courts, which could only condemn ships and cargo and could not inflict actual personal penalties ; and when challenged it was said " that they either hoisted the American flag or threw their papers overboard."

Curiously enough, as regards Brazil the change of heart came from within. The slave trade, as indeed all other overseas trade, was in the hands of foreigners, largely Portuguese men of great wealth. They it was who had always prevented their Government from carrying out its own anti-slavery commitments. They were none the worse for the rise in the price of slaves, for it was said to prevent the native Brazilian from owning them, although they were annoyed at the rise itself. Finally, however, it was realized by the educated classes that, now they were an independent nation, an overwhelming slave population carried considerable danger. In the 'forties, out of five to six million people two-thirds were said to be slaves ; and in Bahia, where the slaves were all negro, there was recognized danger of rebellion. Incidentally the indigenous half-blood Brazilian had developed a great dislike of the European Portuguese. In the southerly portions where climate was more temperate, free labour was already in use. In other parts, men owned slaves as they did horses, to hire out to industry.

The advantages and disadvantages of a slave system now became a subject of debate among politicians where the foreign and indigenous population sided against each other. By 1849 Palmerston had told the House of this free-labour movement with an anti-slavery policy. But the British Sugar Acts of 1846 referred to had increased the demand for slave labour, and for three years after that the number imported, despite our cruisers, stood at an annual average of between 50,000 and 60,000. This was more than Britain could stomach, as they all came in despite our cruisers ; and Lord Palmerston ordered the cruisers to secure slaves even if actually on vessels within Brazilian territorial waters.

The British cruiser *Cormorant* acted vigorously under this order, and took and burned a steam cruiser of 1050 tons in the Rio Frio. She then, despite remonstrance, entered (in June 1852) the River Paranagua, 300 miles to the east and 12 miles up, and saw several vessels of which four were slavers flying the Brazilian flag. Three were captured and the fourth sunk herself. Two were burnt as unseaworthy, and the fourth the captain sent to St. Helen.

Great was the indignation at Rio among the " foreign " and capitalist classes. The British Minister, Hudson, was anxious enough to see the trade suppressed, and thought the action of Captain Schomberg and his *Cormorant* justified. He, after much parley, however, suspended further action by the *Cormorant* in return for a guarantee that definite genuine and effective steps to suppress the trade were taken. Thirty-five days after Schomberg had taken the steamers, the Brazil Chamber passed a Bill which adopted the stipulations in the treaty with Portugal, that slave-trading should be deemed piracy.

The old influences were not, however, to be got rid of so easily. The pirates, hunted out of the vicinity of Rio, had started activity in Bahia on 11th January 1851. Hudson, hearing that seven slavers were being fitted out at Bahia and that many barracoons had been erected there and else-where, announced that all restraint on our cruisers had been removed. That was the turning point, and Brazil, with the good-will of most of the indigenous people and the alacrity of fear from the foreigners, started in earnest. Slaves were seized on landing, caravans sent into the interior were overhauled, barracoons were destroyed, Brazilian cruisers received peremptory orders to assist the British vessels. One large slave trader lost, it was said, eighty-five slave vessels. The slave merchants fled to Europe to use their capital elsewhere ; hundreds of thousands sterling were withdrawn from the trade. Although 23,000 slaves were imported in 1850, the most came early in the year. Next year the number was 3000, and by 1852 it had dwindled to a negligible 700.

At long last Britain had triumphed, and in July of 1851 the Queen's speech announced that Brazil was definitely suppressing the trade. The anti-coercionists claimed this as an evidence that this was a spontaneous act of advancing civilization, and Lord Palmerston, satisfied by the fact, did not deem it necessary to disturb the Brazilian Government by publishing to the world what were his instructions to the cruisers that had so stimulated its good intentions.

The Brazilian trade was practically over, though it was not till 1869 that Britain felt it safe to repeal the Minatory Act of 1845. But abolition did not yet mean emancipation, though the overwhelming shortage of negro women among the slaves in Brazil militated against reproduction maintaining an adequate slave population, and the policy of free labour was obviously on its way, even if lagging behind the more civilized States of the world . . . a set-back came in 1855 when heavy slave mortality due to an epidemic made the position in the sugar plantations critical. The American pirates, with their magnificent clippers, rose naturally enough to the occasion, and several vessels were fitted out. One vessel was captured by the Brazilian authorities with 250 slaves, and many other cargoes were actually kidnapped in Brazil by other dealers for sale ! And that was practically the end of this enterprise, as dealer began to prey on dealer, and dog to eat dog.

THE ASTOUNDING SLAVE STORY OF CUBA

The story of the slave trade and slave life of Cuba and Brazil is interesting and instructive, and in the modern history of the former especially is another instance of the after-effects on world affairs of a slave policy. It has been explained that for many years Spain had not permitted her own people to take part in the importing of slaves, but had never objected to her colonies buying their slaves from those who did. But in 1817 a law was passed permitting Spaniards to trade in slaves. As Cuba was now the principal Spanish colony in the Americas, it was to Cuba that slaves were run in defiance of the British blockade, by the slave clippers of the United States sailing under the Spanish flag and nominal ownership. In 1792 there were but 84,000 slaves in the island; by 1846 the census showed 418,000 whites, 153,000 free coloured people, and 496,000 slaves! It was even alleged that the real total of the latter was nearer 800,000, and again it was said that in 1873 out of a total population of 1,500,000, 500,000 were slaves. The Spanish slave laws compelled manumission after a time, hence the free coloured population which had no doubt considerably increased between 1841 and 1873. The long British vigil, undoubtedly due to the Powers failing to put pressure on Spain, was beginning to have real effect on the Cuba trade by 1840. In 1839 it was believed that 59 slavers had left Havana for the African coast; but in 1841 it had fallen to 31, and in 1842 to 3; while the total of slaves brought back had fallen from 25,000 in 1839 to 11,000 in 1840, and 3140 in 1842. There is no doubt that this result was due not only to faster British cruisers, but to a long-delayed agreement with Spain in 1835, that ships " fitted " as slavers might be seized, and that the entirely evil and incomplete convention that a ship could only be condemned if caught with actual slaves on board was at an end. It had long paralysed our efforts. That it should so long have been accepted, pointed, then as now, to the essential need of an international league if the world is to be properly policed.

In 1840 Spain had sent to Cuba a Governor of a type more consonant with the British conscience, one General Valdez ; partly because both Spain and Portugal had been alarmed at the wave of indignation against both countries, which the inhumanities of their slave trade to the island had evoked. Valdez broke the old tradition of connivance and profit-making by the Captain-General, and though he only stayed two and a half years, he set a standard which his successors could not entirely ignore. After him came a Spaniard of Irish descent, one O'Donnel, who is said to have retired with £100,000, largely the offrakings of the trade. Indeed, with Queen Christina herself extensively interested in concerns that thrive on the trade, a high standard in her proconsuls was hard to expect ! There were many unworthier Captain-Generals after Valdez. In 1846 British cruising activities had reduced the imports to 419, but O'Donnel's efforts made for considerable revival. The old figure of 70 slave ships was never reached again, but by 1847 there were 11, and in 1849 over 8000 slaves arrived, and in 1853 the highest figure for eleven years, 12,500, was reached. British indignation now stirred Madrid to action, and orders were sent out which, if acted on, would have killed the trade. It was not, however, till 1854, under Captain-General the Marquis de Pezuela, that Madrid's orders were fairly launched. All slaves were now enumerated, and all new shiploads confiscated with all un-enumerated slaves. The " enumeration " edict caused real consternation among the hitherto defiant slave traders. Pezuela's activities seized and released 3000 slaves, and dismissed many dishonest and recalcitrant officials. But slave interests were too much for him and he only succeeded in registering 374,000 slaves, a moiety of those held. In the winter of 1853–1854 a cholera epidemic carried off 16,000 negroes, and of course increased the demand. Because of the Crimean War several British cruisers were withdrawn from the African coast, and the slave traders at once returned to work. Concha, the new Captain-General, it is true, did his best, under many restrictions, and the slave traders were very successful in getting far more slaves registered than really existed, so that the illicit importing received a licence, and priests were easily bribed to give a false certificate of baptism. Slave ships arriving were met at sea by steamers bringing false certificates.

As the modern slave ships usually sailed from the United States, the old knowledge obtained by the British agents in Cuba of all probable arrivals was not now existent. It was alleged in England now that capital, crew, and captain were all from the United States (*Hansard*, 1853, cxxvii. 776). Portuguese slave traders expelled from Brazil now came to Cuba to assist the Yankee traders, and it is said they even got passes for enumerated slaves and baptismal certificates handed to the skipper before they sailed from the United States for the African coast. The art of forging ship's papers and slave registers had now been reduced to a fine art, and authority was openly defied on every side.

In 1859 came a most damning report from Commodore Wise, commanding the British cruisers on the African coast, describing the system by which slaves were still raided in the interior and sent down to the coast.

" This expensive cruel system is accompanied by the most terrible heartrending loss of life that can be conceived. In chained gangs the unfortunate slaves are driven by the lash from the interior to the barracoons on the beach ; there the sea air, insufficient diet, and dread of their approaching fate, produce the most fatal diseases ; dysentery and fever release them from their sufferings ; the neighbouring soil grows rich in the decaying remains of so many fellow-creatures, and the tracks are thick-strewn with their bones. On a short march of 600 slaves, a few weeks back, intended for the *Emma Lincoln*, 125 expired on the road. The mortality in these rapid marches is seldom less than 20 per cent. Such, sir, is the slave trade under the American flag."

(The report, dated the 20th July 1859, was written to Admiral Sir F. Grey.)

Lest there should be any doubt of the share of the Stars and Stripes in the trade, let us refer to a letter from Lord John Russell [1] to the British Ambassador at Washington, 10th September 1860, enclosing a copy of a list of 85 slavers that had sailed from American ports in the past eighteen months, and a list of 26 such vessels which landed 12,000 to 15,000 slaves in Cuba. It also stated that of 170 slave-trading expeditions fitted out between 1859 and 1860, 74 were known to have sailed from New York, 43 from other American ports, 40 from Cuba, and 13 from European ports. In 1860 President Buchanan, Lincoln's predecessor, did bring the matter before Congress, but not with a view to amend the law, which was the one thing needed, but rather to vote more money for America's cruisers. This did have the effect of the capture by American cruisers of 4200 slaves, useful if only as illustrating the folly of allowing your own countrymen to so break your laws that you must spend large sums to catch them at it, but not to punish them !

It was computed that in 1859, when there were no British cruisers off Cuba, 30,000 slaves were taken into the blood-spot. A new Captain-General, Serrano, arrived to succeed the quite ineffective Concha, and things now began to move towards the inevitable end that civilization had so long, though most ineffectively, demanded. For 1860 the total landed fell to 18,000, rising again when the result of the American Civil War was the withdrawal

---

[1] Printed by Mathieson in his second book.

of the United States cruisers, and from 1860–1861 the quota rose to 24,000. The accession of Lincoln, however, who was an eager abolitionist, though not prepared to disrupt the whole economical system of the Southern States, was an immense happening for the anti-slave trader. New York had been the great centre of the recent slave trade with Cuba, and Lincoln proceeded to adopt the quite forgotten device of carrying out the United States law. Slave-trading was piracy and punishable by death since 1830, and on 30th December 1862 Nathaniel Gordon, master of the *Eris*, convicted of slave-trading on the Congo, was hanged. This put the slaving fat in the fire.

Lincoln asked for British cruisers to return to Cuba, but it was pointed out that this could only revive the old controversy as to the searching of suspected slavers flying the Stars and Stripes. Then at long last the right thing was done. An agreement was signed agreeing to mutual search, with an equipment article, in which " signs of equipment " were included. It was unanimously signed by the Senate. The knell of African slave-trading had at last been rung. Had this been done when Britain asked for it thirty years earlier, the United States would not be living under the stigma of having been the slave traders of the modern world. In 1862 General Seranno in Cuba had given place to General Dulce. The new Captain-General informed all the " millionaire " slave traders that anyone caught landing slaves would be deported within twenty-four hours. The suppression in the States for a short time switched the fitting out of ships to France and Spain. Nor was England guiltless. The *Nightingale* got away out of Liverpool, but was caught with 500 slaves on her. Hartlepool was said to be building a slave trader. Marseilles and Cadiz became ports of fitment.

In 1865, however, it was believed that no consignment of slaves reached Cuba, and in 1865 the Spanish Cabinet proposed to make slaving piracy also. It may be said that the Cuba slave trade died that year. That year also died Lord Palmerston, who had made abolition his own. The story of Cuban emancipation is quite another matter. For the moment it sufficed that the provision of slaves from outside was killed.

EMANCIPATION IN CUBA

It took the endeavours of Britain nearly seventy years to stop the actual import of slaves to Cuba, but while that trade did die about 1865, emancipation was quite a different matter. *Pari passu* with the import of slaves, a system of manumission by owners had been continually at work, quite inadequate to terminate the slave system but giving an example which might be followed more widely could the conscience of the owners be stirred. There was also a small population descended from the captured contents of slavers who were sent to Cuba as free labourers by the British Navy and the slave courts. It was not till 1880, however, when gradual abolition was decreed, and in 1886, when the abolition became definite, that the difficulties of a colony of free negroes began, in themselves as hard to solve as those of the slave régime. It was not till 1893 that the emancipation of slaves was complete, with Cuba as a free colony of Spain and equal civil rights granted to all. The years following were full with political troubles in which the United States could not shake free. In 1898 the United States cruiser *Maine* was blown up in the harbour at Havana under circumstances of which the truth will probably never be known. A war between the States and Spain ensued which ended with the severance of Cuba from Spain altogether. After a couple of years of American military dictatorship, during which immense progress was made, good roads laid, and the principles of law and order inculcated, Cuba was declared an independent State in 1902.

Since that date progress has alternated with disorder and revolution, but on the whole it may be said that the emancipated negroes have not been entirely a failure as citizens, and with the whole population make a not unhomogeneous blend. To Spain, who had so long neglected the repression of slavery, despite the treaties made with Britain abjuring it in 1817 and 1837, nemesis came in the loss of her valuable possession and colony.

CHAPTER TEN

Slavery on the East Coast of Africa

★

*The East Coast generally—Réunion, and Early Indentured Labour—The
Internal Slaving in Africa—The Trade with Arabia—Zanzibar.*

★

THE EAST COAST OF AFRICA

So far-reaching and so prolonged has been the story of
slave-trading from West Africa to the Americas, that the
tragedy of the east coast has been concealed ; nevertheless
there is as prolonged a story of wrong-doing here as on the
west coast, though happily for East Africa the demand for
labour in teeming India could be met locally and sought no
export thence. It was the labour needs of the great islands
as they became ripe for development—to use the horrible
phrase of the estate agent—Madagascar, Bourbon or
Réunion, and Mauritius, that created the same sort of
demand as sent the slavers to the coast of Guinea. In this
case Zanzibar and its Arabs were entrepôt and suppliers,
Portugal assisting. In the earlier years the French bought
slaves pure and simple from Zanzibar as they had for the
West Indies. In 1848 by the coming of the Second Republic
all slavery in Réunion and the French islands and in the
Mozambique Channel was abolished, at any rate in name.
The form of labour began to trend towards an importation
of the nominally free labourers hired for a promised wage.

But besides the trade from Zanzibar to the French
islands, the Sultan of Muscat, who ruled on that island also,

had a very large and lucrative coastal trade of his own of slaves carried up and down the coast in dhows for sale in Africa itself. Such methods were parallel to the case of Portuguese trade within her own lands, and could not in the earlier years be interfered with. Further, there was the eternal slave-raiding in North Africa to satisfy the Egyptian markets, and to maintain the constant demand of Arabia and the Persian Gulf for slaves. The watching of this trade was for many weary years the duty of the British cruisers and boat patrols, and many were the "scraps" with armed dhows that called for much courage and dash on behalf of the British cruisers and boat parties, and on which many epics might be written. Against them have always been the uncontrolled agents of those Powers who come under Kipling's category of the "lesser breeds without the law."

The whole of the "back races" of the inner Sudan have been the victims of slavery since Egypt became a realm, and till quite lately slavery was ineradicably seated in Egyptian habits and ethics. Among the semi-Arab traders of Egypt and the Sudan the business had been developed for centuries till it rivalled the machinery of a reputable trade, and until quite recent years had furnished the bulk of the material of slave-running to Arabia. Indeed even in its relic to-day, slaves will often acquiesce in appearing as crew or passenger while the cruiser overhauls the dhow. As the story of Victorian activities in the Sudan develops we shall see how ruthless and implacable this trade has been.

Réunion, and Early Indentured Labour

After the French "liberation" there arose a demand from the French planters, exactly as had arisen in the island of Mauritius fourteen years earlier after the British emancipation, for imported native labour. This was responsible for an early version of what is now known as indentured labour, *viz.* labour imported by agreement for a period of years. Well managed, properly paid and cared for, and *accompanied by the labourers' women*, it is unobjectionable ; but rarely in earlier days were such matters seen to, or even thought of. So early as 1829 the French Settlements of Pondicherry and Karikal were expected to provide labour for the island of Bourbon (which became Réunion in 1848), but it was not till emancipation in 1848 produced a crisis that this demand was seriously pressed. So small a territory could not find enough men, and recourse was had to India. The French managed their business badly, the English in Mauritius well ; Indian labour that returned from Réunion to India never came back, the British coolies from Mauritius often did, and often persuaded others to come back with them. The following is an extract from *Six Months in Réunion* quoted by Mathieson, written by the Rev. P. Beaton (1860), an army chaplain who had been in both islands. " I never heard a coolie in Mauritius insinuate that he had not left India of his own free choice. I never met a coolie in Bourbon who did not affirm that he was trepanned in some way. In 1859 there were 180,000 Indian coolies in Mauritius and 30,000 in Bourbon, and many of the latter had come from British India by shady means." It has always been doubted if the slave trade to Réunion had entirely died, and in 1845 it was revived in another form. The treaties with France of that year had not been extended to East Africa. The Imam of Muscat had transferred his headquarters to Zanzibar as Lord Palmerston maintained, to conduct a traffic of negroes to Réunion as free labourers, " *engagés*," to use the French term. But their fate on arrival in what was still a slave colony was lamentable enough. The slave market of Zanzibar was kept filled by Arabs, who brought the slaves from the mainland in dhows, packed to the brim, and if the voyage was at all prolonged most of them died.

In 1832 the Imam of Muscat signed a treaty with Britain by which he agreed to the latter stopping any trade with Muscat. The coastal trade which brought slaves to his own territories was not included.

But the French bought slaves in Zanzibar itself in large numbers. This killed the Sultan's coastal trade and annoyed him because he did not get from the French the customs dues he received from the Arab traders.

Bourbon, however, still could not get enough coolies from India or slaves from Zanzibar, and in 1854 Portugal allowed dealing in her negroes from Mozambique. The demand for " emigrants " such as these set up the old type of slave-raiding in the interior. The French had extended the trade to their islands of Mayetta and Nossie Bé in the Mozambique Channel which in the 'sixties ran to many thousands.

Since British cruisers and consuls were few on the east coast, the " migration " that was a very colourable imitation of slavery went on unnoticed. But France by now was getting herself into considerable disrepute, chiefly by reason of her high-handedness, in protecting with her cruisers her almost-slave-trade operations, accentuated by the absence of British armed vessels during the trouble of the Indian Mutiny. The agreement with Portugal to get her negro " immigrants " from certain areas in Mozambique having been infringed by two widespread recruitments, one of her negro-carriers was seized and condemned at Mozambique and sent to Lisbon. Two French ships then actually entered the Tagus and demanded her release under threat of bombardment.

Britain, who had just seen the Crimean War through in alliance with France, was anxious to help and equally anxious to stop this dubious negro immigration. In France enthusiasm for the Crimean Alliance was waning, and she had become so hostile to her late ally that a disarmed Britain once more had to rearm, start her great volunteer movement of 1859, and fortify the North Downs and her naval ports on the land side. Britain sympathized with the labour troubles of the French colonies, and in the Queen's speech at the opening of Parliament in 1859 announced that facilities would be given for inviting Indian labour to serve them, since the French colonies in India were quite inadequate to furnish enough. The Emperor of the French wrote that if, as alleged, " negroes engaged on the African coast are not allowed the exercise of their free-will and if the enrolment is only the slave trade in disguise, I will have it on no terms, for it is not I who will protect enterprises contrary to progress, to humanity, and to civilization." French foreign relations were in charge of Prince Jerome, who wrote very peremptory instructions to the local authorities. But next year (1860) we find a British minister expressing regret and disappointment at hearing that the purchase of African labour for Réunion was to be revived. And although sanction was now accorded to the enrolment of 6000 natives of India from all-British sources there still came reports that the African stream had not stopped. Indeed it had actually reopened round on the west coast of Africa, under circumstances which at first were received with the approval of ignorance in Great Britain. Enthusiasts talked of a wave of African migration to places demanding labourers, and hailed it as a method of preventing slave trade on the west coast. Indeed so far back as 1851 an announcement that a French contractor in Marseilles had been authorized to buy negro emigrants for the plantations in Guadeloupe and Martinique, was welcomed even by *The Times*. The idea of a benevolent migration sounded so pleasant, so easy to talk of, to simple British folk. It was not realized in our drawing-room circles how difficult it was to organize and supervise, even if

intentions were good—and there were a good many evil
tongues in evil cheeks! Labour thus bought was soon
found to be on its way to Réunion as well as to the West
Indies.

The British struggles against this system, added to a
desire to help France, resulted in 1861 in a treaty authoriz-
ing the general migration just referred to, from India to
Réunion. The French by it undertook to stop their negro-
migration operations. This actually did stop in 1862 as far
as Réunion went, but to the islands in Mozambique Channel
thousands still went in contravention of the spirit of the
treaty and apparently of the Emperor's wishes. Indeed all
through the slaving question do we see that practice is
stronger than precept. Lord Palmerston was perturbed
over the Portuguese action, but the latter's control over
600 miles of eastern coast was largely nominal, and their
resources to cure illicit trade quite inadequate, even if the
desire were genuine.

It may here be explained that in theory the French
practice resulted in buying slaves to make them " free."
Even were the freedom really genuine, the labour well paid,
and after-care adequate, the actual obtaining of the slaves
did nothing to stop the cruelties and raids on villages by
which the chiefs supplied the traders.

Further, at this time negro trade, licit and illicit, was
being carried on under the French flag which all Arab
dhows flew, because it was supposed to give immunity to
search by British cruisers. Indeed it was freely said that
the French cruisers were not concerned in suppressing
slave trade, but rather in protecting slavers from the
British !

So late as 1871 the Rev. Horace Walker, a missionary
and a companion of Livingstone (1860–1869), before a
Select Committee of the House of Commons, said that
Portuguese settlers on the Zambesi eagerly sold off their

slaves at the high prices offered by the French, and bought
replacements more cheaply from the old evil source of the
raiding chiefs.

The British cruisers on the east coast had thus as intricate
a problem to unravel as on the west coast, if of a different
nature. They were, of course, also concerned for many
years in putting down the slave-running of the Arab slave
traders from the Somali and Indian coast to Arabia.

The most extraordinary thing about the whole story is
that even in the year 1865, fifty years after the Congress of
Vienna in which all nations had subscribed to the decision
to suppress the slave trade, only Great Britain supplied any
effective force for the purpose. Moreover we see her
eternally thwarted, not only by the interested nationals, but
by the officials of the very nations who had subscribed to
the convention.

The Internal Slaving in Africa

When we realize that the northern coast of Africa and
Egypt have been for so many centuries in the hands of
Arabs and Moslem Moors, and that the territories over
which their caravans roamed impinged on those of simple
black aboriginal and negroid peoples, we shall not wonder
at the internal slave trade.

From the earliest days of the Pharaohs until a very few
years ago, young men of spirit went a-slaving, as young
men of spirit in England and the States went East and
West. Slaves were to be had for the taking and the markets
of North Africa were eager for the merchandise.

Aeons therefore before the Christian victims of the
corsairs took out their cruel *riposte* on the harmless West
African negroes, rulers of Mauritania and the rulers of
Egypt took the Central African blacks for slaves of all
kinds, and we may be perfectly sure that it was through

the ages much as in Sir Arnold Hodson's report of a few years back. Sir Arnold is now (1937) Governor of the Gold Coast and formerly of Sierra Leone, and writes with responsibility.

" The method of raiding is to surround a village in the dark, the raiders blowing trumpets and uttering blood-thirsty yells, to stampede the inhabitants. The huts are then fired, and the old men and women are ruthlessly speared or shot down, as they rush out panic-stricken, only the younger ones being of sufficient value to capture.''

From Egypt all the way by the Barbary States to Morocco, while the ships of the corsairs took toll of the sea, the land pirates took equal toll of the *Balad-ul-Sudan*, the country of the blacks, a folk more aboriginal than the negroes of the slave-coast hinterland.

Through the Arab and Moorish countries there had grown up the highly organized system of trading, which in the nineteenth century as well as in ancient times is conducted exactly as any other big industry ; the slave raiders who manufacture, the wholesale dealers who buy from them, the lesser dealers with their eye on supply and demand to even their bulls and their bears, while all the while the actual sellers show off the goods—especially the female goods—on whose value they expatiate to the buyers. Since the days of the open Sudan trade dealers are more cunning ; the work is more hazardous, the profit better in individual price, less in the aggregate, and to this day the trade goes on, as slaves from the inner hinterland of Central Africa are smuggled through or openly brought from Abyssinia to the markets of Arabia. The story of Abyssinia in slave-dealing, so open, so ruthless and so recent, will be dealt with by itself. It has been the modern home of the east-coast trade and a powerful source of supply to the emporiums of Arabia.

THE TRADE WITH ARABIA

Not much may be said at this stage of the trade with Arabia and the Persian Gulf. It has gone on between Africa and Asia for many centuries on exactly the same lines, *viz*. slaves are captured in Central Africa and Uganda by Arab and negro-Arab tribes and tribal leaders or slave-trade bands, and shipped from points on the Red Sea coast and Zanzibar to the Arabian littoral. Its victims have been always shipped in dhows, chased by the British Navy or the East India Company's cruisers, for over a century. The subject comes up in the story of the British in the Sudan, in the outline of Zanzibar,[1] and once again in the story of slavery in Arabia to-day. The mere capturing of dhows of slaves by the cruisers and their boat patrols did little to stop the business. So long as the matrix at one end and the buyers at the other existed, so long would the business endure. Capture often stimulated trade, as gins increase rabbits, and the price increased in proportion as difficulties were put in the way of transit. It was not till the British took control of the Sudan and Uganda and over-cast Zanzibar that the trade began to diminish, but the Abyssinian fault prevented the oversea trade from being killed. Arabia as a slave-holding country, eager to obtain what can be brought her, still exists and will be dealt with later. The trade has many facets, and is full of internal drama and tragedy, yet without the encirclement of horrors that centre round the west-coast trade, the old Congo, or the story of Putumayo.

ZANZIBAR

It was not to be expected that the well-placed Moslem State of Zanzibar, since 1837 the undisputed territory of the Arab Imam of Muscat and on the death of Sayyad Ibn

[1] See next Section.

Sultan in 1856 an independent Sultanate, would be free from so profitable a business as the slave trade in negroes, that race so obviously sent into the world to be enslaved ! Zanzibar's position in the centre of the East African coast made it specially suitable as an entrepôt, in which ships for Mozambique and Madagascar, dhows for Arabia and the Persian Gulf, and her own coastwise slave trade could fill up and form depots. It is much connected with the earlier story of the Kawasim, the Arab pirates of the Islam of Kishem, and their daring development following a period of British-made inadequacy in the Persian Gulf. During the time a young Arab princeling of Muscat, one Sayyad Ibn Sultan, was slowly coming to power in the seat of incompetent predecessors and in face of the great Wahabi overrunning of the desert, which had followed on the withdrawal of the Persians from their attempt to dominate Oman.

In 1809 the pirate situation in the Gulf and the Indian Ocean became unbearable, and Sayyad, now ruler of Muscat, co-operated with a British expedition from Bombay. The sea-nests of the pirates were destroyed, but on the withdrawal of the British they revived on land, and the British failure to support Sayyad at Muscat resulted in a worse situation developing, and Sayyad in despair seeking other helpers. By 1817 the pirate force had risen to 64 war dhows and 7000 men, and the British decided that they must be exterminated. They re-entered into their neglected friendship with Sayyad Ibn Sultan of Muscat. So in November 1819 an armada of 9 British warships and 3000 troops arrived at Muscat. The headquarters of the Kawasim pirates at Ras El Khaima was attacked, Sayyad and 3000 Arabs assisting. This ended the pirate power, and cemented our friendship with Muscat ; in 1830 a joint British and Arab force attacked the raiding tribal federation known in our annals as Beni-bu-Ali. This was not successful, but Ibn Sultan received a sword of honour from the British, and next year a larger British expedition arrived and together with Ibn Sultan settled the Beni-bu-Ali handsomely. Sayyad Ibn Sultan was now in a position to secure control of Oman, and being universally hailed as victorious and congratulated by the Porte, was enabled to consolidate his influence all along the coast of southern Arabia and in the Persian Gulf.

From now Ibn Sultan's connection with the east coast of Africa begins. That coast harbours an immensely varying population, negroes and Arab-trading colonies of great diversity being included. For centuries Arab traders had settled and imposed their rule on a backward indigenous stock. In the middle of the seventeenth century the Arab settlers had called on the chief of Muscat to help rid them of the Portuguese. An Arab expedition expelled them from Mombasa, and a widespread massacre of Portuguese rendered the coast free of western influence for close on three-quarters of a century. In 1728 the Portuguese returned and the settlers again appealed to Muscat. An Arab leader was deputed to take over an expedition from Oman, who eventually settled himself as Wali of Mombasa and tributary of Muscat. For the next hundred years the history of Mombasa's Walis is one of uncontrolled local quarrels and successions.

By 1812, however, the rising strong man of Muscat—the Sayyad Ibn Sultan aforesaid—began to take an interest in this runaway fief of Oman. Some ineffective and uncertain interference from Bombay did not improve matters. Ibn Sultan, however, finally—sometime between 1827 and 1829—despatched a strong expedition to Mombasa. Subsequent history is confused, but the place and the island of Zanzibar undoubtedly came under his control, but with no satisfactory results. Ibn Sultan, however, despite advice and discouragement from his British friends, persisted in his efforts, and by 1837 we see him in full possession and control and founding a palace and what is now the city of Zanzibar. Among many activities he introduced what is now the staple product, the clove. Sugar and indigo also occupied the attention of this enterprising leader.

The long and short of a chequered story is that Sayyad Ibn Sultan, a man of vision, courage, and political insight, established himself as ruler of Zanzibar and Muscat, made the hesitating and doubtful British his firm friends, handled French rivalries with considerable diplomatic skill, and died in 1856 powerful and respected. The British friendship indeed had much to do with the final strangulation of the slave trade. Ibn Sultan left thirty-four children, all from concubines, leaving 60,000 crowns to each son and 29,000 crowns to each daughter.

The dominion was divided by his testament into two Sultanates left to two of his sons, *viz.* Zanzibar and Muscat.

It is not to be expected that an Arab mentality would feel any repugnance to the slave trade or look upon it as anything but a source of prosperity to both subject and State, while the Portuguese tradition of the east coast was equally partial to the trade and system. But Ibn Sultan was an unusually enlightened man, and while recognizing in some sort the claim of even negroes to a measure of humane treatment, was soon aware of the strange sensitiveness on the subject felt by his friends the English and was quite prepared to meet them. He however knew, as happily did also our Foreign Office, that to press suppression too quickly meant ruin to his people and danger to his own throne, even to the disappointment of abolitionist enthusiasts. Nevertheless progress was steady, and his shrewd mind soon realized the industrial fact that slave labour was no cheaper than freed labour, if a costing account be cast.

After Ibn Sultan's death British influence in Zanzibar increased still more, a feebler successor requiring perhaps more support than the wise and powerful Sayyad. Between 1858 and 1861, while General Rigby was British diplomatic agent, 8000 slaves were freed, and he and the missionaries did much to organize vocational training for them. This, however, did not touch the main problem. In 1890 a definite British protectorate was recognized by France and Germany. Before this, however, Britain had been very cognizant of the widespread slavery obtaining under Zanzibar influence and protection, and in 1870 the House of Commons appointed a Select Committee. As a result thereof Sir Bartle Frere was appointed a special anti-slavery commissioner and was succeeded therein by Sir John Kirk. The missionary societies were very active in promoting anti-slavery conditions, and were encouraged to start schools for training liberated slaves, while a wealthy young English missionary, by name Arthur West, spent all his private resources in buying in the slave market in Zanzibar. It was now recognized that Zanzibar and its hinterland was hitherto, so far as slavery was concerned, one of the world's plague spots.

In 1876, at the instance of Sir John Kirk, the Sultan issued an edict prohibiting the export of slaves, and in 1890 signed a decree prohibiting slave-holding and slavery. These edicts were largely disregarded, and slaves for the Congo were nominally enlisted, in reality enslaved. The anti-slavery protagonists in England and Parliament generally kept the subject alive, pressing for a railway into the interior and the consequent opening up of the hinterland. The British representative in Zanzibar, however, in the 'nineties, Sir Arthur Hardinge, while keenly alive to the evils of slavery and the Zanzibar contribution thereto, was not prepared to go too fast, to ruin whole businesses acceptable to Islam and in accordance with long existing custom. Other British interests, as well as some recognition that in one sense there was another side to the case which could not be ignored, called for gradualness. The friendship with the Sultan must not be severely strained, nor must our humane inclination go to the points of producing some outbreak among the Arabs. The slave industry must be made to die gradually and people given warning to make a change of habit themselves. The attitude of the greater wisdom did not, of course, commend itself to our enthusiasts, though it was the only wise course. Finally, steady but not overpressed influence produced in 1897 a fresh decree from the Sultan making all slavery illegal. What was now wanted was to see that this edict was enforced. This act was indeed often honoured in the breach, but at any rate our consular officials, naval patrols, etc., had a perfectly clear mandate on which to base their activities. Slavery was illegal and could be suppressed as though it were piracy. The end of it was that slavery slowly died, and the Sultan cordially helped in the various schemes to make released slaves into useful citizens, while the missionary and other enterprises involved and the settlement of the Society of Friends were to meet with considerable success.

From the first decade of the present century slavery and slave-making after many cruel years has come to an end in Zanzibar, owing to British persistence and energy, and due to British wisdom, which achieved this without any rupture with an otherwise valuable ally and protected potentate. To-day trade, cultivation, and the arts flourish with free labour as they had never flourished in the days of slavery.

CHAPTER ELEVEN

The Slave Story of the United States

★

The United States, Slavery, and the Curse—The New Government and Abolition—The Various American Acts and Treaties regarding Slavery —Slave-holding and the Slave States before 1859—Abraham Lincoln, Abolition, and the Civil War—The End of the Sad Slave Story.

★

The United States, Slavery, and the Curse

When the " American Rebellion," that grew to be the " War of Independence," came to its inevitable end, the new Government, like any other in the Americas, started its new life with a vast slave system, whose genesis has been described, deepset in its bones. Of it, Jefferson said, " I tremble for my country when I reflect that God is just." The new nation entered into its independence just as the movement in England for abolition, as distinct from emancipation, was stirring. But the wealth, prosperity, and what might be called " the guts " of the new Republic, lay as yet for the most part in the virile pure British colonists of the Southern or slave States, and the life and revenues of the land largely hinged on cotton production in semi-tropical climes. It was one thing for the Northern States to have no need for slaves, or to abjure slave-holding and to rely as they could on white labour, but it was quite another matter for the warmer South. But there were plenty of folk in the North who abhorred slavery, and to whom the movement in England was most congenial.

L   161

Between the Northern and Southern States, drawn from different origins, and with peculiar features in their lives, there was no great love lost. But however much Puritan and humanitarian feeling in the Northern States might abhor slavery, there was never, through all the long years of the first half of the nineteenth century, any movement of serious import in the North for " Emancipation," *i.e.* the ending of slave-owning, by any means other than evolution and general consent. The struggles and clashes which engendered the feeling that made the Civil War of the 'sixties possible, grew from the difficulties of the status of the new territories, which the continual expansion west-wards had brought into the forefront of politics. The great territory of Ohio had already been legislated for, and it was such areas as Nebraska and Kansas, and the vast region of Texas, that became the cause of so much bitter discussion. How it ended, and how the great curse that slavery brought on our Anglo-Saxon race fell so that they slew each other to the number of close on one million, belongs to the end of this chapter rather than to the beginning.

THE NEW GOVERNMENT AND ABOLITION

The young Government of the Federating States was soon called on by the private abolitionists in England (using the term in its original sense), and a little later by the British Government, to share in the great work of suppressing the slave trade with West Africa, and some reference has already been made to the treaties and activities engendered, and more especially to the turpitude of the United States and other Governments and individuals in fighting against their own humanitarian intentions. It may be, indeed, that the United States Government, in a country apt to give lip-service to great ideas, and having a con-stitution in which the Federating States had given powers but grudgingly to the Central Government, could not " deliver the goods."

It will be remembered that in 1807, shortly after the British Act of Abolition of that year, the United States followed suit, Congress prohibiting the trade, but like Britain, only fixed pecuniary penalties. Great Britain had realized her error in four years. It has been related that the fine leviable at first under the British Act was £100 per slave carried, as well as confiscation of ship and cargo, but in 1811 slave-trading was made a transportable offence. It was not till 1818 that the United States followed our example, at any rate on paper. It not only made slaving a transportable offence, but even imposed the death sentence. This gesture—it was little more—was not unnaturally loudly applauded by the abolitionists. No death sentence was ever imposed, however, in the United States till 1862.[1] In 1824, as has been related, Britain followed suit in adopting the death sentence as for piracy, though her share in the trade was so in hand that further stringency was not necessary.

In the early days of the nineteenth century it was difficult to control the running of slaves into the States, and they were smuggled in constantly from Florida and Texas, there being few to assist and sympathize with the United States legislation and professions. No patrol boats were available and few prosecutions were entered on, nor were any forfeitures recovered under the law of 1807. But there were those who kept the public informed of the scandals, and in 1819 an Act was passed for the use of cruisers,[2] and what was important, the grant to the captors of half the prize-money, and in 1820, as related, the United States declared slave-trading piracy. In 1819, however, it was still estimated that for several years the importation of slaves was between 13,000 and 15,000 a year. A United States speaker indeed

---

[1] *Vide* p. 144.   [2] Never seriously implemented.

declared that the trade was being carried on with all its old vigour and cruelty.

For a while, however, by 1825, the trade to the States was dying away. This was due to two factors besides the cruiser force, one the waning of the cotton trade owing to the fall in world's prices, the other, a new and upsetting development. Several of the Southern States, notably Virginia, started on the exploitation of the slave womb, as men would breed cattle, and stimulated production in every possible way, with the object, long successful, of supplying the trade by the sale of locally produced slaves. This, while carrying some good points, notably the diminution of the slave-raiding in Africa with its horrors of transportation deaths and the improvement in housing conditions of breeding stock, was no improvement to the moral question. It intensified the odious condition that the break-up of families by sale always entailed, mitigated, however, in the plantation life by the usual practice, in prosperity, of keeping families together.

The slump in the cotton trade, as all great commercial trends have always done, upset the conditions of the countryside. It lessened the demand for slaves, and by so much so good, and had it continued the prospects of idle slaves would have induced emancipation ; but it started the trek of slave owners, taking their slaves with them, that raised the issue of the legality of slave-holding in new territories just referred to. Within the slave States, the law dealt firmly and often cruelly with the question of the runaway slave. Under what laws in the new countries, that at first had not attained to the half-way house of a " Territory," were slaves held and punished, when or where did a slave attain freedom ? A complicated question for both moralist and lawyers !

The slave-owning settlers in the old States, finding the bottom fallen out of their cotton-growing life, sought lands and pastures new, sometimes by merely trekking, sometimes by filibustering into Texas, Cuba, and the central American States. As cotton returned to profitable prices, the slaves, who had died down, were now in defect. An agitation arose in the Southern States for reopening the slave trade, and the demand for slave labour was very great. The commerical convention of 1859 that assembled at Vicksburg demanded a return to the old method of labour-raising. Jefferson Davis opposed the motion, but only in the matter of expediency, especially asserting that he had no sympathy with those who " prated " of the inhumanity and sinfulness of the trade. On the other, Stephen A. Douglas, who contested the Presidency with Abe Lincoln, asserted in the same year that 15,000 slaves had been imported. It was openly said, states Mathieson, that some twenty slave-importing depots had been reopened in the South, and that so late as 1860 sixty or seventy cargoes had been landed.

Officially, however, the United States Government maintained its unimpeachable sentiments, and a few years earlier President Buchanan had urged the annexation of Cuba as the only means of stopping the trade. American writers even maintained that for sixty years the slave law had not been violated. But the real story of the trade with Cuba by American shippers and American ships has already been explained !

Although the United States had passed their abolition law in 1807, and their " piracy " Act in 1820, yet they persistently refused to agree with Great Britain for a mutual right of search. That is to say the Stars and Stripes did, as we have seen, openly, blatantly, and inhumanely cover the slave trade. It was not till 1842, as just related, that she even decided to put her own cruisers on to the prevention patrol, although the British had been at it for twenty-five years, and both countries had proscribed the trade in that same year, 1807.

The Various American Acts and Treaties Regarding Slavery

First looking at the story so far as Great Britain's platform was concerned, and the matter of the abolition of the trade with West Africa, we may advantageously summarize the actual Treaties and Acts, unobserved though they were :

1. In 1807 the United States followed promptly the British lead in forbidding the slave trade to her subjects.

2. In 1820 the trade was declared to be piracy and the death sentence established therefor.

3. In 1842 at long last the United States agreed to maintain cruisers to help suppress the trade.

How completely she failed to suppress her illegal slave filibusterers has been explained in the story of Cuba ; and then comes the end when in 1863 Abraham Lincoln, driven to it as a war measure, in the face of the military power and obduracy of the Southern States, actually declared all slaves free in the whole territory of the United States, including those in secession.

Finally in December 1865 a constitutional amendment was ratified, abolishing and for ever prohibiting slavery through the United States.

The misery to all concerned, however, by so sudden and complete a change of life is brought out very strongly in the remarkable American novel of 1936, *Gone with the Wind*. The war having ruined all the estate holders, labour was at a discount, and the freeing of the slaves meant there was no obligation to feed them, no bond that could compel the beaten and forfeited owners to feed and shelter their aged slaves. Abolition for many years meant far more misery to the slaves than slavery did. It is a chapter on which modern American writers prefer to be silent, but it is like the Russian revolution, a standing example of the disasters that follow the attempt to hurry the upheaval of a bad system. On the other hand, in the case of the United States this wholesale method could only have come in the manner it did as a war result.

SLAVE-HOLDING AND THE SLAVE STATES BEFORE 1859

Let us now turn from the failure of the United States to implement their undertakings or control their reckless traders, to the terrible nemesis outlined at the beginning of this chapter that the curse of slavery was to bring on their fair country and bonnie people—the curse of a million dead Anglo-Saxons, husbands and sons.

During the earlier years of the Union of the original thirteen confederating States, nine were slave States, four having denounced slave-holding in their State Constitution and liberated their slaves; but it must be said that the differences in climate was to some extent the deciding factor in the denouncements. Since statesmen from the slave-holding States predominated, various enactments found their way on to the Statute Book of the Union that tended to entrench slavery. Allusion has been made to the real point of disagreement between North and South, as their world spread west, *viz.* did State legislative sanction to slave-holding hold good outside the State, in the new " Territories " which were to become States ? Slave owners had trekked with their slaves to take up new lands and start life afresh. Northerners without slaves were also within the " Territories." At first it was more or less an accepted convention that new States should be formed in pairs, one slave State and one non-slave. Before 1859 eight had been added, four of each category, and Louisiana, because of the Treaty of Acquisition with the French, was also admitted to the Union as a slave holder. The slave States had indeed not come badly out of it, with five out of the nine new States added to their number. Then came the question of

Missouri, partly French, and also partly slave-holding, and with it the " Missouri Compromise." So far back as 1797 a law had been passed by Congress forbidding slavery in the territory north-west of the Ohio.

In 1820 the Missouri Compromise was enacted that settled the dispute regarding slavery in that State, permitting it south of latitude 36.30, but forbidding it anywhere north of that line in any non-slave-holding State or territory. The opponents of slavery disliked this at first, but later came to regard it as a charter of freedom, in view of the strong influence of politicians from the slave States in the United States Government.

In 1845 came the Annexation of Texas, and its admission to the Union after prolonged struggle between the slave and non-slave protagonists, with the right of slave-holding in certain portions thereof.

In 1854 came an enactment of Congress that shook the whole country and greatly increased the arising bitterness. This was the admission of the territories of Nebraska and Kansas to the Union as States, *with the right of deciding for themselves* whether or no they would be slave States— this, too, despite the fact that both were north of the magic 36.30 line! It was in effect the repeal of the Missouri Compromise. No wonder—however logical in itself this measure—that the abolitionists felt they had received a severe slap in the face. This, too, had come on top of the Fugitive Slave Act of 1850, which violated all their ideas as to sanctuary and places of freedom. Yet this, too, was a logical enough Act in itself, so long as slave-holding was in accordance with the law of the land, however repugnant to abolitionist sympathies. Another acerbation, and a severe one, occurred over the Dred-Scott decision (1857). Scott was a slave in Nebraska, where his master had taken him : There he claimed freedom and rights as an American citizen. The Supreme Court by a vote of seven to two declared that the Missouri Compromise itself had already been declared *ultra vires*, and that their constitution did not admit an ex-slave to the position of citizen. Scott himself was purchased and liberated, but the decision of the " old men," to quote Roosevelt, legal enough though no doubt it was, shook abolitionist feeling to its foundation.

The unfortunate affair of John Brown was the last of the series of acerbations and incidents. Brown, a Puritan farmer, had been very much to the fore in the fierce quarrels, and almost civil war, that had been in process in Kansas between the slave and anti-slave factions. He had led forays, slain—nay murdered—slave holders, seen his sons killed, for the glory of God as he conceived it. Mad as ten hatters on the one point, through his introspective brooding over the slave horror, he in 1859, with a large party of abolitionists and negroes, invaded the nearest slave State and seized, not the arsenal even of a slave-holding State, but one of the United States arsenals at Harper's Ferry. A United States force under the great and magnanimous Robert E. Lee proceeded against him. In due course he, the fanatic, was tried and hanged, though here schoolboy and community singers sing to-day the Marching Song of the North, perhaps without knowing who John Brown was.

> " *John Brown's body lies a-mouldering in its grave,*
> *But his soul goes marching on.*"

They who raise spirits from the vasty deep do not find it easy to put them back again. A madhouse rather than the gallows should have been John Brown's fate. But he had caused the death of many men.

It has been said that his bitter mad raid was right in that it abolished slavery. So argued the Inquisition. It added to the bitterness that was to ring the knell of that million Americans, and helped make compromise impossible.

In 1859-1860 occurred the movement to annex Cuba, and the not-unsuccessful revival of slave-running by American adventurers already referred to in discussing slavery in Cuba.

All these decisions and enactments made the slave position more secure, and also served as incentives to the anti-slavery conscience and enthusiasms that were alive in the North. But the old States of the South were full of the best material in the country, old-established and of great tradition, the bonnie and the brave of the Anglo-Norman folks of Britain. Statesmen and politicians of any vision knew that slavery could not be abolished, save very slowly, without disruption. Stop the slave trade from Africa they were slowly able to do, in face of many lawless interests that in a new country of no fixed dimensions fought against them, but " emancipation," which was now taking on the term " abolition," must lie within the womb of time.

It must be remembered that the world was expanding incredibly, and the demands for the cotton of the Southern States after the earlier slump was immense. Labour up-heavals there would mean disaster. Even Abraham Lincoln, with his horror of the whole thing, saw that very clearly. He was never, as is so often said, " abolitionist " so far as the older slave States went, and had intended to move slowly towards amelioration and gradual automatic libera-tion, somewhat perhaps as suggested earlier, on the lines of ancient Greece. The real bone of contention, as just explained, was not slave-holding in the old States, but the question of the Territories, and the new States developing therefrom, as expansion and settlement moved west, and the acerbities that too forward a slave policy had produced.

But unfortunately the temperament of the industrial North and the agricultural South, and the clash of Puritanism and Cavalierism, ran underneath and subconsciously mingled with the different and conflicting needs of their developing economic system.

But deep as even the Norman Conquest had left its trail in the fabric of all folk of British descent, however easily the antagonism in Great Britain itself could be steered, nothing in the past has so altered the world's fabric for British-descended people, and indeed for all the human race, as the aftermath of the slave question in North America. As this is the outline not only of slavery but of its side branches and effects, the story of the falling of North America into Civil War may be somewhat more elaborated before we leave it.

The other great aftermath of slavery beside the de-Normanizing and de-Saxonizing of the United States that has still to embarrass the world, is the presence of the westernized slave-descended negro in the country of many white races.

In the face of an Aryanism as pronounced as that of the high-caste Indian towards the " untouchables," the black people, however clever and advanced, are a thing apart. For the " no-nation " folk, the result of miscegenation, the condition is far worse. However fair and beautiful a woman, however able the man, the curse of an intermingling lies heavy on them—the embarrassing product of a slave system.

ABRAHAM LINCOLN, ABOLITION, AND THE CIVIL WAR

The various enactments just described showed how strong was the political influence of the Southern politicians that fanned the political jealousy felt by the North for the South. The South seemed to have nailed slavery to the mast in a country which stood for freedom. During the ten years preceding the Civil War there had been much bitter writing, and as in all propaganda much traducing. Mrs. Harriet Beecher Stowe's *Uncle Tom's Cabin*, which appeared in 1852, was really an anti-slavery stunt pamphlet, plus anti-slavery propaganda, under the guise of a novel. Only too true in much of its contents, it—like all books of its kind—magnified and traduced and thereby stimulated its effect. You may say that the book was responsible for abolition in its modern sense of " emancipation," or you may say that it was responsible for calling down the curse that set white Americans at each other's throats and encompassed the death of those million Anglo-Saxon victims of the Civil War aforesaid. It has been stated at the commencement of this chapter that the great clash of practical, as distinct from Utopian, feeling on the slave question, was as to whether or no there should be more slave-holding States. A second issue was how far the Southern influences in the legislature, in riveting the slave position firmer rather than tending to gradual liquidation, could be tolerated.

The popular impression that the American Civil War was fought over the question of slavery is wrong, save indirectly ; nor was the slavery question the immediate cause of the Civil War, although of course the clash of mentality and the prolonged mental acerbation over the whole question produced an atmosphere in which civil war became thinkable. Seward, Lincoln's foreign minister, was concerned with making this particularly clear to Europe.

The war was not even fought over the right to secede, which was admitted. It was brought about by a definite act of war by South Carolina, a State that had seceded, opening fire with its big guns on Uncle Sam. The child had fired in anger at its father ! Because memories are short and uprising generations are too busy to learn, a brief outline of how the war actually broke out and fared will not be out of place.

The various enactments that created so much controversy, and the appearance of *Uncle Tom's Cabin*, took place in the beginning of the second half of the nineteenth century, when steam and mass-produced steel were emerging from their infancy, and were for the first time to appear as an overmastering war factor. Those years of the 'fifties were the years when Abraham Lincoln was sowing the seeds of a crop which was unexpectedly to bring him to the Presidency. He had plenty to say during various elections on the slavery controversy ; when he unexpectedly became Republican candidate for the Presidency, he spoke also about the need for the Republican will to dominate State will, and he was uncompromising in his abhorrence of slavery and a slave system. But in his crude, ramshackle way he was a statesman more than a politician. No one realized better than he that slavery was terribly bound up with the economy and wealth of the State, and what was more important, with the productiveness of the land. No one realized more clearly, as his biographers are all agreed, that to force abolition was the way to disrupt the Union. The preservation of the Union was above all things the sacrosanct factor in all statesmanlike minds, however much they deplored the *impasse* of the slave question.

Now Abraham Lincoln's instinct was to " handle " all matters of disagreement, but to the larger part of the United States he was but vaguely known, indeed was hardly a public character at all. To the Southern mind, stirred by the abolitionist propaganda, he appeared in his astounding transfiguration and success as candidate for the Presidency as an arch-leader of abolitionism, regardless of right, wrong, or expediency. While his own addresses contained no such suggestion, no doubt his propagandists put this view about to gain him abolitionist votes. The real contest was between Lincoln, who had come forward as the candidate of those who hated slavery, and Douglas, whose firm platform was that since slavery was lawful throughout the whole of the United States, each territory had the right to continue or abolish it. We need not advert to the numerous great conventions and prolonged discussions nor the various candidates proposed for the Presidency. Lord Charnwood, in his biography of Lincoln, has said : " The fate of America may be said to have depended in the early months of 1860, on whether the nominee of the Republican party was a man who would maintain its principles with irresolution, or with obstinacy, or with moderation," and the ultimate platform of the Republican party was the prevalence of the will of the Republic over the will of the constituent sovereign States. Yet these sovereign States of their own free will had only given up *some* of their sovereign powers to the United States for the general convenience of that confederation. The right to secede was not given up.

When the " little Illinois attorney," with great depth of character and shrewdness, as yet unknown save to a few, was declared President, the Southern States felt that it was time to leave a Union that was so antipathetic to their own ideas.

The Presidential election had been on 6th November 1860. The legislature of South Carolina, which had remained in session over the election, convened a special convention to consider the exercise of the right of secession, and universally —nay, enthusiastically—approved this action, and on 20th December passed the " Ordinance of Secession."

That was while old President Buchanan was still in the chair. The retiring President showed wisdom by holding his hand. But the spirit of compromise had been fading out, although the right to secede was generally acknowledged. The question was whether or no a more powerful North would allow the constituent States to exercise their legal and undoubted right of secession, a right equally undoubtedly belonging to times that were fast passing, if they had not gone. On 4th February five more States passed ordinances of secession, and set about forming a new confederacy. Some men, however, still thought that this legal action might be accepted for a while in the hope of compromise and return. On 4th March Lincoln was inducted to the Presidential chair in the capital, which was almost in the seceding territory, and thus the country lawyer found himself called on to deal with this astounding situation. It is pleasant to realize how Douglas uncompromisingly and publicly showed his support by stepping to his side at the inauguration.

The question was still quite fluid in men's minds as to the secession, and whether to recognize it, for many said that only by military opposition could it be countered. There was no immediate call for precipitate action. Many would have let the slave States " stew in their own juice " for a while. These great issues and controversies cannot be elaborated here. The story of the tragedy comes into the book because it is the story of the liquidation of North American slavery and the falling of the Angel of Death on the descendants of the perpetrators of this great wrong, to the third and the fourth generation.

Except in fire-eating circles there was no immediate demand for war, nor was the Republic equipped for it. Further, the larger number of, and often the more distinguished, officers of the United States Army and Navy were Southerners.

War now arose not from any immediate clash of opinion on slavery, not even from secession, but from precipitate and mad action by South Carolina. It arose because there were what we should call " Imperial Garrisons," *viz.* naval and military stations, as was natural, of the supreme Republican Government located in the territories of the seceding States. In a small way the same situation exists with us to-day in Southern Ireland, where by agreement and treaty the Imperial Forces hold points necessary for the protection of the Empire. South Carolina, a seceding State, made the supreme mistake of refusing to allow the United States to replenish Fort Sumter, and opened fire when the United States Government persisted. Uncle Sam was being interfered with ! Uncle Sam's dander rose ! Again the modern British music-hall tag, " You can't do that there 'ere," described the feeling. South Carolina had given the hot-heads and war-bugs what they were looking for, as the greased cartridges had come to those planning the mutiny of the Bengal Army. The hopes of the statesmen striving for peace were baffled, the feeling was intense that you can't fire on Uncle Sam.

The real inwardness is perhaps best shown in the words which Rudyard Kipling put into the mouth of an old Southern lady living in her daughter's house in Sussex, as she talked at the dinner-table. This is the present-ment.

" I had the privilege of taking Mrs. Burton in to dinner, and was rewarded with an entirely new, and to me, rather shocking view of Abraham Lincoln, who, she said, had wasted the heritage of his land by blood and fire, and surrendered the remnant to aliens. ' My brothers,' she said, ' fell at Gettysburg in order that Armenians should colonize New England to-day. If I took any interest in any damn Yankee, outside of my son-in-law Laughton yondah, I should say my brother's death had been amply avenged ! ' A little later . . . Zigler said, ' Mother's right, Lincoln killed us from the highest motives ! ' "

Abraham Lincoln had been responsible for the death of a million Anglo-Saxon people, tearing at each other's throats ! Not quite fair on Lincoln, who was not an " abolitionist " in a hurry, but a fair criticism on the war-bug, and the curse of fate, the curse incurred by those folk who first put their hand to a slave system in a fair new land.

A slave-dealing Arab sheikh of the interior of Oman (*extreme left*) with four of his followers, each armed with Martini-Henry rifles.

The mixed crew of an Arab dhow, from the Dasht-i-Shan coast of the Persian Gulf, aboard a British examination vessel.

SUPPRESSING THE SLAVE TRADE IN THE PERSIAN GULF

THE END OF THE SAD SLAVE STORY

Since South Carolina had put the torch to the fire, war was inevitable. Uncle Sam sprang to arms, and Lincoln had no opportunity of exercising his undoubted gifts for human compromise. Those four years of war, the brilliant successes of the more military South, the grim acceptance of defeat and disaster by the North and the grim preparation which resulted in final victory, are the saddest of stories to all Anglo-Saxondom. The slow strangling of the debonair and gallant South is a supremely pathetic episode, as war destroyed much of that ancient and attractive civilization. Even more pathetic is the post-war story, both of the whites and the hastily liberated and starving slaves. It is to be noted that after the proclamation freeing slaves in the last months of the war, negro regiments were not unnaturally raised by the North, but not till the last few months of the war.

It has been explained how Lincoln was too great a statesman to have hastily imposed anti-slave measures that could only mean war and secession, had the life of the United States pursued its ordinary course of peace, but once those calamities had arisen, the slate was wiped clean. As an act of war it was important to deprive the Southern States of some of their labour as well as to stimulate his own supporters, and so we have the Proclamation of 22nd September 1862, emancipating all slaves. This is how it ran :

> "That on the first day of January in the year of our Lord one thousand eight hundred and sixty-three all persons held as slaves within any State, or designated part of a State, the people where-of shall then be in rebellion against the United States, shall be then henceforward and for ever free."

This of course was in law entirely illegal, neither the

President nor the legislature had any power to free a single slave. It was an act of war under the sign manual of a commander-in-chief, transferring the property of enemies, like the commandeering of horses and carts, merely to decrease their resources and increase those of the other party.

It has just been said that Lincoln issued this proclamation to stimulate support for him. Nothing was more likely to unite the North, disheartened by constant defeat.

When the four years of war were over, the slave question was practically over of its own weight. Most of the Southern slaves had freed themselves in the destruction of the system of life in the South that the final trample to victory by the United States troops had brought about.

Then the end came fast. On the last day of January 1865, a few months before the end, Lincoln had signed the joint resolution of the two Houses implementing his proclamation prohibiting slavery in the United States. It is famous as the " Thirteenth Amendment." Early in April Richmond fell, Lee surrendered, the Southern States were crushed to powder, and the war was over. A few days later Lincoln fell to the pistol of a mad Southern assassin.

So fell the curse on this great white people, even to the death of the liberator, following that of so many fellow-countrymen. With it went all vestige of illegal slave trade to Cuba and elsewhere. Slavery in the Americas was ended, save in the Spanish islands, and there too its extinction was nearly ripe.

The aftermath of the crime of two hundred years earlier, the establishment of millions of a race capable of great advancement that cannot be assimilated, amid a white America, is yet to dree its weird.

The loss to the United States of those million fathers, and the consequent admission of races whose physiological factors in the *mélange* are not yet fathomed, is another factor due to the war, of which the result is yet to see.

PART III

SLAVERY AFTER 1865

CHAPTER TWELVE

Slavery after 1865, and the New Scandals

★

Slavery after 1865—Liberia—The Congo Tragedy—The Horror of Putumayo—The Cocoa Scandals—The Problem of Benevolent Slavery—Modern Slavery in Abyssinia—Slavery in India.

★

SLAVERY AFTER 1865

With the United States purged of her slave system by practically the uprooting of the Anglo-Saxon race in North America, the world had still a long way to go. Africa was still a home of slave-raiding and slave-making for its own consumption, and for the service of Abyssinia and Arabia. The story of slavery in the Sudan, that fertile matrix of aboriginal slave races, is so much mixed up with the history of modern Britain, with one of our great legendary figures of modern times, and has cost us so many British lives to put right, that it merits a chapter to itself. There is also the satisfaction that something more than the four-leaved clover has grown where the blood of our warriors fell in the cause of humanity. The salvation of the Sudan at British hands is only second to our far greater record of the rebuilding of crashed Turkish India.

In the 'sixties Central Africa was an unknown land, and its opening up and exploration was to carry the birth as well as the death of many horrors. The British fringe on the west coast had all the beginning of enlightenment, but we and the other delinquents of the slave trade had taught the chiefs of the interior how easily wealth could be acquired by the sale of their own people to bondage, and we had to spend many years in eradicating weeds largely of western sowing. As the constant efforts of the British naval patrols drove the ocean slave trade largely off the Red Sea and the Indian Ocean, they forced it to take underground, almost underwater, methods to remain alive ; but a business so thoroughly organized throughout the lands of its vogue has taken years to terminate.

It will be seen that the persistent semi-benevolent slavery of Arabia, as well as the Sudan, took constant satisfying, and has, with that of Abyssinia closely linked with it, persisted to this day. The Amharic rulers, a tribe of Abyssinia proper, during the latter half of the nineteenth and first quarter of the twentieth centuries, succeeded in bringing under a fairly ruthless rule largely unannexed portions of Africa adjoining, and had permitted or been unable to stop a fierce and ruthless slave-raiding and slave factory which must be described. That, as has been said, the conquest by Italy will terminate, though not perhaps as easily as the new masters could wish.

With the opening up of Africa and other parts of the world to persistent trading and exploitation by the West, certain outstanding scandals have occurred, and should be included in this attempt at a general survey of the world's slaving proclivities and demand for labour at all costs. The misdoings of the irresponsible officials of the Congo in Central Africa, and of analogous happenings in Putumayo under the administration of the Peruvian Amazon Rubber Company, are worthy, if a word may be misused, of specific record. Both these stories belong not quite to the slave epoch so much as to a peculiarly callous and ruthless application of *le corvé* and forced indentured labour. The details of the punishments meted out to recalcitrant labourers is what stirred the hearts of the now more sensitive West. The Anti-Slavery and Aborigines Protection and missionary societies had now got an ear that would hear, and humanity had begun to be spelt with a big " H."

LIBERIA

Closely connected with the aftermath of African slave trade is the story of the republic of Liberia, which lies between the British colonies of Sierra Leone and the Ivory Coast.

It has been related how ere long, in the suppression of the trade, the embarrassment of the detribalized released slaves was considerable, and how many were settled in Sierra Leone. So far back as 1816 it was suggested that a State of their own should be established, though this did not actually mature till 1822, when the territory to be called Liberia was taken up.

In 1847 the colony was recognized by all the Powers as an independent republic whose boundaries with her British and French neighbours were finally defined in 1885 to 1892 respectively, when a hinterland of some 200 miles in depth, in which lay valuable forests, was given. It cannot be said that this experiment has ever met with great success, in spite of help and encouragement from the United States and the little republic's neighbours. The treatment of the indigenous native tribes within their hinterland has been inept and unsympathetic in the extreme, and at length culminated in a scandal and state of slave oppression not far removed from the condition of the Putumayo.

THE CONGO TRAGEDY

Cognate to the question of the prevention of slavery had

long been British sentiment towards the question of the treatment of aborigines, and that sentiment was stirred beyond measure by the terrible rumours that were coming through to Europe, in the last days of the nineteenth and early twentieth centuries, of the treatment of natives in the Congo. That story is so long ago now as to be happily ancient history, but both as a matter of drama, of history, and also of the tragedy of high purposes gone wrong, it cannot well be omitted from any story of anti-slavery consciousness.

The story in very brief is this. When Africa was really dark and the slave trade was not yet dead, King Leopold of Belgium conceived the admirable idea of founding a State on the mighty Congo. The Congo Free State, as it was called, now known as the Belgian Congo, is a vast area above the Equator of over 900,000 square miles, drained by the great river. King Leopold, ever a man of large ideas and high principles, fascinated by the human and economic excitement of Africa, conceived the idea of developing this great country under his own direction. To do so without international acquiescence and goodwill was, of course, impossible. The King succeeded in forming an International African Association, a project in which the germs of great good obviously lay. The successors to Wilberforce and Buxton were invited to interest themselves. So it finally came about that at the Berlin Conference of fourteen Powers in 1884 and 1885, the project was actually born.

The famous Stanley expedition into "Darkest Africa" between 1874 and 1877 had already given Leopold ample evidence of the human and economic situation that called for control and the wealth of produce that might be developed. The International African Association assured Stanley, rightly enough, that he had given birth to a grand project in which his experience and assistance were needed.

Stanley himself became agent for King Leopold when the Congo Free State was inaugurated after the Berlin conferences aforesaid. This new State was placed under the sovereignty of King Leopold in his personal capacity, under certain definitions laid down by the Powers in the Berlin Act. The suppression of the slave trade and the moral and material well-being of the peoples of the Congo basins were specially emphasized as the principal objects in mind. Stanley himself described his task as agent thus: " The novel mission of sowing along its banks civilized settlements, to peacefully conquer and subdue it, to remould it in harmony with modern ideas into National States, within whose limits the European merchant shall go hand in hand with the dark African trader, and justice, law and order shall prevail and murder and lawlessness shall for ever cease."

The foregoing reads a little suspiciously as the sort of hot air that the old " Exeter Hall " mentality would swallow, but there is no doubt that Stanley and King Leopold, as well as the Berlin Conference, definitely meant all that was said. Luscious wording did cover genuine intention and hopes. And so this gigantic task, almost impossible for even a nation like ourselves, was inaugurated, with what was practically private capital—and private capital needs returns. There lay the seeds of canker. To start such a concern was needed the wealth of a Britain, a service of power and integrity such as the Civil Services of India, and a disciplined body of officers such as those of the Indian Army or Police. Even then the work must be begun very gradually and confidence engendered. Instead of that there was only available an international Civil Service, of no antecedents, prestige, inherent discipline, nor tradition of high character—impossible to achieve in the given circumstances—and prevented by the climatic reputation that dogged West Africa from attracting the best type of men.

The executives were largely a body of " dago " irresponsibles and " doubtful hats."

In 1889 and 1890 a second conference of the Powers was held at Brussels, which reaffirmed its benevolent intentions and gave King Leopold authority to impose unlimited import duties for the purpose, it was explained, of providing funds for the suppression of the Arab slave traders. But as was inevitable, the sanctioned duties ere long developed into import restrictions that put an end to all free trade.

To open up a country of which the population is both timid and savage demands years of careful penetration and preparation. Backward people dislike work, and since development and cultivation demand labour, pressure of some kind is necessary even in the best-administered colonies in Africa. The African prefers to slumber and let the productive side of life look after itself. Such an attitude can be overcome, but only slowly and by officials who understand the people and gain their confidence.

The authority given to King Leopold to suppress the Arab slave traders further provided him with the equipment for armed forces. With it the native population disarmed before the slave raiders were suppressed, the people in so large an area were left defenceless. For a while, however, the experiment went forward reasonably well. But Free State ordinances began to assume complete right over all the products of the forest, without any regard to the rights or partial rights of the natives. Between 1890 and 1893 the principle was established that the natives owned nothing but their villages and gardens. Incidentally it may be remarked that this was no doubt the principle on which the Saxons took Roman Britain, or the Milesians ancient Ireland from the Iberian ! The outgoings from the Free State's capital resources were very great. Capitalists, naturally frightened, criticized the Governor-General,

Baron Dhanes, and no doubt called for prompt returns. The coming of the bicycle and rubber tyre had meant enormous demands for rubber; in 1897 Congo rubber fetched 3s. 7d. a pound, rising to 8s. 7d., while cultivated rubber even fetched 12s. 5d. The temptation to make money before the plantations being put down all over the world could come into bearing, was great. Rubber! and more rubber! was the cry. But in the Congo more rubber meant compelling the native to bring in increased supplies from the forest, and the Prime Minister of Belgium asserted that all was the property of the Free State and nothing that of the indigenous inhabitants! It was Socialistic principle run riot with a Soviet vengeance! From then the natives were given no encouragement to gather and sell their own produce and were compelled by edict to collect fixed quantities, which meant that force was applied to compel compliance. That force was applied by an unscrupulous subordinate service, imbued with the idea that their own prospects depended on the outturn extracted.

But by the end of the last century and beginning of the present, stories were coming through. Consuls, international merchants, officers of armies and navies, and missionaries began to say what they knew or what they had heard, and the public conscience of Europe woke up. It compelled the King of the Belgians to send out a commission of inquiry composed of three judges—a Belgian, a Swiss, and an Italian.

But the men who knew declared that the King would never dare to horrify the world by the publication of the Report, though the Ministers of various objecting countries had promised that it would be revealed. It was not till after nine years' delay that the Report was extracted. It vindicated thoroughly all that had been said. The truth of the allegations was proved up to the hilt. In vain the King and his friends, the King no doubt genuinely, endeavoured to dismiss the damning evidence as the vapourings of " worthy souls whose reserves of sentimentations are often injudiciously employed "—a delightful phrase coined by Mr. Carton de Wiart in addressing the Belgian Chamber !

The machinery of force employed to make the natives collect the rubber for nothing was as follows : Some 2000 white officials scattered over the country were in charge of areas, each with their force of African soldiery. The usual system was to take the women and children as hostages if the tally of rubber—so many baskets per village—was not forthcoming. If still not produced punitive measures were taken. It was said that the white employés, often the un-desirables of many nations, arrived in debt for passage and outfit, and dare not protest even if they wished to. They themselves were often the victims of climate and un-developed stations, were miserably paid, and received bonuses for rubber obtained, a system well calculated to stimulate pressure on the native. The native guards quartered in the village were termed " sentinels," and of them the Commission reported : " Of how many abuses the native sentinels have been guilty, it would be impossible to say." And again, " they kill without pity." It was also reported that of those forced into the forests to get rubber but half returned. They were ordered to the forest to return with ten pounds of rubber within a week, or else have their house burnt.

The Commission also reported that the women of a village had to feed any soldiers quartered on them. The administration's demands for porters, portage on the rivers, wood for the steamers, etc., were reported as cruel and excessive. But it was the system of black overseers that received the most damning report.

" According to the witnesses, they abuse their authority, and become despots demanding women and victuals, not only for themselves, but for vagabond parasites whom the love of rapine attaches to them like a regular bodyguard. They kill without pity all who offer resistance to their demands or caprices."

The Commission said that this system must be suppressed at once. A British Consul reported that the natives were worked by the administration 304 days a year for 6s. 4d. The Commission reported that the lash was freely used on " collectors of rubber who had not furnished their full imposition."

Numerous reports testified to the horrors of the " hostage houses " referred to. The policy of the administration lay in destroying the authority of all chiefs instead of working through them. It was estimated that in thirty years maladministration had reduced the Congo population from 30,000,000 to 8,000,000. Stanley even put the original population at 40,000,000.

When the truth, with all its sordid details of crime and misery, was known, public opinion in Britain was greatly stirred, and the public held that as one of the signatories of the Berlin Act our responsibility was very definite. Lord Lansdowne had said that the Congo misrule was " bondage under the most barbarous and inhuman conditions, and maintained for mercenary motives of the most selfish character." In March 1908 Lord Cromer declared in the House of Lords, " Never have I seen or heard of misrule comparable to the abuses that have grown up in the Congo State."

The Belgian Press for long supported the Congo authorities—the Church of Rome did not, and the Jesuits repudiated grants of land made to them by the administration. The Belgian public, who had no responsibility and whose experience in colonial administration was nil, were slow in awakening, and it was the publication of the delayed Report that at last brought the matter home to them. The long and the short of the matter was, that despite the furious protests of the now ageing King Leopold, who apparently believed to the end that the administration was grossly maligned, the existing conditions, anomalous enough in any case, were brought to an end. Belgium herself annexed the Congo and became responsible at the bar of humanity and public opinion.

A little later the heir to the Belgian throne, the late King Albert, himself visited the Congo, and his visit, of which no report was published, was no doubt of considerable assistance to the reform of the régime and in the cleaning up of the noxious inheritance. King Leopold had left, it is true, a magnificent inheritance but a terrible reputation ; and to his country, which took over the Congo, a heavy incubus of debt ; and thus *faute de mieux* many of the bad features had to continue for some while. It was not indeed till the old King and his influence had passed from the scene that substantial reform could be attempted, and even in 1911 M. Vandervelde, the Belgian leader in the cause of justice and freedom of the Congo, reported that forced labour still remained in half of the area. Indeed without it all revenue would have crashed. You cannot reform years of injustices at once, as the British found in the old Indian customs. It was Lord Cromer who really wrote the epitaph of the old Congo when he said that at any rate for modern times " any attempt to combine in the same hands the powers of administration and commercial exploitation can only result in maladministration on the one hand, and financial disappointment on the other."

The Congo tragedy is now happily in the limbo of old forgotten things, but the denouncement was a sorry finale to the high aspirations that accompanied the Berlin Act. And since the Congo we have had, as a warning, a worse happening at the hands of a British Company and a " dago " personnel, under the aegis of the Government of Peru, in the horrors on the Putumayo river.

THE HORROR OF PUTUMAYO

The Putumayo is a river in Peru and flows through territories inhabited by Indians. It is a district in which rubber grows freely, and in the great demand for that commodity in the early years of the present century a company, The Peruvian Amazon Company, was formed in London in 1908 to exploit the district. That was a perfectly legitimate enterprise, and the concessions obtained from the Peruvian Government were definite in the right to obtain rubber, but entirely unrestraining in the power to extract labour, by legitimate hire or barbarous force, from the 60,000 Indians of the district. The Putumayo forests were wild, inaccessible, and unhealthy, and the lesser supervisory personnel in such an undertaking was of necessity locally engaged from among the Spanish Peruvians. Companies are formed as the handmaid of industry, but their first duty, within the bounds of honesty and humanity, is to get returns for the investor which will safeguard his capital. The chairman of the Company was a South American who had, no doubt, obtained the concession in the usual manner. It is doubtful if even he realized the difficulty that obtaining labour to work the concession would entail. The story then follows very much the course of the Congo scandals. Dividends, *i.e.* an ample supply of rubber, were needed, and rubber could only be obtained by the exertion of the Indians in the forests in which they lived. The ethical right of the Indians to the rubber we need not pursue, the Peruvian Government was long established and may be considered as competent to grant the concession. South American Governments of the past, seeking development and return, were not likely to be very squeamish over such matters.

That there was something wrong on the Putumayo, something which may at first have been entirely unknown to the British members of the Board in London, was first hinted at by the return to London of a young American in the year following the institution of the Company, Mr. W. C. Hardenberg, a civil engineer with some experience in South America. He brought a written account of his experience in the districts of the Putumayo. Publishers in London fought shy of a story so terrible and damning that nothing but justification to the hilt could protect a publisher from heavy damages.

In those days *Truth* was the hardy exposer of real scandals, and extracts from the journal appeared primarily in that famous paper, and also in some others.

The gravamen of the story lay in the fact that raw rubber fetching 3s. a pound in Europe could only be obtained by compelling the native to collect it in ever-increasing quantities. The Indians were a quiet and docile people, and by good treatment and kindly handling might well have been induced to bring in more and more of the product of the jungles. Such a system meant, as in the Congo, reputable officials, a high-grade native service, and employés of character. It also meant that the establishing of such a system involved a lag in dividend earnings which neither the resources of the Company nor the wishes of its Board were prepared to institute. London no doubt listened to local representations that a little pressure on the Indians was all that was necessary, and the little pressure was applied by armed force, by flogging and torture at the hands of entirely ruthless half-breed subordinates who had their own profit to make. A system of terrorization far worse than any mere slavery arose. Mr. Hardenberg's revelations were, of course, treated by the Company as

192

IN AN ABYSSINIAN SLAVE MARKET

A picture taken prior to the Italian conquest.   The two men on the left are Amharas, those on the right, Gallas.

IN AN ABYSSINIAN SLAVE MARKET

A picture taken prior to the Italian conquest.

imagination, and probably could not bring themselves to believe the extent to which their half-breed machinery would go to carry out their behests.

The public conscience in Britain was roused by the revelations, but action was hard to take. The Company, it was true, was a London one ; but the Government whose concern it was, was Peru. That Government was not inclined to act. But public opinion was becoming insistent, and this was stimulated by a book written by Dr. Paredes of Iquitos and later quoted by Sir John Harris.[1] In it this pregnant passage occurs : " Their insatiable desire to obtain the greatest production in the least time and with the least possible expense (an entirely laudable object, be it noted, under proper conditions) was undoubtedly one of the causes of crime, for the Indians who did not comply with the requirements imposed, were tortured and killed outright, while the stubborn ones were compelled with machite and bullet to fulfil the mandates."

That this was not the fevered account of some hysterical observer with no power of judgment, as sometimes occurs, was amply borne out by a subsequent report of a Select Committee of the House of Commons and proceedings in a London Law Court. The story went on to tell of an entirely ruthless form of torture, flogging, and abandonment of the victims to die, coupled with such scandal as the brazen procuration as mistresses by the Company's personnel of women, of the womenfolk of the very men they had put to death. The Peruvian Senate passed a resolution demanding an inquiry, which their Government refused.

The London Board declined to act, and only after many months decided to send out their own Commission of Inquiry. In the meantime the British Government, on the facts that some 200 British Barbadians were employed

[1] In his book, *A Century of Emancipation.*

by the Company, had a legal pretext for the Foreign Minister, Sir Edward Grey, to despatch their own Consul to the scene. The United States, it appeared, had already got some inkling of the state of affairs and had also sent a remonstrance to the Peruvian Government, who made arrests, but achieved no punishment. The Select Committee examined 27 witnesses and published a most damning report. The report of the British Consul appeared in a Blue-book. A small group of shareholders placed in the hands of the Anti-Slavery Society in London the powers for instituting a petition for the winding-up of the Company's affairs, duly presented to Mr. Justice Swinfen Eady, whose judgment and orders for a compulsory winding-up fully justified all that had been said. And so closed in contumely a venture which had been permitted in this our twentieth century, run from London, and had been conducted with a ruthless cruelty from which a Cortez would have shrunk.

The point for our consideration and eternal remembrance is now, with Russia's punitive lapses to remind us, that human nature, if not warded and guarded, has potentially as ruthless facets as ever disgraced the past.

The Cocoa Scandals

The scandals which Messrs. Cadbury succeeded some years ago in unearthing may now be thrown on the screen of forgotten yet recurring evils. They are specially distressing in showing how little even modern Portugal could control the evil of her own ancient engendering. The revelation indeed went very near to jeopardizing our ancient alliance with her, and the general covenant of protection between the two countries. The Portuguese owned two islands in the Atlantic, the larger one of S. Thomé, discovered by one of their famous navigators, Ioao de Santarem, so far back as 1470, on St. Thomas's feast-day. It is small enough, but twenty miles square, and not far from it is Principe, a smaller island. They were of no great note till 157 years after their discovery, when Portuguese planters took to growing sugar on the islands, a useful but not very lucrative business. In 1822, however, one of them, José Gomes, introduced on to the island of Principe a plant from Brazil, more for ornament it is said than agriculture. Within twenty years the planters were exporting the product of that plant, the cocoa bean, to Europe and America. The islands were soon covered with cocoa trees, as the nineteenth century rolled on, and the world grew and took to cocoa. By 1910 the export had grown to 36,000 tons a year. But it had grown on the bones and the misery of ill-conducted, ill-treated African labour, wrenched in the old Portuguese way from the Africans of their own kingdom and which they were sworn to protect.

The world, however, had failed to take any great notice of the cocoa islands, when one day in the early years of the twentieth century a gentleman called on Mr. Cadbury and offered to sell a cocoa plantation in S. Thomé. The proposition did not particularly interest Mr. Cadbury but he did peruse the papers left with him. He was astounded to find that among the assets of the estate offered was an item, " 200 Black Labourers, £3550." Rumours of slavery still existing in Portuguese West Africa were, it is true, current ; but here was a very definite piece of evidence. 200 slaves at £18 a head !

Now it is of course obvious that an industry of this kind demands labour, and in the interest of the world's food supply should get labour—on proper and acceptable terms. But, unfortunately, through the long years of the efforts of civilization for emancipation, the Portuguese or their planting fraternity have been masters of subterfuge and hoodwinking, and entirely without bowels. They had an admirable system of contract labour on paper. They said their labour agreed to serve for three years, entered their emigrant ships joyfully, and after three agreeable years returned with considerable savings.

In November 1910, however, the stories of this Eldorado had become well established, and our then Foreign Minister, Sir Edward Grey, informed the Portuguese Minister in London at a private meeting of these rumours. In his own words :

"I explained to him that the information I had received from private sources placed beyond doubt the fact that it had been the custom for natives to be captured in the interior by people who were really slave dealers."

In a resulting law-suit in London there was considerable allusion to the Portuguese system of "recruiting." Sir Edward Carson did not mince his words, saying to the jury :

"Have you ever heard of conditions more revolting, more cruel, more tyrannous, and more horrible than what has been deposed as regards the slavery in S. Thomé ? Men recruited in Angola, women recruited in Angola, children recruited in Angola, torn away against their will from their homes in the interior, marched like droves of beasts through the Hungry Country. When they are unable to walk the thousand miles to the coast . . . shot down like useless dogs and useless animals . . . brought to S. Thomé and Principe, never to return to their homes."

This case produced overwhelming evidence that the contract system in question produced the three ancient evils—slave-raiding, slave-trading, and slave-owning. That the evidence in the case was deeply sought and sharply sifted will be recognized when it is said that Sir Rufus Isaacs, Sir John Simon, and Sir Edward Carson were briefed therein.

It was said that between 1888 and 1908 alone, 67,000 Africans were shipped to the cocoa islands. It was further said at the time, that not till 1908 did the first repatriated negroes ever return, and *they numbered* 10 ! Fortunately or unfortunately, evil conditions had their nemesis, for the cocoa plantations were swept with a pest, which almost destroyed the cocoa trees and made human health deplorable. Finally, threatening bankruptcy compelled the return of the African labour.

The British " Cocoa " firms continued to boycott Portuguese cocoa, satisfied that no satisfactory reforms had been instituted. In 1913 the British Government, mindful of their friendship and protection of Portugal, offered to help provide labour if an acceptable system was organized. Not yet has that been possible.

The Problem of Benevolent Slavery

To the ordinary human mind slavery that is benevolent is at any rate far more palatable and acceptable than slavery that is entirely cruel, repressive, and treats slaves as cattle. To the mind that is tense with the desire that no soul-given human body shall be in subjection and the bondage of ownership, benevolent slavery is anathema, as tending to dope both slaves themselves and the outer world to the horror and turpitude of the institution.

The good slave owner of the Southern States of America undoubtedly ran his slave establishments as benevolently as the Roman *potestas* managed his family—nay, better, for he was guided by Christian principles. The romantic affection and devotion that existed in the old slave-owning houses and families, especially in the matter of the house slaves, was full of charm and content. But that but disguised the horror of what might happen should a benevolent master be succeeded by the reverse, with the family slaves still in bondage, or that great difficulty of running any slave system, the treatment of the runaway or intractable slave, occur under a harsh master.

In the *Mui-Tsai* system of China, there are no doubt

197

many cases of that system working well, given the out-pouring of the unwanted girl-child of Chinese fertility. But the room for bad treatment is equally open, and their status always unsecured.

In Arabia the position of the African slave is by no means hard and does not produce fierce unrest among the slaves themselves, and thus to Eldon Rutter, the abolitionist enthusiast, it is the more unendurable and unpermissible. He is, of course, right a thousand times, always however bearing in mind that the endurable slavery does not need the immediate suppression by force that slave-raiding and slave-making calls for, and also that when the evil is not crying in its cruelty, a movement of repression that might upset a large portion of the world and cause much loss of life in the process can wait for the quieter methods of healing—always supposing that it does not slip into oblivion with the outer world.

Similarly the question of slave-raiding among the un-administered hill tribes high up in the Himalayas, and on the borders of Assam and Upper Burma, was for long not sufficiently oppressive to demand a crusade till other more urgent matters had been dealt with, or modern com-munication made interference practicable. Its abolition a few years ago, and the traces still remaining, will be referred to.

Modern Slavery in Abyssinia

The slavery of Abyssinia, which endured up to the days of the Italian conquest, has been alluded to in the opening chapters and at several points in the story, and what it was even up to 1936 must now be related.

It is to be remembered that through the ages Abyssinia or Ethiopia has been a varying quantity, dependent on the power of the Amharic rulers to conquer or control in-dependent or semi-independent chiefs in the hills between the White Nile and the Red Sea or Indian Ocean. In more modern times Theodore, the soldier adventurer, overcame most of his neighbours, till he went mad with power, finally shooting himself as Sir Robert Napier's troops stormed his citadel at Magdala.

In the fluctuating periods that followed, it remained for Menelek II, King of the Shoan province in the eighties, to enforce Amharic dominion to the sea and to the confines of the Sudan; and to bring outlying principalities, ruthlessly enough, within the Ethiopian sway. The people of the Abyssinia of to-day are of many races and several religions : Semites in Tigré in the north and Amhara in the south; Hamitic in the lower coastal country; Negritic and Bantu on the borders of the Sudan, the latter two specially suitable for enslavement. In religion, besides the doubtful Christianity of the Amhara, there is a large Falashie community of Jewish faith, many Moslem tribes and races near the coast—especially the Afar, the Somali, and the Galla. Such a medley in so large and mountainous country, badly served with roads, has produced the conditions that prevented the Emperor's anti-slavery inclination, being of much effect. It may make the endeavours of the Italians equally slow in achieving success. The Bantu and Negritic tribes, as remarked, were obviously provided by Providence for the benefit of the slave trader and raider! but the beauty of the Gallas, men and women, has brought them within the net, a good deal by kidnapping, although within the circle of those that make slaves rather than of those themselves enslaved.

The undoubted fact is that Abyssinia was and probably is at the moment a slave-owning, slave-making, and slave-trading country. It has been so since the beginning of time, and ever since stronger races learnt how to prey on the weaker. In 1926 various authorities and competent observers placed the slave population at 2,000,000 out of a total of 10,000,000. The Emperor, Haile Selassie, who knew perfectly well that his well-intentioned writ did not run to abolition save by long and weary stages, placed the figure at 1,000,000. Some of the great Rases owned thousands of slaves, and on the Sudan frontier it was estimated that every Abyssinian owned at least one. The victimization of the black races of the Sudan by Arabs, as described in a previous chapter, was equally practised by the Abyssinians. The raids on the Anglo-Egyptian Sudan were frequent, ruthless, and a matter for armed punishment whenever possible. Our own Government were, however, aware that it was no use holding the central Abyssinian Government to account, and that the only remedy other than armed vigilance on the frontier was a punitive expedition against the Abyssinian delinquents. For reasons of terrain, distance, as well as diplomacy and foreign relations, such a course was out of the question ; but there was not much sorrow on the Abyssinia-Sudan frontier when the State of Haile Selassie went down.

Now Arabia's slave system has been held up for execration, but let it be noted, Arabia but holds, buys, trades, and breeds. She does not, as Abyssinia did, raid ruthlessly to make new slaves. Perhaps, however, the fact that no black races were within her grip more than her higher morality is responsible. At any rate it was to serve her markets as well as her own that Abyssinia made and traded new slaves.

The method of obtaining slaves by raids was twofold. One the time-honoured one of surrounding villages, often even villages of their humbler fellow-subjects, attacking, killing the old, and marching off the young in those cruel yoked caravans of which so much has been written. The other the easier and less adventurous system of kidnapping, carrying off boys and girls and young people from the vicinity of the villages, a practice at times extended to

Abyssinians themselves even, as distinct from the humbler negroids within their gates. Slaves were freely marched, led, and smuggled throughout the country. Numerous instances have been brought to notice of treatment of the recalcitrant, even of children, that vie with any doing of the worst types of slave owners on record.

In 1930 the enterprise of the Paris *Matin*, despatching a competent Committee of Inquiry of their own, succeeded in producing some remarkable reports on slave conditions in Abyssinia and Arabia. Very remarkable were the reports which M. Kersel, the leader, made in twenty articles ; astounding reports of cruelties, of determined slave-raiding as well as slave-breeding—reports impossible to discredit in their entirety, despite the desire of all modern journalists to electrify and affect their readers. British and French officials have reported freely, while we find Lord Allenby, in his Introduction to Captain Yardley's book *Parergon*, saying of Abyssinian raids into the Sudan :

" Of late years we have shirked responsibilities which are essentially our own. . . . Freeborn people . . . who are virtually our subjects . . . have been seized in their native villages under our very noses and carried off to slavery. The soldiery of Southern Abyssinia have been implicated in these expeditions in search of our people for more years than is pleasant to count. Rape is part of the woman's share of the misery. Their children have been taken from them, their men folk have been mutilated, and their villages plundered by the troops of a so-called friendly State."

This was the country, struggling at its centre for better things it is true, that France and Italy insisted on admitting to the League of Nations, only to hamstring her when ready for the deed. However much we may deplore that hamstringing, and the manner of the doing, is it to be wondered at that many of the world's humanists have welcomed the Italian conquest as a humanizing agent that only external force could bring into being.

SLAVERY IN INDIA

Slavery in India was abolished by decree of the Emperor Akbar in the sixteenth century, but the writ of even mighty Akbar by no means covered the whole land, and in the turmoil that followed the crashing of the great Turkish Empire in the eighteenth century, there were none who very much cared about what was done to the poor and oppressed. There is no very accurate account of how far slavery had advanced, but in a continent whose social system included, and still includes, the strange and difficult convention of the "untouchables," the mere existence of slavery as we understand the term would be of no great account. Such as it was, it was declared by the Company's Government in the Governor-Generalship of Lord William Bentinck in 1825 that slaves could not be legally held in any of the Company's dominions.

It is true that in its early days the Company bought slaves to serve as guards and soldiers, on the west of India, from on the coast of Africa and Arabia, but it bought them to free and to employ as soldiers. If we remember that all the fighting portion of the Egyptian Army in the days of the British Control was composed of freed "Black," *viz.* Sudanese slaves, we shall realize that there was some wisdom in the Company's action.

Slave-making there never had been in any territory under the jurisdiction of the East India Company. The prohibition made in the reign of the Emperor Akbar had doubtless been honoured in the breach as the central power of the Moguls waned, and while martial captives were not held in slavery, the countless folk of the "depressed classes" were always easy to carry off and maintain as slaves of fear, with none to question. The position which such folk hold

in the free India of to-day by ancient prescription and
religious regimentation, often is analogous to a slave condition. Folk of very humble mind, want of will, and devoid
of any form of physical courage, automatically come to
something very near such conditions, and were easily
enslaved by any who thought them worth the constraining.
Such a condition would be easily accompanied by a transfer
for money.

For centuries there has existed in Southern India a
system of bond-slavery for debt, which will be described
later. So important has marriage and procreation as the
practical manifestation of eternity always been in all Indian
opinion, that the most humble and impoverished folk will
spend sums far beyond their means in celebrating the
auspicious occasion. Whence do they get it ? The answer
is that employers, landlords, and others, will always lend
if the borrower will assign himself and children to work as
a bond-slave for keep till the principal be repaid ; often,
once the debt is incurred, does the bond-slave remain
bound for ever. It is difficult to see how, except by some
such method, the indispensable—in the borrower's eyes—
sum can be obtained. The custom is bound up in the life
of the country and it has even a savour of the Arabian
Nights. Variations of the system occur all over Southern
India, and the means of keeping it in reasonable control are
referred to in the last chapter. Incidentally it may be
remarked that the bond-slave has ensured subsistence at
the hands of the lender till the debt be paid ! It is analogous
to another custom of the country which has a good as well
as a bad facet. Humble labourers become in debt to the
village *buniahs*—*i.e.* traders and moneylenders—for marriage.
He takes all their wages when they are in work, feeds the
family in kind and perhaps clothes it, and gives a few
pence as tobacco money. When the family is out of work
he still provides subsistence, and in a country where no

unemployment insurance or public assistance exists the system has manifest merits. Perhaps what will not bear closest scrutiny is the debtor's account, in which wages are entered up against interest on capital and advances in kind or cash. It has the merit of making the labourers carefree, if poorly nourished, and absolutely dependent. At any rate his children have been married with the pomp decreed by custom !

The ways in which the sense and tradition of slavery have remained in the countryside is to be seen in an old-established irregular regiment like Skinner's Horse, largely recruited from the neighbourhood of Delhi. Like all the irregular regiments its officers and troops were *silledars*, *viz.* provided their own horses and equipment, and, in early days, even arms. Members, however, might be allowed to bring relatives and dependants, mounting and equipping them at their own expense. Men thus accepted by the Commanding Officer were known as *barghirs*. A man of Skinner's Horse who had brought such always referred to them as " my slave " or " slaves." The " slave " holders were usually Turks settled in the vicinity of Delhi, to whom the principle and tradition of slave-holding was familiar. The only real slavery, and that of not too obnoxious a kind, save in the case of slaves held for sacrifice, occurred here and there, and still occurs, in the unadministered inaccessible hill tracts that fringed the Indian side of the Himalaya. These tracts, such as part of Lushai, Assam, the Naga Hill, etc., like the tribes of the North-West Frontier, have never been administered by an Indian ruler or their British successors. The Himalayan tribes, though not administered, have had to be controlled, because they would raid, and slave-raid too, those villages and plains under British administration.

The folk of this North-East Frontier, like those of the North-West, would never have been interfered with had they been capable of refraining from raids into British territory, or from exacting more than fair toll on any trade routes that might traverse their land. For many years, since the British were not prepared to burden the Indian taxpayer with the costs of roads and administration for freeing a comparatively small number of slaves, they very properly contented themselves with preventing new raids, or punishing the perpetrators thereof by punitive expeditions. As time rolled on and communications slowly developed, Government felt better able to cope with the problem, and were able to subscribe to the general activity that the League of Nations was stimulating by taking measures to so influence the tribe concerned as to actually liberate their slaves, for which compensation was paid. This meant that the general political influence had been extended in the independent and unadministered tracts. In 1925 and the succeeding years Sir Harcourt Butler, the Governor of Burma, was specially able to bring about the release of slaves in the Hukong Valley. The task, however, for the same geographical reasons, is not yet complete.

CHAPTER THIRTEEN

The Sudan and the Tragedy of Gordon

★

Egypt, the Sudan, and Central Africa—Gordon and the Equatorial Province (1874)—Gordon made Governor-General of all the Sudan (1876)—The Removal of the Khedive and the Departure of Gordon (1879)—The Rise of the Mahdi—The Return and the Death of Gordon—The Avenging and the Restoration of the Balad-es-Sudan.

★

EGYPT, THE SUDAN, AND CENTRAL AFRICA

IT is to Egypt (the age-long home of slavery), the Sudan (the " country of the blacks "), and Central Africa, that we must now turn for a fresh glimpse at the ancient evil, and the new effort in suppression. For many generations Egypt had stayed her journey south—so far as Empire went—at Wadi Halfa, whence the desert, spreading far east and west of the Nile, ran south for close on 200 miles. In ancient times, it is true, the Pharaohs had been at Khartoum and had built pyramids at Merowe, but this was but ephemeral, and the desert kept the races far apart. But since the early years of the nineteenth century the desire for Empire seemed to point for a short time to a new semi-Turkish Empire under Mehemet Ali. Nubia, Kordofan, and Senaar were added to Egypt, and the bogey of the desert laid. Between 1853 and the 'seventies, Egypt had pushed her military posts and attempted control from a point 120 miles south of Khartoum to within a couple of miles of the Equator on both the lakes Albert and Victoria Nyanza. But the line of conquest had not followed the Nile alone, for it had penetrated far into Darfur and but fifteen marches from distant Lake Tchad. European traders and adventurers established posts far up the Nile, defended by armed blacks led by Arabs; at first to protect their trade in ivory, then plentiful and cheap. But it soon appeared that a trade in slaves was even easier and more profitable.

Colonel Gordon, when Governor-General of the Equatorial Provinces, wrote : " About the year 1860 the scandal became so great that the Europeans had to get rid of their stations, they sold them to their Arab agents, who paid a rental for them to the Egyptian Government."

The wretched blacks, of course, were none the better off. Both European traders at Khartoum and the Egyptian Government supplied arms, and the Arabs carried on their slave-raiding and trading to a far greater extent. Captain Speke, the explorer out of Devon, wrote : " Those vile ruffians on the White Nile . . . the atrocities committed by these traders are beyond civilized belief " ; and Dr. Sweinforth, writing of those days also, said that the land where hundreds of Dinka villages had stood on the eastern bank of the Nile had been turned into waste by the ravages of a notorious trader, one Muhammad Kher. Sir Samuel Baker laid the wasting of the Dinka country at the door of men high in office in the Egyptian Government, and wrote : " This country had been quite depopulated by *razzias* made for slaves, by the former and present Governor of Fashoda." In 1864, and again in 1872, he had visited the country, and he wrote : " It is impossible to describe the change that has taken place since I last visited this country. It was then a perfect garden, thickly populated, and producing all that man could desire. The villages were numerous. . . . The scene has changed ! All is wilderness ! . . . Not a village to be seen. This is the certain result of the settlement of Khartoum traders. They kidnap the women and children for slaves, and plunder and destroy wherever they set their foot." [1]

Colonel Gordon also wrote as he went up the Sobat river, " all driven off by the slavers in years past ; you could scarcely conceive such a waste or desert."

Such half-hearted orders as might now and again emanate from distant Cairo had no effect, but ere long the slave traders became so powerful and had such large armed forces, that in the seventies the Khedive awoke to the possibility of a rival power, for a slave trader, one Zobeir [2] Rahamat, had assumed almost princely conditions. He was said to own more than thirty armed slavery stations which penetrated far into Central Africa. In 1869 the Egyptian Government tried to curb his power. Egyptian troops sent against him were defeated and Zobeir became more important than ever.

GORDON AND THE EQUATORIAL PROVINCE (1874)

This living horror and scandal of the slave trade in the Sudan, far more cruel and more ruthless than even that on the slave coast in West Africa—existing as it did long after slavery disappeared in blood and cannon smoke from the United States of America—was to bring to the anti-slavery stage a man whose name will remain in history and legend for many centuries. It is not necessary or desirable to dwell in detail on the meteoric career, brilliant services, or tragic end of the great Charles Gordon. The main story is an epic of years of endeavour to govern humanely—on behalf of an inefficient and corrupt Egypt—a vast continent, and to eradicate a cancer that was destroying simple lives by the tens of thousands ; but some outline of what he attempted, and for a while did, is part of the world's slavery

---

[1] *Ismailia*, vol. ii. 136.

[2] Zobeir is the popular spelling of a name that once was often in the British news. *Zebehr* is a more accurate but less familiar rendering.

story. Moreover it leads to the astounding cataclysm of the Mahdi and his successor the " Khalifa," and the clinching of the fetters of slavery and massacre till 1898, when Lord Kitchener's brilliant campaign laid the spectre of cruelty and slavery in the Egyptian Sudan—*Balad-es-Sudan*, " the land of the black "—let us hope for all time.

In 1868 Khedive Ismael was anxious to open commerce in the distant provinces of the upper Nile that there was none to dispute with him, and to diminish the slave trade that was already reflecting discredit on Egypt. He commissioned, on the suggestion of the Prince of Wales, Sir Samuel Baker, a well-known traveller and sportsman, to suppress the slave trade and to extend the Egyptian dominion to the then newly-discovered Equatorial lakes. Sir Samuel, in accepting the appointment, had stipulated that he should be succeeded by an Englishman, and when after four years his appointment terminated, Nubar Pasha, Ismael's Armenian Minister, then in Constantinople, was looking for a successor, he there found Gordon a guest at the British Embassy. A year later Gordon, with approval of his Government, accepted the offer of the succession to Baker.

In February 1874 he was in Cairo, and while taking a liking to the Khedive was appalled at the mass of corruption surrounding him. The Equatorial Province, whose boundaries were still undefined, lay south of Khartoum, and Gordon was now its Governor-General, but it proved to consist of the land on either side of the White Nile from the Sobat river, 300 miles south of Khartoum to the Lake Victoria Nyanza.

The work of Baker had lain largely in marching and discovery, and Gordon found himself, with a small international staff that he collected in Cairo, with the whole work of reconstruction to do.

Proceeding via Suakin and Khartoum, Gordon eventually

established himself at the northernmost portion of the province, and set about the difficult matter of procuring troops and personnel. A port on the Sobat would give him some power to arrest the slave convoys coming down the Nile. Now followed three years of intense struggle against conditions, with few reliable followers, sickly and inefficient Egyptian troops, and in the neighbouring province of Khartoum an Egyptian Governor-General hand-in-glove with the slave traders and doing everything to nullify Gordon's efforts at good government and abolition. For those to whom the story of Egypt of the nineteenth century is a closed book, it may be stated that Egypt comprised a long-established overlay of Turks and Albanians who held, and indeed hold to this day, most of the posts of authority. They are the ruling and governing classes imposed by conquest in the past, on the tame and unmanly Egyptian, who himself—and in few countries have the old peoples so remained—is the descendant of those whom the Pharaohs ruled. They were largely converted to Islam by the conquering Arabs of the seventh and eighth centuries, from the Christianity that had come to them earlier.

The Khedive, surrounded by his Turkish and Albanian Pashas, concerned in extracting loans from Europe to be largely wasted, had little real power to carry out his good intentions. Service in the Sudan, deadly in heat and malaria, was loathed by all Egyptian officers, officials, and soldiers, save as an opportunity for making money by illicit means, of which the slave trade was the easiest. While Gordon could find some who sympathized with his mission to extend Egyptian rule to the Equator, there were none who sympathized with his desire to ameliorate the lot of the blacks, or suppress the slave trade. The only men of action and energy were the Arab slave traders themselves, some of whom he employed, often to his own undoing, and the actual black slaves, many of whom he bought, as Baker had done, to make soldiers. For many subsequent years black ex-slaves furnished the only fighting portion of the reconstituted Egyptian army under British officers, and to-day the same races furnish the bulk of the rank and file of the Sudan Defence Force.

During his Governorship of the Equatorial Province, while carrying out the extension of the Khedival authority, his principal anxiety was to establish posts on the western border of the province against the slave trade from Darfur and Kordofan. After three years of astounding activity and ubiquity, while the peoples were again beginning to flourish, he realized that there was no possible continuity to be attained, while even such successes as he achieved were marred by the opposition and corruption that he experienced from the Khartoum Province that lay between him and Egypt itself. It should be mentioned that his only staff on which he could rely were Europeans of various nationalities whom he had picked up in Egypt and the Sudan, and one or two Americans of that body of American officers who had entered the Khedive's service after the termination of the Civil War.

A whole book might be written of the slave trader Zobeir, who had established himself in the distant province of Darfur, killing the Sultan, and had become almost a slaving prince and ruler in the heart of slavedom. With him and his myrmidons Gordon's troops had had many tussles. Since Zobeir seemed like to remain as Sultan of Darfur, the Governor-General of Khartoum, Ismael Ayub Pasha, proceeded to the capital, El Fasher, with a considerable force and took over Darfur in the name of the Khedive. Both men sent reports to Cairo, and to settle the dispute Zobeir was summoned and retained there. He was eventually made a Pasha and in 1877 was sent in command of an Egyptian force to support the Turks against Russia. He was never allowed back to Darfur, however, while his son later made his peace for a while with Gordon. Zobeir's influence against Gordon in slave-supporting circles was great and proficient, and eventually in 1884 Gordon—in a fit of remorse and opportunism—asked for him to be sent to Sudan as one who alone could cope with the rising Mahdi. His absence while Gordon was at the height of his anti-slavery campaign was a gain, and the work of suppression proceeded apace. But, great for the moment, or comparatively great, as had been Gordon's successes in his own province, and implicit as was the ineffective reliance that the Khedive reposed in him, no one knew better how his work could but be but chalk on granite, and that the longer he stayed the greater must be the relapse. Slave traders avoided his ports in Equatoria, but had all Khartoum open to them.

In 1876, therefore, after three years of astounding energy, Gordon resigned for the first time the service of H.H. the Khedive, arrived in London in December, and was shortly after invited to return to China, where his earlier reputation had been made.

Gordon made Governor-General of all the Sudan (1876)

The Khedive, however, whose ability and wide vision at times transcended the influence and intrigues of his corrupt Pashas, was aghast, and offered Gordon the complete control as Governor-General of both the provinces of the Equator and Khartoum and the seventeen Governorships involved. That meant that every stronghold of slave-trading would be at his mercy, could he but secure sufficient force, money, and honesty to carry out the crusade. Never perhaps had such power, might, dominion, or territory been offered to the hand of a single man, or put in the hands of one better qualified to make use of them. Never, too, was such a

THE LIBERIAN SCANDAL

(*Above*) A group of shackled slaves from the hinterland.
(*Below*) A Gio king (*seated*) with his slave musicians and dancers.

" call " given to mortal man. So the hero returned to his
sceptre, eager to destroy the slave traders, to protect the
people, and to make a human land of what was almost a
continent. Neither then, when the Sudan was beginning to
be in men's minds as a reality—nor now, when the British
Governor-General and his mixed indigenous and British
Civil Service rule it as it has never been ruled before—was
or is the magnitude of the land realized. The fact that
from Cairo to St. Petersburg is about as far as from Cairo
to Gordon's Equatorial Province, may bring it home to us.

The news of Gordon's supreme and overriding appointment and the magnificent full-dress marshal's uniform the
Khedive had sent him flashed through the countryside to be
received with mixed feelings. The slave-trading ruler and
the great slave merchants set their hearts hard for a tussle,
and poured out the gold of opportunity into Cairo as
Zobeir had done before. All corrupt officials quaked in
their shoes as the Governor-General rode into Khartoum
from the Red Sea on his camel that was to become the outward, visible, and ubiquitous sign of his energy, courage,
and benevolence. The Khedive wrote, and meant it, " use
all the powers I have given you, take every step you think
necessary ; punish, change, dismiss all officials as you
please." And Gordon did so ; communing all the while
with God, his Bible, and his Prayer-book.

Now slavery then was the breath of life to not only the
Sudan but Egypt. Almost every Egyptian kept at least
one slave. In the Sudan seven-eighths of the people were
slaves, and Gordon set to work as if all the wealth, all the
power, troops, and honest officials were behind him. He
issued an historic decree : slavery in the Sudan would be
abolished in twelve years, but all Europeans in the Sudan
must forthwith give their slaves a paper of enfranchisement,
and in future only employ freed or free men. And forthwith the slaves, often content enough to remain, carried

213

their enfranchisement papers round their neck, and the spirit and desire for freedom, if only in principle, spread.

The feature of Gordon's first year in the Sudan was his ubiquity. A large Egyptian army of great inefficiency existed in the Sudan other than in Baker's and Gordon's Equatorial Province. Shortly after his arrival at Khartoum some 16,000 were isolated and surrounded by a rising in Darfur. With only 300 men Gordon started off, finally riding on his camel alone with an orderly into the camp of Egyptian troops, many miles ahead of any escort, *wearing the great gold coat as a Marshal of Egypt,* to which he rightly attached an almost mystic importance. His camel and his coat became his mascots and the fetish by which he ruled, and no other rule was then possible.

Zobeir's son Suleiman tried rebellion. Gordon with his gold coat and 2000 rubbishy Egyptian troops rode to see him, passing through the ranks of 3000 efficient slave-trading soldiery, and won for a while. The Abyssinian frontier and its brigand chiefs, Somaliland, Massawe, the Red Sea littoral, all saw the ubiquitous one ; seeing for himself, ordering, compelling, executing, building a magnificent façade of personal prestige, hailed by the miserable blacks as their deliverer, flouting and destroying the slave-traders, with little real force, no finance, and a weak international staff to help him. But you cannot rule continents by " go look see " and personal magnetism and courage alone, and Gordon was soon driven to his palace at Khartoum to finance, to tax-gather, to get his army efficient, and to spend unwilling days among files.

The actual slave conditions in his Empire as Gordon described them were heartrending in the extreme. Writing at Edowa on 31st March 1879 he says : " This evening a party of seven slave dealers with twenty-three slaves were captured and brought to me. Nothing could exceed the misery of these poor wretches. They had come across the torrid zone from Shaka, a journey from which I on my camel shrink. I got the slave dealers chained at once, the men and boys were put in the ranks, the women were told off to be the wives of the soldiers, the children were to be sent to Obeid " (where he had a settlement for them) ". . . when I had just begun this letter, another caravan with two slave dealers and seventeen slaves was brought in, and I hear others are on the way. Some of the women were quite nude. I have disposed of them in the same way, for what else can I do."

This passage again illustrates the point mentioned in the case of the West African release, viz. what to do with your released slaves when such have no known home or country and no labour-market available. To be the allotted wife of a soldier, however, did mean food, rest, home to one who had no home, and had long known neither comfort nor mercy.

Gordon resumes : " Both these caravans came from Shaka, where I mean to make a clean sweep of the slave dealers." Now Shaka was Zobeir's stronghold, run by son Suleiman. " These captures make the total of caravans captured since June 1878, sixty-three."

In June he writes, after saying how he had cursed Yuzuf Bey for all the grinning skulls of slaves on the slave route : " Just as I write these words they came and told me that another caravan of eighteen slaves had been captured with two camels. They were mostly women and children— such skeletons some of them . . . in less than two days I have caught seventy. There is no reason to doubt that seventy a day have been passing for the last year or so."

Next day, in his journal again, 17th June 1879 : " This morning we started at 1 a.m. and halted at 7 a.m. Soon after we caught nine slave dealers, twenty slaves, a camel and two donkeys. Some of these poor slaves are mere skeletons. No female child, however young, passes un- scathed by these scoundrels ! ! ! " (The three exclamation marks are Gordon's own.) [1] As the law did not permit death to the slavers, all Gordon could do was to flog and strip them and send them like Adam to the desert. Next day at Tiashig he captured 100 dealers and 500 slaves, and in this particular expedition saved some 1700 in all.

In the diary of 19th June he puts down the slave trade between 1875–1879 as from 80,000 to 100,000 souls. " This evening a caravan of 122 was captured." The slavers, hearing Gordon was there and the water inaccessible for them, had abandoned them and fled.

In 1885, in an introduction to his work *General Gordon's Journals* (*viz.* the Journal of his career in 1884), Mr. Egmont Hake writes thus of the days of the Governor-Generalship : " He [Gordon] saw that Circassian Pashas, the Bashi-bazouks, the Arab soldiery, the slave hunters, were by their action fast goading the people to revolt—on every hand he found caravans of packed slaves, hungering and parching in the sun ; and bands of slave hunters, dogged by the vulture- like dealers, waiting and watching for further prey, and over all these rogues the miscreant spirit of Zobeir." [2] It was not long before son Suleiman in the last year of Gordon's reign was in open rebellion, at Zobeir's instigation, in some hope of saving his position as the slaving king, but was captured with all his chiefs by a magnificent feat of Gordon's lieutenant, Gessi Bey, after an astounding cam- paign against the rebels. Since he and they were found to be planning treachery, Gessi shot the lot, and the whole Sudan breathed again as Ismael sent his congratulations.

[1] From *Colonel Gordon in Central Africa*, pp. 346 ff.
[2] " Sebehr," in *Gordon's Journal.*

Countless slaves were released, nor were the slaves in their hands all blacks !

THE REMOVAL OF THE KHEDIVE AND THE DEPARTURE OF GORDON (1879)

But over the Khedive's devoted and none too wise head storms of finance were gathering. The State of Egypt was too rotten, and rightly or wrongly, at the instance of the powers, Ismael was removed by decree of the Sultan, and Tewfik installed in his stead.

With Ismael gone no one rendered even lip-service to the cause of anti-slavery in the Sudan, and in August 1879 Gordon, almost at the end for a while of health and energy, resigned his Governor-Generalship. Ismael had been far away, but he never failed in his affection for Gordon or limited his authority.

That month Gordon, indignant at the treatment of Ismael, was in Cairo to find all his influence gone, none to care for the Sudan, and much misrepresentation regarding himself. He handed his resignation to Tewfik, who—at first pleased, while all the slave-trading interest rejoiced—soon found a different opinion from that instilled into his ears, and implored him to remain. This Gordon, on the verge of a breakdown from nervous exhaustion, would not hear of. He however accepted a special mission to Abyssinia to stave off a war, and was successful, returning to Cairo after four months, and strongly urged the appointment of a prince of the blood or a European to succeed him. Expressing his views freely and stormily, Gordon finally left Cairo for England in January 1880, and with his departure the curtain rang down on the reign of humanity in the Sudan.

Had a competent successor been appointed or had Egypt cared for anti-slavery, the immense work that Gordon had accomplished would have lived. Had the Powers of Europe cared, even then there was something to be saved ; but the worthless Raouf Pasha was appointed in his place, and the nemesis of the years of Egyptian and Turkish villainy was now to appear, and appear in strange cataclysmic form.

THE RISE OF THE MAHDI

We have now come to that stage of the history of the Sudan which long made it a household word in England. Under Raouf Bey the Sudan was fast slipping back into the hands of oppressive Pashas and slave traders, when there arose in Egypt and in the Sudan two simultaneous but distinct moves. In Egypt in 1881 Arabi, the Egyptian colonel, led a revolt of the army against Turkish misrule and European influence, a movement which, however righteously conceived, would only have made Egypt a bankrupt shambles. In the Sudan an Arab, the son of a boat-builder, who had long been acquiring a reputation as a religious thinker and holy man, a *faqir*, sprang into fame by proclaiming himself the long-expected Messiah in Islam, the Mahdi. The economic condition of the country made anything better than the reviving rule of the Pashas.

In May 1881 he issued a proclamation that all who opposed him opposed the will of God, and promised boundless relief from Turkish and Egyptian rule.

The effete Egyptian troops and gendarmerie sent to arrest him were destroyed ; the *faqir* demanded the sub-mission of all. At once, people, slave dealers, and Arabs flocked to his standard. His principal henchman, one of his three Caliphs, was Abdullali of the Baggara Arabs, those Bedouin horsemen, slavers all, smarting from the blows of Gordon and Gessi. To them the Mahdi made his *hejira*, his flight of safety and power, to the Nubia mountains 200 miles south-west, recognizing that he must fight the Egyptian

Government. Everywhere the Egyptian troops were being defeated and destroyed and all Turkish Pashas slain or ousted. And there was reason to think that these two movements kept some touch in the early days. The sympathy of England and of many others went with those who knew the sordid evil record of the Turkish overlay in Egypt and the Sudan. Folk, especially the Sudan folk, were struggling to throw off an unbearable yoke refastened on their necks since Gordon left. The Mahdi, like the Wahabi, would march to Constantinople and plant once more the true pure faith in corrupt Stamboul. But the identification of the Mahdi with the Baggara was but to fashion yoke far worse on all but the Arab tribes.

As the Sudan authority fell away before the Mahdi, Egypt became alarmed, and with Egypt the British, who after the defeat of Arabi by their forces had taken reconstruction in hand. They had at first essayed a semi-reform of the Egyptian Army, as distinct from the root and branch affair that was to come later. Ex-British officers and those of other nationalities were endeavouring to bring some sense of discipline and honour. The famous Colonel Baker of Plevna renown was reconstructing the gendarmerie, but as yet no British officers on the active list were allowed to join the Egyptian Forces. The Sudan had now a more effective Governor, Abdel Kadir Pasha, a Sudanese who had served, of all places, with the French in Mexico, and had actually commanded Baker's Equatorian bodyguard known as the " Forty Thieves."

His arrival at Khartoum inspired confidence, but the days when efficiency could have served were gone. The sands of safety had run out. Four months after the issue of his great proclamation, the Mahdi in Nubia had destroyed a force of 1500 sent against him from the Nile. Six months later a force of 3000 soldiers sent against him from Khartoum, under Gessi's lieutenant Yussuf Bey, was destroyed, with few survivors ; and in the summer of 1882 the Mahdi boldly marched for the Nile and El Obeid, which lay half-way between his retreat in Nubia and Khartoum.

Khartoum was now hastily fortified. El Obeid was a town of 100,000 inhabitants and the Egyptian Commander who had fortified the town hurled back the attacking of the *Dervesh*, the " poor men," as the Mahdi named his followers, with very heavy loss. The Mahdi's movement being more religious than political for the present, survived this repulse, and tribe after tribe now joined him. Thus beleaguered, the small Egyptian garrison of El Obeid fell, on 17th January 1883.

The news of the Mahdi's successes was received with consternation in Cairo, and the Khedive decided to send 10,000 of the re-formed army under Colonel Hicks, a retired British officer, but Mr. Gladstone's Government washed their hands of any adventures in the Sudan. He would not even allow advice for or against the expedition to be tendered. By October 1883 Hicks, much hampered, proceeded against the Mahdi, and by some mischance, never fully understood, the whole force was destroyed in wooded ravines in the desert. The news naturally increased consternation in Cairo, and ere long it seemed quite possible that an invasion of Egypt by the Dervishes might ensue. The problem soon became that of saving the lives of all European and Egyptian residents in the Sudan, indeed of evacuating the whole of both Provinces, since Turkish Egypt was never fit to hold either. And then thoughts of both Egyptian and British went back to their former hero : Chinese Gordon, Gordon of the two Sudans.

The Return and the Death of Gordon

The earlier stories of Gordon's career in the two Sudans have been related because they are an integral part of

RESCUED MUI-TSAI CHILDREN IN A HOME AT YUNAN-FU, CHINA

the anti-slave endeavours of the British. The story of his return and death are not an integral part of that same story but only follow as *sequelae*. Nevertheless, it is such a familiar theme in the world that its outline is needed here as a decorous completion of one of the dramas of history.

While the Sudan under Raouf Bey was rushing to that revolution of a desperate people, spoilt by the years of Gordon's restoration for any Turkish villainy, Gordon was in many parts of the world and greatly sought after. The Viceroy of India, the King of the Belgians, the Basutos, all made some claims on his services ; and then, a Major-General, he sought his own leisure in the Bible lands. Thence after much discussion and *pourparlers*, during which the abandonment of the Sudan seemed both to Egypt and Britain the only possible policy, Gordon accepted the mission of endeavouring to withdraw Egyptian troops and nationals, but with, as we now know, a practical *carte blanche* to try any other course that gave promise of better results.

That he had expected by his own prestige to straighten out the trouble is pretty certain, and that he had misgauged the basic changes in outlook engendered by the Mahdi's fanatical and inspiring claims and his successes.

It was too late to evacuate, and Gordon stayed to die in the ruins. That he was nearly saved by Herbert Stewart's desert column, we know ; and that a more prompt decision could have saved him. But it was not to be, and he died, as we also know, in his capital on the early morning of the 26th of January 1885, while two small steamers under Sir Charles Wilson with twenty redcoats were struggling through the rapids, fifty miles away. Two days later they arrived to see no flag flying, to learn that Gordon's head had been taken to the Mahdi, and that 10,000 of his people had been massacred to make a Dervish holiday. All the civilized world wept at a tragedy they could have prevented.

In Khartoum itself, nemesis for some, sheer cruelty and ruthlessness for most, was the immediate sequel. 10,000 folk were massacred; first the few Europeans, the Greek, Copts, the Egyptian Government officials. The Austrian Consul, Hansal, was beheaded. The Greek Consul, Leonhides, first had his hands cut off and was then beheaded. The tailor, Klein, had his throat cut from ear to ear beside his family, his eldest son was speared over his body, his eighteen-year-old daughter was carried off to a harem. Only boys were spared who could be slaves, and women suitable for the harem. Old women were cruelly tortured to reveal their treasure. The young women were all collected—white in one slave zareba, black in another. The Emirs had the choice of white or black. The wives and daughters of the Turkish pasha and the oriental Christians often entered the harems of their fathers' and husbands' murderers, in the old old custom of the East. Amina, daughter of a murdered notable, husband of another, a woman of rare beauty, went to the Mahdi—for whom it was said she developed a passion. It was a sorry tale of tragedy unspeakable.

With the Dervish spear that pierced Gordon's heart on the steps of his palace, the blacks of the Sudan were plunged into such tyranny and slave-dealing at the hands of fanaticism and ruthlessness that the world now can never realize.

The Avenging and the Restoration of the Balad-es-Sudan

For thirteen years Herbert Kitchener, of the same corps as Charles Gordon and of the Anglo-Egyptian Army, worked and watched and built; and with the British Garrison and the Egyptian Army, largely recruited from escaped slaves, slowly drove the Dervishes further north, till thirteen years after the culminated blow fell at Omdurman opposite Khartoum. Muhammad Ahmed the Mahdi was dead, and power and savagery were centred in the hands of his successor, his Caliph and henchman, the Abdullali of the Baggara tribe aforesaid, the " Khalifa " of history. His hosts were destroyed by Kitchener's Anglo-Egyptian Army, largely European and black, fighting with superb fanatical courage, at Omdurman across the river from now desolate Khartoum . . . that second day of September 1898, in which thousands lay dead on the ground. The Khalifa himself escaped from the battle to the same mountains to which the Mahdi himself had made his *hejira*.

Fifteen months later he once more advanced on Khartoum with an army that he had scraped together. There, trapped in a forest sixty miles from Abba, the Mahdi's island of origin, he was defeated by Wingate and slain, with most of his pirates.

It ended once and for all the story of the Mahdi of Allah and the fierce ruthless puritanism that passed with him, of his Khalifa who released all the old forces of slaving to die before the drive and energy of Kitchener. With the holocaust of Omdurman came peace unbelievable to a sore-tried land. In a very short while the condominium of Britain and Egypt under a British chief has brought wealth, education, learning, and prosperity. The story of the freeing and settling on land of the vast population of slaves, is a story in wisdom and administration that will fill a book in itself, and stands for all time as a memorial to the energy and humanity of British administration. Progress, machinery, communications, hospitals, cotton - growing, Manchester goods, weaving, have come fast on the land. Simplicity, alas, has gone to a great extent, and the zeal of the Moslem puritan ; and for these the land may be poorer ! But it has peace, and peace after aeons of misery. If you want to moralize and to dream on the rough-hewing of destroying, read Allan Bergman's *The Mahdi of Allah*.

CHAPTER FOURTEEN

Slavery and the League of Nations

★

*The Declaration of 1815—The League takes a Hand—The Convention of
1926—Adherents and Non-Adherents—The Work of the " Committee of
Experts " of the League—The Liberian Scandal.*

★

THE DECLARATION OF 1815

IN 1815 twenty-six nations round the council table at the
Congress of Vienna declared themselves entirely opposed
to slavery in any form, and expressed their determination
to put an end to it as soon as may be. Not only would
they and their nationals not engage in it but they would
eradicate it from their territories. And little resulted
therefrom !

The Congress of 1815 was a unique occasion, since the
whole world had been torn by a war for over twenty years,
the primary reason of which was the emergence of Napoleon
Buonaparte from the events of the French Revolution.
From this war, although prolonged and evil, much good had
emanated in the overthrow of old systems. Now with the
war spirit exorcised, the broken nations assembled, as in
1919, to make a new world. There are many who will
tell you that the experts of the Vienna Congress made a
far better job of it than the amateurs of Versailles a hundred
years later. Their protocol laid down more successfully
than that of Versailles the humane and statesmanlike
objects of the new peace and the new Europe, with as few

P   225

wounds as possible to be licked. On the whole they made a remarkably good job of it, as it was not till forty years later, with another Buonaparte on the throne of France, that the war-god really walked again. Further, the concert of Europe, in the hands of the big five, seems to have been an effective body. When therefore such a Congress, representative of every State that mattered, signed a convention deploring and renouncing slavery, the anti-slavery protagonists in England, a body to which public opinion in that land was yearly becoming more akin, were justified in expecting something more than lip-service in the great cause. How they were disappointed, nay betrayed, and how for years the British Navy was hampered has been recalled.

It was apparent that what was missing was some central body who could constantly put before their respective Governments any failure to implement an agreement, and who could if necessary indicate how to further their Governments' admirable sentiments. Without that Great Britain and the small Nordic States through several generations stood alone, while Britain bore both the financial and the moral burden !

The League of Nations, when it was formed, provided in one of its sub-committees, that for which we had been waiting during over a hundred years of disappointment. Not only anti-slavery, but aborigines protection, anti-white slavery, anti-drug traffic, and anti-contagious disease causes, were all looking for a machine that alone would induce finality and combination in matters that all civilization had at heart. Let it here be repeated as forcibly as possible, as has been suggested earlier, that however Utopian the conception of a League of Peace may prove to be among great nations struggling to live, its services to civilization and the desires of the whole world in the causes just enumerated are alone " worth the money ! "

THE LEAGUE TAKES A HAND

The international agreements of modern times, the Berlin and Brussels Acts, deal purely with the suppression of the slave trade and not with slavery in itself. But with the close of the World War, the entirely illusory hope that it was " a war to end war " gave scope for all the great thoughts of humanitarians to come uppermost. Among such the anti-slavery protagonists were not idle, and since the world had sufficiently progressed, every State at the Peace Conference was found ready to give its sympathy to the abolition of slavery once and for all. In 1919, therefore, the crown came to the memory of Sharpe and Buxton and all who had worked with them, in the shape of a new Convention signed at St. Germain, by which all signatories pledged themselves " to endeavour to secure the complete suppression of slavery in all its forms." Those who are well versed in the subjects know, and those who have read even the brief outline contained in these pages will equally realize, the supreme importance of this agreement—this nailing to the mast of the flag of the cause of personal freedom. Further, it included a clause which the champions of " aborigines protection " had dear to their hearts : the suppression of forms analogous in some of their aspects to slavery and slave-holding—such as serfdom, debt-slavery, and indentured labour under bad conditions. These matters were specifically included in the terms of the mandates to the Powers taking over control of the territories and tributaries of which Germany and Turkey were deprived. This Convention of 1919 superseded the Berlin and Brussels Acts so far as the signatories thereof were concerned. In 1924, the League of Nations being now at work, a committee was appointed to investigate the matter further, and continued to sit at intervals till 1925, and it recommended a new and more comprehensive Convention, which is now the authority on which the League acts. It proposed that all nations, whether members of the League or not, should be invited to subscribe thereto, and that it should be of world-wide reference, and not only applicable to Africa as were the previous Conventions of the greater Powers.

THE CONVENTION OF 1926

This Convention was approved and definitely adopted by the Seventh Assembly sitting in 1926 with a view to its immediate submission to the Member-States for their ratification. It was accepted without demur by fifteen of the States : the British Empire, India, Bulgaria, Denmark, Haiti, Hungary, Latvia, Norway, Portugal, and Spain. India made the necessary reservation with regard to the masterless and unadministered inaccessibles within her gates. Belgium, France, Germany, Italy, and the Netherlands did not ratify at once, but were expected to do so before long.

It will be noticed that the accessions of many of the members meant little, from the nature of local conditions, but moral support ; but those of Portugal, Spain, Belgium, and Haiti were important factors. Afghanistan, Ecuador, Egypt, Germany, Mexico, Turkey, and the United States, not members of the League at the time, were invited to accept the Convention.

In framing the Convention so that it could be widely accepted, considerable thought had to be given to the history, mentality, and economic condition of the nation whose accession was desired. In fact the greatest common measure was all that could be attempted. It also included provisions concerning forced labour, and since needs of nations were various and in some insistent, it was here that the mean between practical and useful politics and humanitarian theory needed careful manipulation. The

SLAVERY IN NORTHERN BURMA

A girl slave of " the Triangle," lying between the main branches of the Irrawaddy.

League now proceeded to transform its Committee of General Principles into a " Standing Committee of Experts " to examine the more technical details of the subjects and their ancillaries, as well as to keep the League informed of the reports of progress which all signatories were to be asked to furnish to the Committee.

It is not necessary to give here the text of this great Convention in full. It consisted of twelve Articles, and the preamble is of paramount interest in view of all that had passed, often too ineffectively, before :

. . . .

" Whereas the signatories of the General Act of the Brussels Conference of 1889–1890 declared that they were equally animated by the firm intention of putting an end to the traffic in African slaves ;

" Whereas the signatories of the Convention of Saint Germain-en-Laye of 1919 to revise the General Act of Berlin of 1885 and the General Act and Declaration of Brussels of 1890 affirmed their intention of securing the complete suppression in all its forms and of the slave trade by land and sea ;

" Taking into consideration the report of the temporary Slavery Commission appointed by the Council of the League of Nations on 12th June 1924 ;

" Desiring to complete and extend the work accomplished under the Brussels Act and to find a means of giving practical effect throughout the world to such intentions as were expressed in regard to Slave Trade and Slavery by the signatories of the Convention of Saint Germain-en-Laye, and recognizing that it is necessary to conclude to that end more detailed arrangements than are contained in that Convention ;

" Considering, moreover, that it is necessary to prevent forced labour from developing into conditions analogous to slavery ;

" The High contracting Parties have decided to conclude a Convention and have accordingly appointed as their plenipotentiaries :

.   .   .   .   .

who, having communicated their full powers, have agreed as follows : "

Then follows the twelve Articles, and the first fulfils the great want felt for several generations by all those handling the subject, a definition of " slavery." The word can obviously have a restricted and also a very wide meaning, and whatever might be considered as *not* coming within the official meaning of the term, it was more essential for thorough control to understand what *did*. It must be remembered again that the views of the Powers varied, and in fact the Portuguese plenipotentiaries had limiting views to expound when the question of " forced labour " arose, in view of the age-old condition obtaining within the old Portuguese Empire and the conscience of her people in the matter. A fairly satisfactory and comprehensive definition was, however, arrived at, and this is it.

Article I

" For the purpose of the present Convention, the following definitions are agreed on :

" 1. Slavery is the status or condition of a person over whom all or any of the powers attaching to the right of ownership are exercised.

" 2. The Slave Trade includes all acts involved in the capture, acquisition or disposal of a person with intent to reduce him to slavery ; all acts involved in the acquisition of a slave with a view to selling or exchanging him ; all acts of disposal by sale or exchange of a slave acquired with a view to being sold or exchanged, and in general every act of trade or transport in slaves."

Article II provides for the suppression of trading and the abolition as soon as may be of slave-holding.

Article III provides for the prevention of slaving ships being outfitted in their waters or trading under the flag of the High Contracting Parties.

Article IV provides for mutual assistance in achieving the object laid down.

Article V refers to the question of compulsory or forced labour, which has for some time occupied a leading place in the considerations of humanitarians. Forced labour for government purposes in undeveloped lands is often a necessity, and all Governments have refused to listen to any other point of view, but all are agreed that it is desirable to make the conditions involved as humane as possible.

In this Article all the signatories undertake to ensure that the administration only shall exact forced labour, or when this is not immediately possible, to end the practice of the conscription of forced labour by private persons as soon as practicable. When other people than the administration are allowed to compel labour, it is agreed that the remuneration shall be adequate and that labourers shall not be removed from their homes.

The remaining Articles provide for the adequate implementing of their undertakings by the signatories, and for the settlement of disputes between them concerning the meaning of the Convention if they cannot mutually agree. Each signatory may by Article IX, at the time of accession, reserve difficult parts of their territories from any of the provisions, and may accede in their respect at a later occasion. It is also, of course, provided (Article X) that individual signatories may denounce their accession in a formal manner should they so elect.

Adherents and Non-Adherents

The actual state of ratification and adhesion in 1937 is as follows : of the thirty-six States who signed the Convention, twenty-nine have definitely ratified it, and seven have not yet done so. Fifteen non-signatory States have definitely acceded, while twenty-two more may accede. Thus forty-three States have definitely bound themselves, with of course power to withdraw, to observe the Convention, *viz.* :

Twenty-eight Members of the League who have
Acceded and Ratified

Austria	Italy
Belgium	Latvia
Great Britain, her Dominions,	Liberia
and India (total six)	Netherlands
Bulgaria	Norway
China	Poland
Cuba	Portugal
Czechoslovakia	Roumania
Denmark	Spain
Estonia	Sweden
Finland	Yugoslavia
France	And one non-member,
Greece	Germany, making 29

Fifteen States who Acceded Later

(Ten being Members of the League)

Members—

Afghanistan	Irish Free State
Ecuador	Mexico
Haiti	Nicaragua
Hungary	Switzerland
Iraq	Mexico

Non-Members (five)—
Egypt (since become a Member of the League)
Monaco   Syria and Lebanon
The Sudan   United States of America

Signatory or Acceding but Non-Ratifying States (eight)
Albania   Iran
Columbia   Lithuania
Dominican Republic   Panama
Ethiopia (now defunct)   Uruguay

It will of course be recognized that many of the accessions are merely factors of good-will and moral support, while others are those of States within whose confines the ancient evil still obtains—places where the plane and the automobile have not yet brought control, or which are within the legitimate reservation of a State who must give attention to the need of *festina lente*.

There are still twenty-two States who have not yet acceded, but who no doubt will, some of which are of importance in the matter. One of them, Nepal, has lately abjured her ancient system to free her slaves.

Twenty-two Non-Acceding States
Saudi Arabia   Luxembourg
Argentine   Nepal
Bolivia   Paraguay
Brazil   Peru
Chile   Salvador
Costa Rica   San Marino
Free City of Danzig   Siam
Guatemala   Union of Soviet
Honduras   Socialist Republics
Iceland   Venezuela
Japan   Yemen
Liechtenstein

The Work of the " Committee of Experts "
of the League

The Committee of Experts have now (1937) made four reports to the League, and each year some definite progress, some real steps here and there, some further adherence in principle, some interesting and practical reports from the Governments of the signatories, are recorded. Since the great mass of the lands in which slavery was rife, and in whose inaccessible spots British authority has been ceaselessly at work, are within British spheres of influence, it is but natural that the League's report should consist very largely of appendices giving the reports of the various British Governments on the matters they are tackling. They make a fascinating continuation to the long story of British effort for the last century and a half, and the inoculation of the whole civilized world with the sentiments of our country.

Indeed it may be said that apart from some meagre statements from French West Africa and Spanish North Africa the report is entirely made up of the ample British reports, from Governments obviously deeply interested in the matter, but at the same time fully cognizant of the pace at which they can move, not as already said always as fast as the benevolent theorist could wish. And the report even takes on itself to make criticisms in this respect which might be resented by any nation other than the good-tempered British.

Article II (Para. 2) of the Convention enjoined on the Secretary-General of the League the duty of bringing the Convention to the notice of non-signatories, whether members of the League or not, and the assembly of the League in 1930 passed a resolution directing the Secretary-General to press those of the original signatories who had not yet ratified to do so. Albania, Iran, Panama, and Uruguay, all replied after some time that the matter was under reference or discussion; the Dominican Republic and Lithuania did not reply.

This Committee of Experts normally meets every two years, but in 1937 held an extraordinary session in view of the many reports submitted that needed presentment and consideration.

The above brief outline shows how satisfactory in principle this first universal charter of humanity is, and how little excuse any State can have in not acceding to the Convention. The Secretary-General of the League is charged with bringing it again and again to the notice of States who have not as yet accepted it, and this fact emphasizes that already commented on, that for the first time there is an accepted and acceptable machinery for acting as humanity's remembrancer.

THE LIBERIAN SCANDAL

Some mention has been made of Liberia, the negro republic on the west of Africa, beloved in its day by negrophiles and experimenters and recruited from various sources of emancipation. It has led a not unchequered existence since its inception over a century ago, looked on somewhat askance by British and French administrators in the vicinity as a nest of extravagance and futility. In 1931, however, it was suddenly borne in on the civilized world that rumours long current were true, that it had developed into a slave State on most oppressive lines, and an example of what black could do unto black, as bad and cruel as the earlier white unto black; a standing example to negrophiles, that however great the good in the negro character, it cannot develop the gift of managing itself on western lines without some measure of control! These fears were adumbrated by the famous negrophile, Clarkson himself, a century earlier, who said that uncivilized ex-slaves could not themselves teach civilization, and protested also against the United States dumping their negro " scum " in Liberia after emancipation in their own Northern States.

There is no doubt that the American negroes of Monrovia, its capital, had had great difficulty in controlling their hinterland tribes. They have often had to use armed force, and have been unable to control slave-holding in the hinterland even if they wanted to. The whole of their own system, electoral and otherwise, has been a travesty of good or honest administration. During the years between 1852 and 1916 they have had eight Caffre Wars, and risings have often been suppressed only by the presence of an American cruiser on the coast. Now the allegations on which the League of Nations Committee reported in 1931 began to come before the League so far back as 1923. Lord Lugard himself reported to the League that women were still sold even in the west area, the price varying from £3 to £40. A boy cost £5. He then recommended that the President of the Republic of Liberia, who had dealt with the earlier scandals, should be invited to deal with this. The information given was entirely in accordance with the report and complaints made by the British officials on the neighbouring frontiers, and indeed at the British conference of Provincial Commissioners held in 1924 it was said :

" We are of opinion that on the Liberian frontier the importation of slaves continues, and is not diminishing. We are also of opinion that masters or owners of slaves thus introducing slaves into this Protectorate should be considered as trafficking in slaves, for in practice this most frequently occurs, and though we are aware of this fact it is obviously most difficult to trace, follow up and prove, as such traffickers have means of covering up their tracks and the purpose for which they enter this territory. . . ."

Nothing more damning than this could well be recorded

so far as the traffic is concerned. Further, it was estimated that there might be an increased domestic population of 500,000. The hinterland chiefs, not discouraged by the American negroes, were enslaving and trading away their own folk and their neighbours'.

It is not surprising then that the League of Nations became more and more insistent.

By 1930 these rumours resulted in an interpolation and protests at the meeting of the League of Nations. The Liberian representative indignantly denied the implications and invited inquiry. A small international commission was appointed by the League consisting of two members from the United States, together with Mr. Edwin Barclay, a former President of the Liberian Republic. Their report was rendered in 1931, which not only confirmed the indictment, but brought to light a far more serious state of affairs than had been suspected.

Indeed in the House of Lords in March 1932, Viscount Snowden said : " The revelation of that Report shocked the moral conscience of the whole world."

Reference has been made to the considerable hinterland of Africa attached, by agreement of the Powers, to the small maritime state of liberated slaves. The report said that 2,000,000 of ordinary indigenous Africans suffered oppression and cruelty at the hands of but 15,000 " Americo-Liberians."

So definite and concise was the report that the Government of Liberia actually accepted its findings without reserve. It found that what were practically both slavery and serfdom were in existence and that force from without was used against the recalcitrant individual or tribe who resisted the working of the system. A system of " pawning " introduced by the Government itself was responsible for much of it, where fines imposed were paid by the man fined pawning himself and family as slaves, with the proviso that only a third party might redeem them. It was bond-slavery in a particularly ruthless form. There was also an instituted serfdom, which presented some of the worst features of that method of life. The acceptance of this report by the Government is perhaps indicative of a want of power to put things right without interference from outside—a not uncommon feature in feeble or helpless executives—and the reforms promised *may* have by now, under the constant scrutiny of the League, been achieved. But it is probable that for a few years an impartial authority is the only complete remedy.

CHAPTER FIFTEEN

The Analogous Problem of Indentured Labour

★

Labour in General—The Kanaka Labour Scandal—The New Hebrides Labour Scandal—Indian Indentures—Debt Bondage and Peonage—The League of Nations, Debt Bondage, Peonage, and Indentures.

★

LABOUR IN GENERAL

ANALOGOUS and a corollary to the slave question comes that of indentured—or perhaps we might say misindentured —labour ; coloured labour that is persuaded and sometimes compelled to leave its homes for work abroad under what seemed on enlistment adequate terms.

The story of indentured labour in modern times throws a convincing explanation on the whole story of male slavery from the beginning—female slavery being another story based on the polygamous tendencies of man. We see at once that the moment the more lordly races turn from nomadism to land settlement, or to any form of manufacture, they require labour. They desire personally to continue in the pleasure of nomadism, which might always be called do-nothing-ism, while enjoying the comforts of agriculture and even manufactures, a having-it-both-ways life—and very nice too ! It at once means putting constraint on races with an equal desire to do nothing, but with less courage and power to resist than their stronger neighbours.

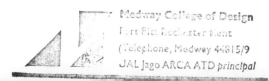

It has yet to be proved that neolithic man did not succeed in using the less developed remnants of Palaeolithic and Anthropoid man for his purposes. Those purposes were undoubtedly the development of civilization and progress and the mastery of nature—the development in fact of what phrasists like to call the " dignity of labour." In modern times, with a huge population in the West and in the advanced eastern communities demanding raw material and food, and capital seeking outlet and places of employment, with slavery out of fashion and virtue regnant, the demand for slaves turns to the demand for enlisting native labour. In the early days the French tried to get Indian labour from their own Indian territories for work in Réunion, and finding their own population too minute, obtaining it from British India by leave of the East India Company (*vide* Chap. X).

This brings us to two facets of the native labour problems : that of those crowded communities as in India, where the fertile womb has made living conditions difficult, and who have long acquired the habit of labour ; and secondly, those communities to whom regular work is not habitual, and for whom humanists demand the right to live in their own primitive way. In this book it has more than once been suggested that in the conditions of the modern world the transference of native population from crowded lands to empty ones might have some justification, always however with the proviso that the transfer is done under conditions of humanity, after-care, and definite rights. Any such ideas of transfer were in any case torn in bits and frustrated by the genesis of the African slave trade.

Indentured labour, when offered to a people anxious for work, eager to acquire some modicum of savings, and quite prepared to go overseas, is an entirely desirable condition given the necessary concomitants. It is welcome both to the empty country which is filled and the crowded country-

CHILD SLAVERY IN HONG-KONG

Two young servants who, under the Mui-Tsai system, are virtually slaves in the house of a well-to-do Chinese.

side thus eased. But what are the necessary concomitants ?
They are :

> No compulsion ;
> Honest recruiters ;
> Definite prospects ;
> Fixed periods of indenture ;
> Adequate passage arrangements ;
> Suitable accommodation ;
> A paternal welfare and after-care system ;
> Medical care and supervision ;
> Prompt return on expiration of agreement.

Under such conditions indentured labour may be most
satisfactory. Indeed under British Governmental arrangements Indian labourers finish their indentures, bring home
their savings, and enter joyfully into fresh indentures.

But even if all the conditions just enumerated are
adequately met, two great difficulties still remain. In the
first place there are two people to the agreement. Under
a proper system of control the employer fulfils his. What
about the employee, the indentured labourer, giving his
due meed of labour for his wages and keep ? It is perhaps
over this important side of the question that cruelty to
slaves and such horrors as those of the Putumayo have
arisen. Assuming that the task to be performed is reasonable, how are the lazy and recalcitrant to be dealt with ?
To return them as unsuitable when the bringing them has
been costly hardly commends itself. Hasty supervisors
take readily to birch and lash. It is a problem which all
indentured labour schemes under Government control have
to solve, and which accentuated the horror of actual slavery.
In the armed forces of a nation, officers have statutory
magisterial power to exact due performance. In the case
of indentured labour, only some form of magisterial
stimulant duly accepted at the time of enlistment can

fill the case. The *ex parte* fining by employers can rarely do so.

The other difficulty is the sexual one. If whole families can be taken and accommodation provided the trouble does not arise, but such may add impossible expense to the indenture. Eastern convention will often admit the departure of a labouring concubine while the lady of the household stays at home and receives remittances. That is satisfactory for the labourer provided with a concubine, but not for all. Humane consideration now makes us realize that this is a prime factor where masses of men are congregated, lest far worse befall. Nelson arranged companions for his fleet while blockading Toulon. The French, during the World War, accommodated their soldiery overseas when beyond the reach of the husband's train, and could not understand British reluctance to participate.

The proposal to use Chinese indentured labour in the South African mines after the South African War, which aroused such a commotion and opposition in Britain—partly fictitious, partly political—had this very real sex difficulty at the bottom of the objection by humanists and moralists. The Chinese deprived of domestic life develop strangely. Those despatching Chinese labour to the war fronts in the World War even despatched women with them, whom the military authorities had reluctantly to refuse, while recognizing the point involved.

Another facet of the modern native labour question, as in the earliest days, is that of the demands of an agricultural community, settled among or near a nomad or cattle-rearing native community who will not labour. The settler demands a taxation that shall compel the natives to work to gain money to pay their taxes. Traders endeavour to create desires that can only be satisfied by those with money to spend. Aborigines protection societies naturally combat any pressure on native inclination. A Colonial Government may have to decide that, in the interest of a community increasing owing to the immunity from transfer and disease conferred by the Pax Britannica, an enlarged outlook is now essential and must be engendered. Under a good Government, tribal chiefs will usually agree to help persuade their peoples. It is the business of the Secretary of State, and if necessary Parliament, to be sure that undue pressure by settlers is not responsible for a labour policy that is not popular among the natives.

The foregoing sums in brief the ethics underlying the question of indentured labour. The story of the scandals which have arisen in the last century through inhuman or badly administered indentures may now be outlined.

The Kanaka Labour Scandal

For a great many years, from the 'sixties onwards, the Aborigines Protection Society endeavoured to arouse, and finally did arouse, public opinion in Britain and in Australia in the methods of recruitment and the callous treatment of Kanaka labour. Kanaka is the generic name for the inhabitants of the islands of Polynesia, *i.e.* the South Sea Islands. In the general search for labour to develop the resources of the growing world of the mid-Victorian era, the labour-mongers had hit on these teeming islands. The trade was originally started by Peru, while so early as 1850 we learn of a French agent kidnapping Kanakas from Kingsmill Island and selling them in Réunion as *émigrés*: In later years they were to be recruited voluntarily for various parts of the world requiring labour, such as Queensland, the New Hebrides, and Peru. Unfortunately the so-called enlistment soon developed into nothing less than kidnapping, and unfortunately too no one stained their escutcheon more than the British Government of Queensland, in the days when the Australian public was often far

243

rougher than now and more eager for development *coûte que coûte.*

It was Peru, across the Pacific, that first thought of Kanaka labour for her plantations of cotton, sugar, and the like. The islands were not too far off for the purpose. The actual trade, for trade it practically was, began about 1850, and perhaps the first case was the kidnapping referred to of some Kingsmill Islanders by a Frenchman for the island of Réunion. By 1860 atrocious stories were coming to England concerning Kanakas in Peru, who were, it was definitely said, kidnapped by Peruvians for the mines and guano islands of that country.

In 1860 Lord Russell protested to the Government of Peru, who assured him that the trade had been abandoned and that immigrants would be returned. In 1866, however, missionaries in Samoa reported that the kidnapping for Peru was still in progress. The British Government protested again, but was shocked to find that its own people were doing the same and that its position of protest was seriously undermined. In 1867 a member of the Legislative Council of New South Wales and the owner of a cotton plantation in Queensland was engaged, with others, with not only importing Kanaka labour, men obtained by fraudulent means, but not paying them until the end of their three years' indenture, and it was said then only in goods. The senior naval officer lodged a protest with the Governor of Queensland. In 1869 the Aborigines Protection Society took a deputation to the Colonial Office, but the Governor of Queensland denied that kidnapping and abuses existed. The Queensland Government had indeed passed an Act to regulate the traffic, but it appears to have been wholly disregarded. A new Colonial Secretary, Lord Kimberley, protested, only to be met once more by indignant denial of any abuses. Then in 1871 a tragedy occurred which brought matters to a head. Bishop Patterson, in his ship the *Southern Cross*, was set on and murdered ; and then it transpired that some time previously the traders had painted a coolie ship like his, and sent a man dressed as a missionary to say that their beloved Bishop was on board sick and that they must come and see him. Once they had crowded on board, they were seized and carried off. When the real Bishop arrived he was murdered as a foresworn kidnapper. As a result of the indignation the British Parliament passed the Pacific Islanders Protection Bill, which, however, had very little effect; while more stories of imposition, fraudulent treatment, and disregard of regulations filtered home. In 1877 a Queensland Government Committee sat which issued a whitewashing report. Still the abuses continued, and in 1885 a Royal Commission sat in Queensland. At last, in 1890, so damning was the evidence, that the Queensland Government abolished the system of importation.

It was, however, equally certain that Queensland needed native labour very badly, and it also seemed quite possible to draw up an honest and humane system of importation and repatriation. In 1892 Field-Marshal Sir Henry Norman, then Governor of Queensland, gave the Royal assent to a new Act under regulations which did seem to promise all that was required. Polynesians were given better protection, though arrangements for their due return were still said to be unsatisfactory.

The matter was debated in the House of Commons in 1892, when Mr. Byrne pointed out that the House could not control the doings of a colony with the position of Queensland, but as the situation was still unsatisfactory they could control the matter at the Polynesian side, and this was what was eventually done. It may have been overdone, but the finale was that the restriction imposed made the employment of Kanakas so costly that the whole business died out. That also was a disaster, for a cheap and climatically suited labour was a real need in Queensland, to which, by that time, to the annoyance of Australian opinion, thousands of Chinese were flocking for the gold-fields.

It was a nemesis, for had the Kanaka labour been properly organized by a Government cognizant of its responsibilities and competent to control, an efficient service beneficial to both sides might well have been instituted. While we are horrified to think that such scandalous slavelike conditions, both in recruitment and treatment, should have arisen in late Victorian times, we have had an example of how matters of transportation and administration can go on through the ignorance of well-intentioned authority.

Incompetence alone may cause some of the worst conditions in wild and undeveloped lands; without any turpitude, and with a self-satisfied Government and some unscrupulous employé, scandals may easily arise. In Queensland, while the conditions of the Congo and the Putumayo were happily not reached, the whole matter was a scandal of inhuman treatment, which no modern British Government should have tolerated for a month.

THE NEW HEBRIDES LABOUR SCANDAL

But equal scandals were developing in another portion of the Pacific for which England was far less culpable, but which endured much later, and which for fifty years exercised the conscience of missionaries and the humanity societies. The group of the New Hebrides, islands far closer to the eastern coast of Australia, which comprised Queensland, than ever the Kanaka matrix was, were in 1906 placed by agreement under the control of an Anglo-French condominium, a condition of responsibility that can be very unsatisfactory. This convention would, it was hoped, put an end to a labour scandal of much earlier origin similar to that of the Kanakas. The conditions, however, especially so far as the French conscience went—a conscience which in effectiveness had developed a good deal later than that of the British—were deplorable so recently as 1913. The modern British missionary is normally of a class with far greater understanding and depth of vision than in earlier times, and reports from missionary authorities are to-day worthy of the fullest consideration by those in authority. In 1913 a conference of the Protestant Churches held in the New Hebrides passed a resolution calling the attention of the British Empire to the deplorable condition of things existing in this group of islands. The French judges, it was said, knew no language but their own ; native cases went through a double translation in court ; justice was rarely executed on a French offender, and so forth. On the other hand British courts gave the native the fullest protection, and penalties were enforced against British nationals by the British courts with due severity. The contrast was most marked. The resolutions went on to say :

" Whilst on British plantations fair conditions of life, work, and payment, are generally maintained, the majority of French plantations furnish examples of an exploitation which can only be denominated slavery."

In March 1912 a French paper put the case clearly enough :

" The recruiting of native labour goes on in flagrant violation of the convention of 1901, under abominable conditions. Slavery is in fact re-established. . . . alas ! it has become impossible to obtain voluntary labour. So one of the most disgusting forms of slavery has been established in order to procure labourers." Then follows a description of the methods of kidnapping employed. Allowing for the sensation-mongering of modern press methods, such a situation existing so recently as just before the World War is disconcerting, and again shows how readily modern civilization can relapse. It has also been stated that the native population of the New Hebrides had been reduced by the labour system from 600,000 in 1882 to 65,000 in 1911, which even if exaggerated must denote an astounding state of affairs. Happily this disguised slavery of the last decade of the nineteenth century has passed away never to return so long as ordinary vigilance is maintained.

INDIAN INDENTURES

The "teeming millions" of British India have long evinced the desire to leave their homes a while to improve their position, and we have already seen how they flocked to the ill-treatment even of Réunion before the Government of India interfered. To British colonies, such as Natal, Guiana,[1] and Mauritius, they have gone readily, and for many years the Government concerned has seen to it that conditions were humane, sanitary, and fair. That it is so is vouched for by the fact that many such labourers often return to them and go back for fresh periods of indenture. In 1917 the actual indentured system was put a stop to and anything in future would be free migration under suitable supervision for a simple and sheeplike folk, while all emigrants were placed under a Controller of Emigrant Labour—a very important step under modern conditions. After the war a special mission from India proceeded to study the conditions under which Indian labour in Fiji and the Pacific, going as it did freely, actually existed. Their report was a valuable one in that it indicated steps to take and conditions to watch which ensured progress as well as profit to the migrants. In 1922 it was thought advisable in the interest of labour to permit emigration of unskilled labour only to countries approved by the Government of India.

There is and was a widespread system of indentured

---

[1] Though even here there were grave scandals in the past.

labour existing within India itself, of which the control is naturally entirely in the Government of India's own hands. This is the provision of labour from Madras and Bengal, entered into eagerly enough, to provide labour for the tea plantations in Assam and on the slopes of the Himalayas, which has grown during the last fifty years to a very considerable proportion. What began on a small scale, easily managed by private enterprise, grew to such proportions that scandals, possible when numbers are large, might easily have arisen, and in some cases certainly did. Innumerable Government reports showed conditions that called for regulation, and rules and laws have now long been in operation. The Indian villages from which the labour was drawn live under simple and crude though not poverty-stricken conditions. But what was permissible under the long-established conditions of village life was not suitable for mass migration. In addition to terms of employment and repatriation and the due observance of such, conditions of accommodation, sanitation, prevention of cholera, and ordinary medical and welfare care, became essential. Until these were properly organized and adequate overseers appointed—something more effective than the callous Indian subordinates—conditions began to prevail which needed the rigorous attention and control of Government. Fortunately plenty of experience was available, and internal labour indentures are now a satisfactory feature in Indian domestic economy. It was not always so.

In this question of modern Indian emigration, usually of course for labour, it is interesting to note the large numbers of Indians serving overseas, chiefly but not entirely within the British Empire. In 1930, just before the slump, these totalled close on 2,500,000, of whom 800,000 were in Ceylon, 628,000 in Malaya, 281,000 in Mauritius, 279,000 in British Guiana and the British West Indies, 165,000 in South Africa, 73,000 in Fiji, and 69,000 in East Africa, while about 100,000 were in foreign lands. It must not be imagined, of course, that all these are labour coolies for the plantations ; the figure includes many merchants, traders, and professional men. Such grievances as from time to time attract notice are not those of physical or monetary ill-treatment, but refer, as South Africa, to the political status of educated Asiatics.

With so large a population abroad economic conditions have to be watched. The slump of 1931 disturbed the conditions of Indian labour overseas and the Controller of Emigrant Labour had his hands very full. For instance, throughout the labour world abroad, it was necessary to reduce wages. In Malaya the local Governments decreed a 20 per cent. reduction. India could but acquiesce, but was able to arrange that all who did not accept a lower wage should be repatriated. This brought 73,000 home from Malaya alone, just as the same typhoon of depression brought thousands home to Britain and shelter from Australia and Canada.

There is no need to pursue further a matter which only comes into our story at all because it is the comparatively triumphant ending to a story that supervened on the British Act of Abolition in 1834.

Debt Bondage and Peonage

Debt bondage and peonage mean different things in different countries ; in all detestable, in some cruel and abominable. The debt bondage of India, so long mixed up with age-old customs, has already been referred to, while some systems, however inexorable, have not been tainted with physical duress.

This matter of debt bondage was first authoritatively dealt with in the report of the Temporary Slavery Commission of the League of Nations of 1925. The following extract from their report describes the condition with some exactness :

" Sometimes this enslaving is voluntary on the part of the debtor, sometimes he is compelled to submit to it ; sometimes it is for the life of the debtor and does not terminate on the death of the creditor whose rights pass to the heir ; sometimes it terminates when the debtor finds means of repaying his debt ; or when the creditor considers that the labour given, deducting the cost of the maintenance of the pledged person, is equal to the amount due."

Now the last sentence describes a debt bondage,[1] which if undesirable is at any rate capable of being justly administered, but it appeared that in countless cases the creditor keeps the debtor always in debt—by chicanery or by encouraging him to indulge in goods or food that he covets, and having the amount " put down in the bill." This, of course, meant that a contract which had originally some appearance of equity would be converted into bondage for life, and in an inadequately administered country, as with slaves, the bond servant (a status, be it noted, known to Holy Writ) who is idle or recalcitrant must be under duress of some kind, at best by a magistrate, at worst by a master with lash and instruments of torture.

The report of 1925 brought to notice that debt bondage, or peonage, is especially prevalent in South America. The peon is practically a serf, *adscripti glebae*, and is sold with the land. It remarks, " the peonage system is one of the exacting problems that South American nations must face," and describes how the peon is constantly in debt to his overlord. " The debt hanging over him reduces him to practical slavery . . . the peon is tied to the land . . . in settling the property, the peons pass to the new owner. Theoretically free, they are practically unable to break away from their yoke."

[1] As in parts of India.

In Venezuela for instance, it is said that every farm has thirty peon families, and large ones as many as a thousand. They are to all intents and purposes the property of their master, having no knowledge of any rights that appeal to doubtful authority might give them. Shown from time to time their accounts, the articles they have received in dress and maintenance keep their accounts well on the wrong side ; escaping is severely punished at the owner's discretion, and police usually arrest and bring back absconders.

Similar to peonage is a system of pledging for debt in vogue in parts of Africa. How this was imposed by the Government of Liberia as a method of paying fines for offences has been explained. All over the Asiatic and African world this custom prevails in many different forms. In its worst forms it is far inferior to the old serfdom that existed throughout Europe, and being without the reasonable justice that a Christian principle and priesthood helped to secure, turns into slavery and atrocity. The League of Nations Slavery Committee happily takes full cognizance of it, and by the aid of the watch-dogs—missionaries and the anti-slavery societies—is able to detect where the lip-service activities of some Governments fail to come up to their professions.

Once again, however, let it be repeated that peonage as a debt bondage may be a necessary condition of development in certain backward countries, and as explained in the case of India may be greatly bound up with custom ; and further, it is the only known method of obtaining any credit for the penniless. Under such conditions it is more than incumbent on the administration of the country where it obtains to see that such a state of bondage is properly regulated. To get some picture of what it might mean, figure to yourself a young agricultural labourer wishing to marry without means to furnish a home. A farmer might say, " I will fit you up : I will build you a house, and you must then undertake to work for me, receiving food and clothes and only a small pocket-money until your debt is paid." If such an arrangement were so regulated that the wage to be credited were fixed and properly registered, and the law admitted action against a debt-bondsmen for laziness, or against the master for ill-treatment, it might be said that such a system had its advantages.

THE LEAGUE OF NATIONS, DEBT BONDAGE, PEONAGE, AND INDENTURES

But while the note of triumph that has been sounded applies to the British Empire, all is not quite so advanced in the rest of the world ; and the League of Nations, in view of the watching brief assigned it in anti-slavery and aborigines protection matters, has a good deal to say in this matter of indentures. Spain, Portugal, South America, are all concerned with providing plantation labour, and where that labour comes from outside the jurisdiction concerned the world as a whole, through its agents the League of Nations, is at once interested. The League's report this year (1937) of the work of its expert committee on slavery, includes reports submitted by the courtesy of the Governments of Madras and Orissa on the ancient debt bondage system as existing and resulting in those Provinces of India, while a memorandum from Sir George Maxwell, Secretary to the Expert Committee, is also printed, which describes how debt bondage in the Malay States was first regulated and then abolished by the rulers of Kedah, Perlis, Kelantan, and Trengganu, to which he was for some years " adviser." Reform first began by the registration of all debtors in bondage, their liability and the amount being duly recorded in a document given them. The amount of diminution of the debt by service was fixed at a monthly rate, and this meant that only those heavily in debt would remain bound after two years. Sustenance was to be given by the owner of the bond. By this method all would be freed in time, and what was important, the freeing was due at varying dates, according to the amount of their debt, thus avoiding any simultaneous disappearance of the bonded labourer. Eventually the States themselves paid up the balance of those with long periods still to go, and the system came to an end. Embarrassment at the loss of bound employés was soon counteracted by the fact that bound labour was proverbially lazy and hired labour was not, giving further proof of the law that " slave labour was always uneconomical."

In most of the districts in Madras the bondage is not for a long duration, save in the Nilghiry Hills, where a very primitive race serves the Badagas and other landowners for life, with all his family, in return for an advance of twenty to thirty rupees. This bondage is dying as other employment attracts this class of labourer.

In almost every case it is the need of money for marriage expenses that sends the labourer into debt bondage. In the State of Hyderabad there exists the Bhagela system, which has been the custom for centuries—the Bhagelas being another depressed and probably aboriginal folk admitted to the outside edges of the Hindu system of life. Here, as elsewhere, the Baghelas entered into debt bondage and have thereby secured an existence for themselves, which under the conditions of India so long prevailing, they might not otherwise have got. The Hyderabad Government, desirous of modernizing and humanizing the system, made a regulation that after 7th February 1937 all existing debts would be considered liquidated. By it any fresh agreements were to be stamped and registered, and would provide for the proper crediting of definite rates towards liquidation, thus avoiding victimization. Like every other beneficent regulation in India, it does provide opportunities for oppression by dishonest and unscrupulous officials (who are not rare), but it is obviously the right step to be taken.

A Hyderabad official touring the Bhagela districts before the regulation came into force, remarks that he found fear among the landowners that they might lose cheap labour, and among the Bhagelas themselves that the indispensable marriage money might be hard to obtain in future.

CHAPTER SIXTEEN

The Slavery that Remains

★

General Aspect—Slavery in Arabia—Slave Arabia To-day—The Mui-Tsai System among the Chinese—Mui-Tsai in China To-day—Remnants in the British Empire—Some Results of a Slave Past—The Ringing to Evensong.

★

GENERAL ASPECT

WE have now come to the end, as far as yet revealed, of a story as old as time ; of the exploiting of humbler, weaker, or in some way inferior folk, by races better equipped for the struggle of life. The real end of the world's slavery story is not yet, nor can it be said that it is even in sight. It is believed that there are at least 4,000,000 people in 1937 who are entirely enslaved, and who are but chattels in this largely Christian world. These 4,000,000 are for the most part held in Arabia, Abyssinia, the interior of Northern Africa, and in China. It may happily now be said that, except in recently reft Abyssinia, where transition must take time, there is now no territory of a European Power in which slavery of the old complete type now exists. There are, as shown, in out-of-the-way pockets of the British and French Empires, certain customs and tenures of slave nature, not necessarily unbenevolent, the too prompt ending of which is politically inadvisable. It has taken the best part of a century for the European and American slave-holding nations to emerge from the cocoon of the old unholy weaving !

TRANSLATION

This Deed of Sale is made by Poon Shi of Mak Family.

In consequence of urgent need for fund to meet family expenses, I am willing to sell my own daughter, Ah Mui, 10 years of age, born in the afternoon, 23rd day of 11th moon, Mo Ng year (i.e. 25/12/18), to Chan Yee Koo through a go-between. In the presence of three parties, it is mutually arranged and agreed that the purchase price is to be $141.00. After this sale, Chan Yee Koo shall have the right to change the name of the girl. If the girl is disobedient, Chan Yee Koo shall be allowed to resell her, and the mother shall have no recourse. In the event of any misfortune befalling the girl, there is no blame to either party.

It is also made perfectly clear that the girl has never been betrothed to any other family, nor is there any mortgage on her. In case any question arises as to the origin of the girl, the seller, Poon Shi of Mak Family, is held responsible, and it in no way concerns the buyer.

This is a straightforward sale and purchase between two parties, and lest verbal contract is invalid, this deed of sale is made and delivered to Chan Yee Koo as proof thereof.

Poon Shi of Mak Family hereby acknowledges receipt of the purchase price of $141.00 in full, without any deduction.

Finger print of Poon Shi
of Mak Family . . . . .

Go-between, Poon Shi of
Chan Family . . . . . .

Dated
The Republic of China, 13th June 1927.

DEED OF SALE OF A MUI-TSAI SLAVE GIRL

The gravest and most pronounced slave-holding and slave-breeding that yet exists has its home in the Arabian countries, where the system is as old as slavery itself, and can fade but slowly.

Mui-Tsai, which is really *Pei-Nu* (slave), in China is a problem, but is on its way to be solved, and in British spheres it is dying. Genuine slavery in China itself must wait till skies are clearer. In India there is nothing, though the work of release has still to go in some of the most inaccessible mountain slopes of the Himalayas. In Africa, while in British spheres it is gone, and in French spheres is going fast, there are many corners in the interior where motor and plane cannot yet carry the message of freedom ; but again *ça marche*. The Arabian situation will stand some further examination, as it is there that the blot is still inaccessible.

SLAVERY IN ARABIA

It has just been said that in Arabia slavery is as old as time ; and still to-day, in this year of grace 1937, there are many hundred thousand slaves, real undisguised slaves, called by no camouflaged name and sold as chattels at their owner's will. The slaves are men and women brought in the past, and still smuggled in smaller numbers, from the black races of the Sudan and even from negro Africa by Arab and half-Arab dealers. But since both men and women are bought and sold as slaves, the slave womb is kept busy both by slaves and Arab masters. Tens of thousands have been born slaves of slave mothers in Arabia ; and wearing as they do the Arab *kefiyah*, *agal*, and the *abba*, have all the appearance of Arabs save for the negro features of varying degree. The negro woman is very popular as a concubine in the summer, for her black skin keeps surprisingly cool, while that of an Arab does not. When, during the World War, the British Forces came to the

Tigris, the word went round that "now the British had come all slaves will be free"; especially were the authorities petitioned not to free the women because of the advantages of this coal-black skin.

But taken as a whole the Arab slavery is of that benevolent kind that is very properly anathema to the anti-slavery gospel. Like that of the Southern States it does not cry to high heaven for vengeance, and therefore gets a toleration which its soul-destroying effect by no means merits. Slavery in Arabia is a perfectly legal affair, sanctioned by Turkish rule, by custom, and by the Moslem religion.

Until the World War, Arabia was nominally—very nominally for the most part—under Turkish rule. Even had Turkey done lip-service to any anti-slavery advances she would have been powerless to carry it out, save within hail of her Hejaz railway and her military centres.

Until very recently the desert Arab, the Bedouin, and the people of the centre, were all quite aloof from the outer world. Slaves were and are part of the ancient system. The patriarchal sway holds among the Arabs of the desert as strongly as in Ancient Rome. Hordes of slaves and slave children, often his own, appeal to an Arab, to be ruled—often kindlily enough, but quite definitely ruled—fed, clothed, and supplied, and entirely unpaid. The head of the Arab family likes to have them all about awaiting his orders. Since the slave is usually friendless and homeless he has no other anchor in life save the patriarch's tent.

No slave can leave his master. His only change, as in other slave systems, can come from being sold. In the desert slaves are both cheaper than free labour and far less trouble. As concubines slave women are equally inexpensive, and therefore dear to the Semite instinct of the Arab. A Moslem wife receives a dowry from the husband, that is both law and custom; and while a modern wife may be divorced easily enough, her dowry is her inalienable right and goes with her. The slave concubine who is a disappointment may be sold off, and may even yield profit. These slave concubines, and the slave children born of them, are therefore useful assets in every way, apart from the other charm just mentioned. It is not, therefore, to be expected that from within will come any great movement of conscience to rid themselves of so comfortable a system. In the desert, however much modern contacts may touch the fringe, the life of the *bedu*—that is to say the flock-master's life—must continue. The desert does not yield water that could ever make the cultivator's life universal. The *bedu* turns *fellah* sparingly, from taste and from opportunity ; incidentally he loses something of the admirable aspects of his peculiar character thereby. He may acquire others.

There is nothing in Moslem religious teaching that militates against slave-holding. On the contrary, the existence of slaves is especially recognized as the law of life, from the fact that the freeing of slaves is enjoined as a meritorious act. As the existence of slaves was in full swing in the days when the Pentateuch was written, so when the Qoran was put together years later, it dealt with it as a recognized institution, and one can but infer that while good and fair treatment of slaves was enforced, and their liberation was considered meritorious, condemnation of the institution was not thought of.

In the days when the Arab conquests were absorbing Central and Western Asia and North Africa at an astounding rate, and this teaching of the Prophet, born in the pot-holes of the desert, was raging across the world like the roar of a forest fire, the Arab tents were full of slaves— largely slave women and children. The freeing of slaves was easy to practise, there were plenty more where those came from, and the slave-born produce of the vigorous desert loins, brought up in the faith and inured to arms, were readily absorbed into the desert community of soldiers fighting to spread the faith. Indeed the alarming rate at which the desert was swamping the old civilization was probably due to the enormous accession of children. When we read of a Moorish king who had six hundred sons, all of whom lived at least to an age when they could become horsemen, we can imagine the rate of increase in an Arab encampment well supplied with slave women, as well as the urge for more food lands that such productiveness stimulated. The spread of the faith eastwards in Asia or north of Africa had a basis of economics as well as of fervour.

Slave Arabia To-day

The primitive desert life of the sixth century is the desert life of to-day, despite the attack of motors and planes, and the travels of the adventurous Philby, Bertram, of Freya Starke, and Rosita Forbes ; they illuminate, but they do not change.

It is well to quote from Eldon Rutter's lecture of a few years ago to the Central Asia Society, because it does re-assure us that a state of affairs which is impossible to remedy save in the slow march of time is not unbearable. We know that the slave-raiding which produces new slaves by capture, the world, largely the British world, has almost brought to an end.

" Now I shall have to show that slavedom in Arabia is in its physical aspect a slight thing. Regarded in a material way only, the lot of a slave in Arabia is quite as happy as that of thousands of human beings in the most advanced countries of the world. This is because social conditions are still in, not exactly a primitive state, but an old-fashioned state. Such conditions make for content-ment simply because the essential difference between the life lived by prominent citizens and that lived by the less fortunate, even by servants and slaves, is not very great. In the more advanced countries the difference between the life lived by the rich and that lived by the poor has now for several centuries been enormous. In mediaeval times it was not so, a rich man did not live in a pauper-proof mansion. He was accessible to everybody. This is the position in Arabia to-day, and there the levelling influence of Islam has preserved one set of manners for rich and poor alike. Moreover, the many injunctions to release slaves which are contained in the Qoran have certainly given rise to a feeling among the more pious Muhammadans, that they hold their slaves on sufferance. They treat them kindly, even affectionately."

He adds that the slavery of that kind makes contented slaves, " and that is precisely why I regard slavery of the easygoing Muhammadan kind as the worst of all forms of slavery."

There speaks the believer in the sanctity of the human soul, and the human body " made in the image of God." He adds, however, that this comparatively humane sub-jection really requires a vocabulary of its own, and does not merit the same term as even the slave life that was to be seen on many plantations of the old sea-board slave States. The *rigg* or slavery of Arabia, and the position of the *'abd* or slave, is not within the same four walls as " slavery " in its worst form.

With this description of the life, it is not to be wondered at that a slave from Abyssinia, a victim of some raided and destroyed village, lends himself willingly to the slave trader's desire to disguise him as a sailor or merchant during his passage across the Red Sea.

Mr. Rutter in his lecture describes the scene at Mecca, the meeting-place of the Moslem nations. He is visiting as close as may be the House of Allah, the great place of pilgrimage to the world of Islam at Mecca, that town set in an inaccessible valley, with its walls of bare rocky hills.

"We do not come as pilgrims, but as investigators of slavery. We therefore take particular notice of a score or so tall negroes in immense turbans who are standing or walking near the House of Allah. These men are called *Aghas*. They are eunuch slaves and are employed as police in the great Mosque. There are about fifty of them altogether, and their duties are not very heavy. They were first established in the Mosque in the eighth century." They are employed because squabbling women have at times to be ejected.

"No man is supposed to touch a woman who is not his wife or closely related to him, but an eunuch is not classed as a man in the proper sense of the word. Most of the *Aghas* have been presented to the Mosque by Muhammadan princes. Nowadays they are chiefly purchased as boys by the chief *Agha*. They are not owned by any person but are slaves of Allah. They are in fact presumptuously presented to God by their fellowmen, a sort of bloodless human sacrifice . . . the last thing they would be likely to desire would be their freedom from this, to them, honourable and prosperous slavery."

The streets and precincts are full of slaves ; some, well-dressed and carrying daggers, escort their masters as a bodyguard. "We may see, too, a few old slave women. They are recognizable by the poverty of their clothing and the lack of proper veils, but we see nothing of the several thousands of younger women slaves who are kept close in the shuttered houses of the city. . . ."

"We make our way through the dusty ways which surround the mosque, and presently come into a narrow street called the *Suk-el-Abid*. This is the slave market. It is very narrow, and the tall houses on either side allow very little daylight to reach the roadway. Against these houses there are stone benches resembling the display counters of shops, and so indeed they are, for these houses are the shops of the dealers in human beings. The slaves are sitting on the benches—some silent, others talking together, some even joking and laughing. The crowd moves slowly apart. . . .

" The most desirable of the slave girls are not exposed to view. They are kept inside the houses, where prospective buyers are taken in to view them. There are also street auctioneers called *dallal* . . . among these *dallal* are a number who specialize in the sale of slave girls, and they conduct the buyers to the house where the slaves may be inspected. The best slaves are sold among the citizens by private treaty this way." Men are unscrupulous in Arab life as elsewhere, for whereas an owner with slaves should care for their old age, there are the heartless and the hypocritical who manumit their slaves when they are too old to work and too old to sell. Thus Eldon Rutter.

" As we move along in the cloisters we see two or three very old men and women who look like dreary black skeletons. If we go to the mosque at sunrise we shall see some of these. If we go at sunset they will be there too. And if we pass by at midnight we shall see them there still, sleeping on the stones in their rags. They are manumitted slaves, free men and women. They have no home but the mosque, and no food but what they receive in alms, turned out ' to seek the bounty of Allah,' as their masters would say."

So much for even a " benevolent slave system," though it is but fair to say that good masters maintain their old slaves till they die . . . a sorry death."

One more extract to add to the *lacrymae rerum*.

" There is yet another repulsive blot on human manners which is rendered possible by Arab slavery. Mekka [1] is

---

[1] Save in quoting, the older spelling of " Mecca " is used.

always full of students who settle in the cities for years to study theology—some of these marry slave women belonging to the Arabs. Any child of these so-called ' marriages ' is born into slavery, and becomes the property of the woman's owner. The father is usually too poor to buy the woman's freedom." Rutter adds, " I do not think I have anything more barbarous than that to report out of all I have seen and heard of Arabian slavery."

So much for Arabian slavery to-day. Is there any remedy ? It may confidently be said that so far as the land of the Hejaz, and Ibn Saud's own country, the only remedy lies in the pressure that the 300,000,000 Moslems of the world to whom Mecca is the Holy of holies might bring to bear—but even that is not much where the ordinary slave-holding of the desert is concerned.

Ibn Saud, whose personal name is Abdul Aziz—Saud being his father's name, and Ibn, meaning son—the King of the Hejaz, touches the western world on one side and the fanatical hordes of the desert in which his fanatical Wahabis the *Ikhwan* [1] live on the other.

By Article VII of the Treaty of Jedda of 1927, he has undertaken to co-operate with the British for the *suppression of the slave trade*. That he has done ; but interior slave life, as we have seen all through the story, is another matter. It is the old question, the old difference between *abolition and emancipation*.

Now of the potentates who hold sway over the wilder Arabia, we have Ibn Saud of Saudi Arabia as the most important, while the King of Transjordania runs him close, the King of Iraq, who has *bedu* tracts " between the rivers " and west of the " Good Frat " or Euphrates, and the Imam of Sanaa, the King of the Yemen, but none of their writs run very freely outside the towns and the *fellah* colonies. The League of Nations Anti-Slavery Committee reported

[1] Brothers.

264

in 1937 that King Abdul Aziz Ibn Saud had announced the suppression of the slave trade from Africa, that is to say would endeavour to prevent his people being customers to the slave dealer of Abyssinia and elsewhere. Up till 2nd October 1936, by treaty and consent, the British representative at Jedda had the right of manumission of slaves who presented themselves in the consular area. But in prosecution of a co-operative policy, and in connection with the general activity regarding slavery of the League of Nations, the British Government has renounced that right from that day, consequent on the promulgation of slavery regulations by the King of Saudi Arabia. These regulations are immensely important in principle. In practice they depend on the extent to which the Saudi writ runs within the confines of his dominions. The principal provisions are as follows :

It is absolutely prohibited :

1. To import slaves from any country by sea.
2. To import slaves by any land route, unless the importer proves by a Government document that the slave is recognized as such in the country from which he comes.
3. To enslave any free person.
4. To buy or obtain possession of any slave who has been imported or enslaved in contravention of the regulations.

It will be evident that the above is a great step forward, but that it does not touch slave-holding because no monarch or government can go against the inherent mentality of its people, as Haile Selassi well knew. It may give a great fillip to slave-breeding, and it gives, like all such regulations in the East, and to a lesser extent everywhere, an opportunity to the venal official to exact gratification for carrying out the permissions that are inherent in the regulations.

They are, however, a considerable step in advance, and definitely support the British anti-slavery patrol. But the League of Nations report in welcoming the regulation speaks as if the customs stations between say the Yemen and Saudi Arabia are as complete as those on a continental border.

However that may be, the King's promulgation proclaims him as one who accepts definitely the world's decision to have no new slaves made or imported. The next step in years to come should be to free the womb, and declare that no man or woman can be born a slave. But desert opinion is not yet ready for that.

The Mui-Tsai System among the Chinese

Among the systems bordering on, and indeed often entering the condition of slavery, of which a good deal has been heard of late years, is that called in euphemy *Mui-Tsai* or " little sister " in Southern China ; and by less pleasing but more accurate term of *Nu-Pei* or *Pei-Nu* in Northern China, which means quite unequivocally " slave girls." The system is the direct result of intense fertility, the difficulty of disposing of daughters, the small value placed on human life, where life is so easily engendered, and the inextricable poverty that must surround the existence of those who are born in greater numbers than the circumstances of their country can maintain. In India, the unwanted daughter was freely in the past, and still is at times, exposed to die. In all countries such things occur among the very poor, and wilder peoples. In China for centuries parents have sold their unwanted children openly, and probably feeling quite truly that whether as " adopted child," " little sister," or " slave," their lot would be better than they themselves could offer.

Such a system, in a country whose ancient system of

control had snapped before a new one could possibly take its place, was, and is, obviously hard to put an end to. In China the Central Government, however genuinely *doctrinaire* in anti-slavery, has a writ that runs feebly, and is hampered by an undeveloped national conscience that does not gird at the evil.

The system of *Mui-Tsai*, using the euphemy of the Canton province by which it is more familiar to western thought, has the advantage that, used by folk of any kindly nature and conscience, the lot of the *Mui-Tsai* might be much better than that of the starving village child. But in any but the best hands it has every opening for cruelty and slavery of the worst nature, from the cruel beating and slipperings of ill-tempered mistresses, young and old, to sex outrages of every kind. Of late years philanthropists and missionaries, and in the case of British colonies that have Chinese inhabitants, the Governments themselves, have been more and more aware of what was, and might be, behind the lattice of the Chinese quarters. Modern China herself has in theory become aware of the evils of this ancient custom. In the British colonies, such as Hong-Kong and Malaya, ordinance followed by action has been possible, the general line being to insist that all *Mui-Tsai* shall be registered, thus making the mere holding of an unregistered *Mui-Tsai* an offence. Detection of breaches of this regulation and of ill-treatment is the work of inspectors, usually women.

With this has come the establishment of places of refuge to which a *Mui-Tsai* may be sent in safety while complaints are being investigated, and hostels where freed *Mui-Tsai* can be held and helped to normal life. Without such the transition from a bad mistress to a brothel would be almost a certainty.[1]

The facts of the case at once show the difficulties that

---

[1] Refuges are badly needed, but the war must make *Mui-Tsai* worse.

remedies arouse. Among other palliations has been that of the restoration to parents, where possible, of freed *Mui-Tsai*. As an example of the machinery and the methods required might be mentioned the *Children's Ordinance* 1927, the *Women and Girls' Protection Ordinance* 1930, the *Mui-Tsai Ordinance of* 1913, to all of which amendments have been found necessary as the intricacies of the problem, even in so easily handled an island as Hong-Kong, became more evident. In Malaya the problem of controlling *Mui-Tsai* is far more difficult, for the term includes three separate categories : that of the administered Straits Settlements, of the Federated Malay States, and of the " Unfederated " Malay States, while each of these have four, five, or six components. In the Straits Settlement, similar ordinances to those referred to in the case of Hong-Kong were introduced in the same year. Both Malay and Hong-Kong have reported their progress to the League of Nations, but it is somewhat odd to read the comment of the League of Nations Advisory Committee of Experts on the excellent reports from Malaya, since not only is it written in a tone which only Great Britain would tolerate, but is well calculated to annoy Malaya, whose administrators no doubt know their job and its difficulties, and prefer to make their own reports their own way.

Mui-Tsai in China To-day

In China itself, with its countless millions, the problem is a very different one from the comparatively trivial populations of the British colonies that have Chinese settlements. In January 1936 the Chinese Government promulgated a regulation prohibiting the keeping of *Pei-Nu* (such being the official Chinese term for *Mui-Tsai*), and followed this by inaugurating hostels and charitable organizations to assist in emancipation and settlement. How far

China, amid her far more urgent problems, and her war-clouds, can see that her regulations are observed, save in her more controlled towns, only the future can show.

The problem in the International Settlements, by the very nature of the unavoidable anomalies, has been very complicated, and not till China herself promulgated her regulation could the administration of the International Settlement take anything more than charitable action.

Since the Chinese regulations are so recent, it is at present only possible to state that in Kulanzu (Amoy) and Shanghai the Municipal Councils are now taking steps, and taking their advice from the experience of Hong-Kong. It may be expected that unless the whole attitude of the Chinese is against the *Mui-Tsai* Regulations of their Government, matters will move rapidly in the International Settlements, who have fortunately that most necessary requisite for any action, an efficient police. The Shanghai International Settlement has already appointed an English lady Inspector of the *Pei-Nu*. But the problems of turning the *Pei-Nu* or *Mui-Tsai* into free labour are those of enabling the girls to invoke the help of the law, and to shelter them while they protest from vindictive masters and mistresses.

THE REMNANTS IN THE BRITISH EMPIRE

But since Britain leads in the anti-slavery van her own vestiges of slavery should be prominently recorded. They are not many, but may be summed up here :

1. Actual slavery, the results of slave-raiding and slave-breeding in most inaccessible pockets of the Himalaya and the upper basin of the Irrawaddy, where at present administration and police columns cannot act.

2. A debt bondage of ancient custom among the depressed and aboriginal races of India.

3. A harmless hereditary slavery that is entirely un-

269

supported by law, but is willingly maintained and observed in some portion of old feudal India, and is breakable at will.

4. Traces of debt bondage and serfdom with occasional slave-raiding and slave-holding in the less accessible hinterland of our African Crown Colonies.

For an Empire on which the sun never sets that is not a very damning total, and is one which will be very soon liquidated.

Some Results of a Slave Past

In opening this study it was remarked that the slave system, both of ancient and modern times, has left indelible marks on all the world's framework ; though the view, often expressed by historians, was referred to, that without it the world could never have attained a civilization of industry, art, and production. It may be true that only by compulsion were Piltdown and Java men brought to higher things, or the neolithics given a notion of crafts other than flint. Whatever truth there may be in this view of a life that lies so far away behind the mists of Time, and however much we realize that the slave system was so universally accepted that it is referred to in both the Old and New Testaments, we may be quite sure that the foul slave systems of Greece and Rome were no part of any law of development.

Whatever be the manner in which slavery originally came into the world, the fact remains that many of our incongruities and difficulties of social structure to-day are descended from the slave systems of the past. In nearly every country in Europe, for instance, some unsatisfactory condition, fixed in the days when slave-holding was part of the system, still exists. It is probable that some of the fierce and unreasoning passions that Communism is able to raise are due to an old inherited slave complex. The bitterness of the Irish, which has been given an anti-English twist, is just as likely to be due to an instinctive memory of the slavery that Milesians and other Celts imposed on Formorian, Iberian, and other predecessors, as to any injuries at the hands of the Norman English; just as the first invasion of Ireland by the Normans was due to anger at the slave-raiding carried out by the Irish on the western shores of England. Right through the story of European development similar conditions can be observed.

Our imaginations may well be struck by the thought that the Pyramids were built by slave labour ruthlessly driven. But among the most startling results of slavery is the conglomeration of races in Southern Italy descended from the vast slave populations settled there as serfs; and in the West Indies, whole populations almost entirely due to the freeing of alien negro slaves. Through the whole of South America there is a negro blend that was never intended by nature. We have also seen the de-Saxonization of the United States as a result of the heavy slaughter in an internecine civil war bred of a slave policy, and the anomaly of 12,000,000, often prosperous enough, blacks dumped in the middle of 90,000,000 whites, with the savagery and mutual fear that produces negro and anti-negro outrages in the Southern States. The extreme good of the present development in the Sudan, the giant loss of life that preceded it, the great expenditure and the tragedy to our country of the Gordon period, are all the direct results of slavery. We might almost say that our entirely good, if at times inept, measures of abolition induced the Great Trek in South Africa, cost us the friendship of the settler Dutch, and not even very indirectly led to the blood and cost of the South African War.

The foregoing instance a few of the more immediate and memorable *sequelae* of slave life, and a little reflection on some of the world's other great problems will show how they can be traced to slave causes.

It is not too much indeed to say, that wherever man has offended against the rights of man, there in due course to him or his children has come a nemesis as marked as it has been terrible.

THE RINGING TO EVENSONG

In trying to cover the story of thousands of years of slavery, it has not been possible to mention, except in the slightest way, the great deeds of the original torch-holders in England. From Sharp and Wilberforce and the generations of Buxtons to the Convention of St. Germain in 1919, from Castlereagh and Palmerston to a Foreign and Colonial Office thoroughly alert, is a long story of high endeavour, and the spirit of the pioneers, like the body of John Brown, still " goes marching on." Unfortunately the end is not yet, though save for the disruption of civilization by destructive wars, which still persist, one might hope that complete emancipation was just round the corner. However-so-soon it may come or however-so-long we must wait for the end, we can feel that the international body now formed is not likely to lose its grip, nor our British Society to fail in its watch-dog rôle over the care of the African races by the Governments concerned.

It is all a sorry story to look back on, but Britain may fairly feel that, thanks largely to the great souls who made her slave-conscious, she has at any rate tried to wipe out her share of the ancient evil in the eighteenth century. As part of the penitence the interest of the British people as a whole in emancipation is still demanded.

THE END

INDEX

Eunuchs, 12
discovery of Semiramis, 13
in Arabia, 13
how made in China, 14
referred to in both Testaments, 14
and vengeance on the Mogul, 15
guards at Mecca, 262

Falashi Jews in Abyssinia, 199
Florida, slaves smuggled from, 163
France and slave trade, 111
flag covers infamy, 110
cruisers active, 113
and East Coast of Africa, 147
French Empire, remnants of slavery, 256
French papers:
modern anti-slavery zeal, 247
the *Matin*, 201
Frere, Sir Bartle, in Zanzibar, 159
Fugitive Slave Act, the (U.S.A.), 168

Galley slaves, 70
Gengis Khan, 55
Ghorids, the, 48
Ghuz, federation of, 48
Ghuzni, dynasty and powers, 47
Gordon, General:
and Equatorial Provinces, 207, 208
resigns, 212
returns as Governor-General of both provinces, 212
and slavery in Sudan, 215
and Zobeir, 215
resigns again, 217
returns to evacuate Sudan, 220
his death at Khartoum, 221
Granville Sharp and London negroes, 120
first society's chairman, 122
Greece, ancient, slavery in, 17
Grey, Sir Edward, and Putumayo, 194
Guinea Coast. *Vide* Slave trade

Haile Selassie could not control slavery, 5, 201
Harem slaves:
description of, 59
Sultan's harem, 60
Harris, Sir John, his book, *A Century of Emancipation*, 193
Hawkins, Sir John, and slave trade, 85
Hebrews and slaves, 11
Hicks, Pasha, disaster of, 220
Hodson, Sir Arnold, his book quoted, 154
Horace, son of a slave, 27
Hull, Sir William, protests in Parliament against coercion, 131
Hungry Country, the, 196
Hyderabad State and depressed labour, 254

Iberian serfs, 30
Ibn Saud and slavery, 264
Ilek Khans, the, 47
Indentured labour:
early condition, 148
in Mauritius, 149
in Réunion, 149
modern problem of, 240
requisite conditions, 241
sex problem, 242
Kanaka scandal, 243
in India to-day, 248; figures, 249
India, slavery in, 202
bond slavery in, 203
backward tracts, 204
Turkish days, 204
Ireland, 38
slave trade in, 79
Islam, rise of, 44
and Central Asian slave system, 45
Italy shoulders the White Man's Burden, 5

Jamaica, slaves in, 92, 104

Napier, Sir Robert, in Abyssinia, 199
Napoleon and slavery, 109
New Hebrides labour scandal, 246
exposed by French newspaper,
247
Nicosia, capture of, 57
Niger Expedition of 1839, 124
Norman, Field-Marshal Sir Henry,
and Queensland labour, 245

O'Donnel, Captain - General of
Cuba, 141
Oliver Cromwell and white slaves,
87
Oman, 156
and Ibn Sultan, 167
Omdurman, battle of, 223
Ottoman Turks, slave-makers, 56
Ouloudj, corsair, 68
at Lepanto, 71
becomes head of Ottoman navy,
74
Ouverture, Toussaint L', 103
Ovando, Nicholas de, Governor of
Haiti, 84

Palmerston, Lord, becomes anti-
slavery champion, 135
and Zanzibar, 149
Pastures Green, 4
Patterson, Bishop, murder of, 244
Pei-Nu. Vide *Mui-Tsai*
Piali, corsair admiral, 68
Portugal and slavery, 109
peculiar position, 111
and British cruisers, 112
problem of, 134
Putumayo, the horror of, 191

Qoran, the, and slavery, 259
Quakers and anti-slavery, 123
Queen Elizabeth and slave trade, 86
Queen, the, in chess, 50
Queen Semiramis and eunuchs, 13
Queen Victoria's Jubilee, 16
Empress of India, 50

Queensland and Kanaka labour, 245
Qutb, the, 49
Qutb-ud-Din Aibuk, 49

Rome, slave system of, 20
servile wars, 30
revolt of gladiators, 31
Rovers, Sali :
stories of, 78
and Charles I, 79
Rutter, Eldon, on Arabian slavery,
260

S. Domingo, 103
Sabakhtegin, 48
Sali rovers, the, 64
raids in England, 79
Saxons and slavery, 39
Seljuk Turks, 48
Serfdom, 32
in Britain, 37
Shah Alum blinded, 15
Sierra Leone :
slave settlement, 118
story of, 120
Skinner's Horse and their "slaves,"
204
Slave freed :
problem of, 117
sent to Sierra Leone, 118
difficulties of disposal at sea, 118
Slave kings in Central Asia, 45
in India, 49
dynasty of Delhi, 49
Slave market at Delos, 25
in Mecca, 261
Slave past, results of a, 270
Slave trade with West Africa,
origin, 73
British enter trade, 85
in Muscat, 147, 149
Slave women :
in Rome, 21
rape of, 21
as Turkish concubines, 59